D0092877

DATE DUE

| | | | |
|---|---|---|---|
| | | | |
| | | | |
| | | | |
| | | | |
| | | | |
| | | | |
| | | | |
| | | | |
| | | | |
| | | | |
| | | | |
| | | | |
| | | | |
| | | | |
| | | | |
| | | | |
| | | | |
| | | | |
| | | | |
| GAYLORD | | | PRINTED IN U.S.A. |

CRIMINAL RESPONSIBILITY AND PARTIAL EXCUSES

# Criminal Responsibility and Partial Excuses

GEORGE MOUSOURAKIS
*School of Law*
*University of Queensland*

## Ashgate

### DARTMOUTH

Aldershot • Brookfield USA • Singapore • Sydney

Published by
Ashgate Publishing Ltd
Gower House
Croft Road
Aldershot
Hants GU11 3HR
England

Ashgate Publishing Company
Old Post Road
Brookfield
Vermont 05036
USA

**British Library Cataloguing in Publication Data**
Mousourakis, George
    Criminal responsibility and partial excuses
    1.Criminal liability - England 2.Criminal liability - Wales
    3.Justification - England 4.Justification - Wales
    I. Title
    345.4'2'04

**Library of Congress Cataloging-in-Publication Data**
Mousourakis, George
    Criminal responsibility and partial excuses / George Mousourakis.
        p.   cm.
    Includes bibliographical references.
    ISBN 1-85521-943-3 (hardcover)
    1.Criminal liability--Great Britain. 2. Justification (Law)-
-Great Britain. 3. Criminal law--Philosophy. I. Title.
KD7890.M68 1998          98-24988
345.41'04--dc21          CIP

ISBN 1 85521 943 3

Printed and bound by Athenaeum Press, Ltd.,
Gateshead, Tyne & Wear.

# Contents

vi

# Introduction

Criminal law theory recognises a distinction between two types of legal defences: justifications and excuses. Justifications challenge the wrongful and unlawful character of an act or omission which, on the face of it, violates a criminal prohibition. When a justification-based defence is raised the argument is that, in the circumstances, an act which would normally constitute a criminal offence should be considered right or, at least, legally permissible. The circumstances of justification, in other words, are understood to alter the grounds for the moral and legal assessment of the relevant act. Self-defence and related defences are often referred to as examples of justification-based legal defences. Excuses, by contrast, do not deny the wrongfulness or unlawfulness of the act or omission at issue. What these defences call in question is the attribution of the wrongful act to the actor. An accused who pleads a valid excuse cannot be held blameworthy and culpable for having committed a criminal offence. Examples of this type of legal defences include insanity, duress and, arguably, necessity. Modern commentators agree that, by contrast with German and other Continental criminal law systems, the distinction between justification and excuse has not been given enough weight in the development of criminal law doctrine in common law jurisdictions. It is argued that much of the confusion surrounding criminal law doctrine could have been avoided had the importance of the distinction been recognised at an earlier stage in the development of the law.[1] Nevertheless, the increasing literature on the theory of justification and excuse and the frequent references to the relevant distinction in judicial decisions and legislative enactments in recent years manifest a renewed interest in the benefits of this approach to conceptualising criminal liability.[2]

---

[1] See especially G. Fletcher, *Rethinking Criminal Law* (1978), ch. 10; "The Right and the Reasonable" *Harvard Law Review* (1985), p. 949; "The Individualization of Excusing Conditions", *Southern California Law Review* 47, (1974), p. 1269.

[2] As Professor Yeo points out: "The criminal theory concerning justification and excuse can no longer be ignored by the courts. Its primary contribution is

1

This book examines the question of criminal liability in terms of the fundamental distinction between justification and excuse. Its governing task is to explore the implications of this approach for criminal law doctrine, using provocation and related defences to focus the issues. It is believed that the partial defence of provocation offers a particularly interesting site because of its potential interpretation as excuse- or justification-based. Provocation, when pleaded as a partial defence to murder, does not lead to complete acquittal, but to the reduction of homicide to the lower offence category of voluntary manslaughter. Besides its role as a partial defence to murder, provocation is also considered as a factor in the mitigation of sentence in relation to criminal offences other than murder. The defence is understood to rest upon two interrelated requirements, namely the wrongful act of provocation and impaired volition or loss of self-control. Given that the former element pertains to justification whereas the latter to excuse, the rationale of the defence seems difficult to locate. Is it the wrongfulness of the victim's provocation, entitling the actor to some form of punitive response, that underpins the actor's plea for mitigation? If this were true, provocation should be viewed as a partial justification. Or  is it, rather, the fact that the actor had lost his self-control at the time he committed the offence that provides the reason for reducing culpability? If this were accepted, provocation should be regarded as a partial excuse.

Chapter 1 offers a general account of the theoretical distinction between justification and excuse and explores its implications for the theory of criminal liability. Moreover, this chapter considers how the concepts of justification and excuse relate to the defence of provocation and maps out some of the main themes around which the subsequent analysis will revolve. Chapter 2 examines how the role of excuses in the criminal law is explained and justified from the point of view of different theories of criminal responsibility. In this chapter three of the most  influential theoretical approaches to the question of excusing in law are described and assessed. Chapter 3 offers an account of the partial defence of provocation as it operates in English law. Following an outline of the distinction between murder and manslaughter and its

---

consistency  in the development of the law, a goal which the courts themselves proclaim  as  most desirable. Without the theory to guide the courts, aspects of the  law  of self-defence, duress, necessity and, until only recently, provocation have  developed  in  an inconsistent fashion". S.M.H. Yeo, "Proportionality in Criminal  Defences", *Criminal Law Journal* 12 (1988) 211, p. 227. See also his *Compulsion in the Criminal Law* (1990), ch. 1.; J.C. Smith, *Justification and Excuse in the Criminal Law* (1989), ch. 1. And see the decision of the Supreme  Court  of  Canada  in *Perka v The Queen* [1984] 2 SCR 232, 42 CR (3d)112, 13 DLR (4th) 1, (1985) CCC (3rd) 385.

history, the main problems surrounding the doctrine of provocation are highlighted as they emerge from the discussion of important cases. Chapter 4 examines more closely how provocation can be conceptualised as a partial justification or as a partial excuse and discusses problems relating to the traditional understanding of the defence as a concession to human frailty. It is argued that the true basis of the provocation defence lies in the excuse theory. The wrongfulness of provocation provides an explanation for the actor's loss of self-control as a basis for excusing rather than a reason for directly reducing the gravity of his crime. Chapter 5 looks at the problem of cumulative provocation and the possibility of setting up a combined defence of provocation and diminished responsibility when evidence suggests that the accused was suffering from an abnormality of mind and was provoked. Finally, chapter 6 takes up problems of possible overlap between provocation and self-defence, and examines the rationale of the partial defence to murder that may arise in some cases involving the use of excessive force in self-defence. Although, throughout the book, the analysis focuses on developments in English criminal law, the references to other criminal law systems included in the work add an important comparative perspective to the discussion of the issues.

# 1 Introduction to the Theory of Justification and Excuse

## Distinguishing between Justifications and Excuses

Criminal law doctrine proceeds from the principle that a person cannot be convicted and punished for an offence unless two basic elements are established: the conduct or state of affairs which a particular offence prohibits and the state of mind which a person must have at the time of such conduct or state of affairs. The first element, which is said to represent the external or objective or conduct element in crime, is traditionally referred to as *actus reus*; the second, which is sometimes described as the internal or subjective or fault element in crime, is termed *mens rea*. Under the latter term fall the mental states of intention, knowledge, recklessness and, arguably, negligence. Of course the *actus reus* and *mens rea* elements differ from one criminal offence to another. To determine what must be proved before an accused is convicted of a particular offence one needs to consider the legal definition of that offence as found in the applicable statutory enactment or, in the case of a common law offence, in the relevant case law. However, proving that the accused brought about the *actus reus* of an offence with the requisite mens rea is a necessary but not a sufficient condition for conviction. Criminal liability and punishment depend, moreover, upon the absence of certain excusing or justifying conditions.

The legal excuses serve to relieve a person of criminal responsibility even in some cases where the person admits that he or she intentionally or knowingly committed the unlawful act. In general, a person is not subject to criminal liability if, at the time of the offence, he was mistaken about some material fact relating to the circumstances or possible consequences of his action, unconscious of what he was doing or unable to exercise control over his bodily movements, insane or subject to certain forms of coercion. But not all criminal law defences hinge upon the concept of excuse. Criminal law also recognises legal defences based on the idea of justification. Justification-based defences are seen as complementing or modifying the prohibitory rules of the criminal law by allowing for exceptions in the application of the rules under certain legally prescribed circumstances. In these circumstances an act which would normally be described as criminal is deemed objectively right or, at least, not unlawful. This is usually explained on the grounds that the harm caused by the person acting under a justification is outweighed by the fact that, by doing so, he or she has avoided an even greater harm or has furthered some greater societal interest. Thus, by contrast with claims of excuse which focus on the subjective state of mind of the actor, claims of justification primarily focus on the objective character of the act in the circumstances.[1] Examples of legal defences operating as justifications include self-defence and defence of another, defence of property and prevention of crime.

Central to the theory of justification and excuse is the distinction between primary or prohibitory norms and norms of attribution. The former impose general duties of conformity with minimum standards of conduct on  members of society who are required to guide their conduct accordingly if they are to avoid the sanctions provided when these norms are infringed. These primary or prohibitory norms are complemented or modified by norms of justification which allow for exceptions to the application of the primary norms in prescribed circumstances. For example, the primary norm against committing acts of violence is complemented or modified by the provision which licenses the doing of such acts in self-defence or in defence of another. Justifications operate on the assumption that, when done under the prescribed circumstances, the act in question, harmful though it may be, should be assessed differently than when done under normal circumstances, i.e. under those in which the original prohibitory norm would apply.

By contrast with the primary or prohibitory norms, the norms of attribution are specifically addressed to judges and juries as these norms lay down grounds for legally excusing someone who has violated a legal prohibition. Unlike claims of justification, the norms of attribution do not  modify the primary norms. Their role is not to guide

---

1　　As J.L. Austin notes: "In the one defence [i.e. justification], briefly, we accept responsibility but deny that [the act] was bad; in the other, we admit that it was bad but don't accept full, or even any, responsibility". "A Plea for Excuses", in *The Philosophy of Action* , A. White (ed.) (1968) 19, p.20. And see Eric D'Arcy, *Human Acts* (1963), p. 85: "If an act is justified the agent is responsible for it, but the act is, in the circumstances, not wrong. If it is excused, the act is a wrongful one, but the agent is, because of some special circumstances, not responsible for it, and hence not guilty...An excusing condition, therefore, primarily affects the agent; a justifying circumstance primarily affects the act: its species description, or its moral appraisal".

conduct but to allow for exceptions in ascribing moral blame as a prerequisite for legal culpability. According to Professor Fletcher

> Wrongful conduct may be defined as the violation of the prohibitory norm as modified by all defences that create a privileged exception to the norm. The analysis of attribution turns our attention to a totally distinct set of norms, which do not provide directives for action, but spell out the criteria for holding persons accountable for their deeds. The distinction as elaborated here corresponds to the more familiar distinction between justification and excuse.[2]

Justifications are concerned with the objective evaluation of conduct. The conditions which give rise to claims of justification are understood to alter the grounds for the moral and/or legal assessment of a *prima facie* wrongful and unlawful act.[3] An act which, in absence of the justificatory conditions, would normally be described as an offence is now considered to be right or, at least, legally permissible.[4] As Eric D'Arcy notes:

> [T]o say that a decision, belief, practice, rule, or act was justified is usually to imply that one's first reaction was to say that there was something wrong with it, though subsequently (on learning the circumstances, or in the light of the consequences) to decide, agree, or admit that it was right: wc say that something is justified only when we think, or expect that someone will think, that it needs

---

2   Fletcher, *Rethinking Criminal Law* (1978), p. 458.

3   In the words of Professor G. Williams: "A defence is justificatory (for the purpose of the criminal law) whenever it denies the objective wrongness of the act... Normally a justification is any defence affirming that the act, state of affairs or consequences are, on balance, to be socially approved, or are matters about which society is neutral". "The Theory of Excuses", *Criminal Law Review* [1982] 732, p.735. See also G. Williams, "Offences and Defences", *Legal Studies* 2, 3, (Nov. 1982) 238.

4   There has been some disagreement among legal theorists as to whether justifiable conduct should be seen as praiseworthy or as merely permissible. According to P. J. Fitzgerald, "to justify an action is to show that there are circumstances such that the action, which might ordinarily be disapproved of, is in this case to be commended", *Criminal Law and Punishment* (1962), p. 119. Similarly P. Robinson argues that justifications require that "harm is outweighed by the need to avoid an even greater harm or to further a greater societal interest", *Criminal Law Defenses* (1984), p. 83. This approach has been challenged, however, on the grounds that justified conduct means conduct that is permissible, and not all permissible conduct can be said to promote a greater societal interest. See, e.g., Fletcher, supra note 2, pp. 769-770; J. Dressler, "New Thoughts About the Concept of Justification in the Criminal Law: A Critique of Fletcher's Thinking and Rethinking", *Univ. of California at Los Angeles Law Review* 32 (1984) 61; D. N. Husak, *Philosophy of the Criminal Law* (1987), p. 189.

justification...The effect of a justifying circumstance is to *justum facere* an (otherwise wrongful) act, so that it becomes good, or at least permissible: lawful.[5]

It is important to note here that raising a justification-based defence presupposes that a person finds himself accused of something. In other words, one cannot plead a justification unless some form of conduct is identified on his part which, on the face of it, meets the external requirements of a criminal offence.

In order to bring to light the rationale of a justification-based defence one needs to consider the possible moral grounds for excluding wrongfulness under certain circumstances. Various moral theories of justification have been proposed. A well-known utilitarian theory, based upon the so called principle of *lesser evil*, postulates that in a situation of unavoidable conflict of interests an act which preserves the greater interest is justified, notwithstanding its being in a narrow sense harmful. Although the act may cause harm, and as such it should in general be avoided whenever possible, in the circumstances the harm is outbalanced by the need to prevent an even greater harm or to promote a superior societal interest. Fletcher argues that all claims of justification "can be reduced to a balancing of competing interests and a judgment in favour of the superior interest".[6] However, no jurisdiction gives the individual the exclusive right to determine subjectively which of the conflicting interests is to be sacrificed, for the power to assess the relative interests rests with the legislature or the jury as representing the community's views.[7] It is society which, directly or through its

---

5   *Human Acts* (1963), p. 81.

6   G. Fletcher, supra note 2, p. 769. And see P. Robinson, "Criminal Law Defenses: A Systematic Analysis", 82*Columbia Law Review* (1982) 199, p. 213.

7   According to the American Model Penal Code, for example, "The balancing of evils cannot, of course, be committed merely to the private judgment of the actor; it is an issue for determination in the trial", Para 3.02, Comment 5 (Tent. Draft No. 8, 1958). And as pointed out by Dickson J. in *Perka v. The Queen* (1984) 13 D.L.R. (4th) 1, "...no system of positive law can recognise any principle which would entitle a person to violate the law because on his view the law conflicted with some higher social value... To hold that ostensibly illegal acts can be validated on the basis of their expediency would import an undue subjectivity into the criminal law. It would invite the courts to second-guess the legislature and to assess the relative merits of social policies underlying criminal prohibitions. Neither is a role which fits well with the judicial function", quoted in J. C. Smith, *Justification and Excuse in the Criminal Law* (1989) pp. 14 ff. Against this view Fletcher argues that the norms that a court or an individual may rely on to justify conduct are not

representatives, determines the relative values of the interests at stake. Thus, only when the actor's determination agrees with that authoritative assessment can he rely on a justification-based defence. The theory of lesser evil is supplemented by the *forfeiture* theory of justification. According to this, inflicting harm on a wrongdoer is justified because, other things being equal, acting wrongfully entails a partial relinquishment of the wrongdoer's rights. The defence of self-defence is often explained on this basis. According to Professor Williams

> Self-defence is classified as a justification on the basis that the interests of the person attacked are greater than those of the attacker. The aggressor's culpability in starting the fight tips the scales in favour of the defendant.[8]

Another, non-utilitarian, moral theory of justification revolves around the *rights-enforcement* principle, or the principle of the *vindication of personal autonomy*. This theory claims that a person is justified to cause harm, if necessary, in order to protect his recognised rights against unwarranted interferences. Having a right means having the moral authority or permission to prevent violations of that right. From this point of view, the justification e.g. of self-defence has to do with the right of a person whose rights or sphere of autonomy are threatened, to repel the aggressor and restore the integrity of his domain. Again, the use of force remains wrong and is to be avoided whenever possible. The assertion of the need to defend a right, however, will normally provide a justification for the use of force and the causing of harm. The principle of lesser evil or the forfeiture principle have no part in this theory. As Fletcher points out "...in contrast to the necessary defence as a variation of lesser evils, the aggressor's culpability appears to be irrelevant; what counts is the objective nature of the aggressor's intrusion".[9] Although the above theories of justification may appear to hinge upon fundamentally different moral principles, these principles are often relied upon as

---

reducible to the body of enacted rules. Supra note 2, pp. 790-795; "The Right and the Reasonable" *Harvard Law Review* (1985) 949.

8    "The Theory of Excuses", supra note 3, p. 739. And see P. Robinson, *Criminal Law Defences*, supra note 4, pp. 69-70.

9    G. Fletcher, supra note 2, p. 862. See also S.H. Kadish, "Respect for Life and Regard for Rights in the Criminal Law", *California Law Review* 64, (1976) 871, pp. 883-884. D. Hoekema proposes a distinction between first-order and second-order rights. Every first-order right, such as e.g. the right to life, is supported by a second-order right, i.e. a right to defend against violations of one's first-order rights. See Hoekema, *Rights and Wrongs* (1986), p.113.

complementing rather than contradicting each other when claims of justification are being assessed.

However, justifications are not concerned exclusively with external conduct and its consequences. They are also concerned with the actor's state of mind or even his motive in acting. For example, in common law jurisdictions the question of whether the force used in self-defence was reasonable is decided by the trier of the facts in the light of the circumstances in which the accused decided to use force as he or she believed them to be.[10] Thus where a person uses defensive force under the mistaken belief that he is about to be attacked his actions will be judged as justified or not by reference to that belief. Further, it is accepted that, even if a person's actions, from an external point of view, appear to satisfy the requirements of a justification-based defence, his harm-causing conduct should not be regarded as justified unless he was aware of the circumstances rendering his actions justifiable. Thus a person who, while attempting to commit an offence, unintentionally brings about the lesser of two evils, cannot escape criminal liability on the grounds of a justification. On the other hand, it would be sufficient for the purposes of legal justification that a person's acts objectively meet the requirements of a justification-based defence, irrespective of whether he was aware of that fact or not, provided that no criminal intention or fault on his part can be established.[11]

Usually the legal definition of a justification-based defence is formulated so as to include certain limitations on the defence reflecting prior judgments as to what is reasonable, hence justifiable, conduct in certain circumstances. For the defence of self-defence to succeed, for example, it is required that the force used must be necessary, i.e. in response to a sufficiently specific and imminent threat, and reasonable, i.e. proportionate to the attack. The requirement of proportionality limits the amount of force, and hence the harm, that may be used in defence of a legally recognised interest. Justification is precluded if the harm caused by the actor, although necessary to protect the interest at stake, is too grave as compared to the objective value of that interest.

---

10   See, e.g. *Palmer v R* [1971] AC 814.

11   For a fuller discussion of the interrelation of objective and subjective requirements in relation to justification see G. Fletcher, "The Right Deed for the Wrong Reason: A Reply to Mr Robinson", 23 *University of California at Los Angeles Law Review* (1975) 293, reprinted in *Justification and Excuse in the Criminal Law*, M. L. Corrado (ed.), (1994), p. 305. For a different approach see P. Robinson, "A Theory of Justification: Societal Harm as a Prerequisite for Criminal Liability", 23 *University of California at Los Angeles Law Review* (1975) 266, reprinted in *Justification and Excuse in the Criminal Law*, ibid. p. 283; *Criminal Law Defenses* (1984), pp. 27-28.

By contrast with justifications, excuses focus primarily on the actor rather than the act. When a person pleads an excuse, the wrongfulness of his or her act is not denied. What is called into question is the internal relationship between the wrongful act and the actor, as required for holding the actor blameworthy.[12] With regard to excuse-based legal defences the context within which the harm-causing conduct takes places does not itself excuse; it only provides an acceptable basis for explaining the excusing condition relied upon. Moral excuses as well as excuse-based legal defences fall into three different categories: involuntariness, moral or normative involuntariness and irresponsibility.

The conditions that give rise to the first type of excuses negate cupability by precluding the attribution of *authorship-responsibility* for a *prima facie* wrongful act. The category of involuntariness includes situations in which a person is regarded as having no control over his or her bodily movements as e.g. in a case where A pushes B's knife-holding hand down on another person's back. Cases of physical compulsion, such as this, are relatively easy to identify because we can actually see the external force being applied. But in the same category fall also situations in which the condition that causes the actor's loss of bodily control is internal, as e.g. in certain cases of somnambulism or when a person suffers an epileptic seizure.[13]

The category of moral or normative involuntariness includes cases in which a person is capable of exercising control over his bodily movements, i.e. of acting in a strict sense, but he is not free to choose the course of his action. In these cases the person's freedom of choice is so constrained by circumstances that acting wrongfully appears to be unavoidable. Two kinds of situations are regarded as giving rise to excuses of this type: situations in which the constraint arises from a defect of knowledge, and situations in which the constraint arises from a defect of will. The former furnish the basis for the excuses of mistake of fact and accident, the latter of those of duress and necessity. From a different point of view, however, one might argue that claims of

---

12  As L. Heintz points out "[t]he central moral force of excuses is to mitigate or remove blameworthiness. Excuses do not have the moral force of removing obligations nor do they remove the accusation or charge 'you ought to have kept the obligation'. One who is sincere in requesting to be excused has already admitted that his conduct was in some way wrong (deficient or substandard)", "The Logic of Defences", *American Philosophical Quarterly* 18 (1981) 243, p. 245.

13  Excuses expressed in the form "I was not in control of my bodily movements" deny that the harm-causing conduct was the product of conscious determination and thus, in a sense, question the alleged wrongdoing as a matter of fact. The legal excuse of automatism offers the typical example of such an excuse.

mistake and accident should not be included in this category of excuses. As Aristotle has remarked, actions done under mistake should be treated as involuntary in the same way that unconscious or compelled actions are involuntary.[14] Like in the involuntary act defence, it may be said that the conditions of mistake and accident preclude moral and legal responsibility because they deny the alleged wrongdoing as a matter of fact by negating the necessary mental element (intention accompanied by knowledge) required for its description. From this point of view, if A shot and killed B by accident, i.e. without knowing that he was shooting at another human being, A has not committed homicide simply because the very description of the relevant wrongdoing presupposes that the actor is aware of what he is doing. On the other hand, when a person adduces an excuse based on a defect of will he admits that he committed the wrongful act with both knowledge of what he was doing and intention, but claims that he did so only because, in the circumstances, he could not have done otherwise.[15] An excuse of this type operates on the assumption that the actor was not free to choose.[16] The legal excuses of duress and necessity provide the typical examples here. The main difference between the two is that, in duress, the threat e.g. to the actor's life or limb that precludes his acting otherwise comes from another person, whereas in necessity it emanates from non-human factors.[17]

However, excuse-based legal defences do not rest, exclusively, on subjective considerations, but are based also on objective requirements. Jurors are invited to compare the accused's response with the way a person of reasonable firmness would be expected to act if faced with a similar predicament. What amounts to excusable conduct in the circumstances is usually left to the jury to determine on the basis of generally accepted moral standards and commonsense considerations. Often, however, the legal definition of a defence specifies minimum conditions that need to be satisfied before conduct could be considered reasonable and therefore legally excusable. For example, with regard to the defence of duress as it operates in English

---

[14] Aristotle, *Nichomachean Ethics* 1110b.

[15] According to Aristotle, under normal circumstances the actor "would not choose any such act in itself", ibid at 1110a.

[16] As Dickson J. pointed out in *Perka v The Queen* [1984] 2 SCR 232, at 249, in such cases "[the actor] has control over his actions to the extent of being physically capable of abstaining from the act. Realistically, however, his act is not a 'voluntary' one. His 'choice' to break the law is no true choice at all; it is remorselessly compelled by normal human instincts".

[17] For a similar approach to the classification of excusing condition see Michael Moore, "Causation and Excuses" (1985) 73 *California Law Review* 1091.

law, this minimum condition pertains to the requirement that the actor must be faced with an immediate threat of death or serious bodily harm.[18]

Finally, the excuses based on the notion of irresponsibility operate on the assumption that holding a person morally and legally responsible presupposes a certain degree of rationality and maturity. Persons who, due to their mental condition or age, are incapable of making rational judgments or of exercising control over their conduct are not subject to blame. The legal defences of insanity and infancy provide the examples here. Whereas a person acting under duress or necessity is excused because he acted as any of us would when caught in similar circumstances, the insane person is excused because he has shown himself to be so different from the rest of us that the normal criteria of moral and legal responsibility no longer apply. On this point the criminal law relies on the concept of mental disease to mark out the insane and therefore legally excusable offender. In this respect it is asked whether, as a result of a mental disease, the accused was unable to appreciate the nature and character of his actions, or to exercise control over his conduct.

As criminal law is concerned not only with punishing wrongdoers but also with highlighting and reinforcing societal values and expectations, it should be capable of identifying the moral character of actions and the moral basis for exempting certain persons accused of offences from criminal liability and punishment.[19] In this respect, describing a defence as a justification conveys the message that the relevant conduct is approved or, at least, tolerated. On the other hand, labelling a defence as an excuse draws attention to the fact that, although the actor is free from blame, his conduct remains wrongful and as such is to be avoided. A failure to recognise the distinction between justification and excuse will result in sending confusing or contradictory messages to the community.[20] Besides its great moral significance, the distinction has important practical implications. It has been recognised, for example, that as duress and lack of *mens rea* operate as excuses, a person who assists another in the commission of an offence should be convicted as an accessory even though the principal offender is excused on such grounds. By contrast, other

---

18   *Howe* [1987] 1 AC 417.
19   According to M. Moore, by moral values and expectations we mean those "attitudes of resentment, moral indignation, condemnation, approval, guilt, remorse, shame, pride and the like, and that range of more cognitive judgments about when an actor deserves moral praise or blame", "Causation and Excuses" (1985), supra note 17, p. 1144.
20   See P. Robinson, "A Theory of Justification: Societal Harm as a Prerequisite for Criminal Liability", supra note 11, pp. 276-277.

things being equal, an alleged accessory would be free from criminal liability if the person accused of an offence as a principal successfully pleads a justification-based defence. Moreover, it is recognised that legally justified or authorised conduct cannot be resisted by force — e.g. one cannot justifiably use force to resit a lawful arrest, for this would undermine the greater interest being protected, i.e. the enforcement of the law — and that third parties are generally entitled to assist a person whose action is deemed justified. On the other hand, because excuses do not deny the wrongful character of one's conduct, a person may use force to resist an attack by an excusable aggressor.[21] Moreover, whether a defence is classified as a justification or as an excuse may have important consequences as regards the issue of compensation of those harmed by the accused's conduct. If the defence is regarded as an excuse a person harmed would have a strong claim for compensation. By contrast, if the defence is classified as a justification the victim's claim for compensation would be significantly weaker. [22]

## Justification and Excuse in Common Law Jurisprudence

At early common law the distinction between justification and excuse was fully recognised and had important practical implications, particularly in the context of the law of homicide. A successful justification-based defence resulted in the full acquittal of the accused. On the other hand, an excuse-based defence resulted in the usual sentence for homicide — death — and the forfeiture of the accused's property. The excused person, however, could escape execution if he was granted a royal pardon. The Statute of Gloucester, enacted in the thirteenth century,[23] provided that killing another in self-preservation, like the killing of another by misadventure or accident, was excusable and therefore subject to royal pardon. The distinction between justifiable and excusable homicide was elaborated further by the commentators of the 17th and 18th centuries. For example, in his *Commentaries on the Laws of England* William Blackstone distinguished between justifiable homicide as it is committed "either for the advancement of public justice...or...for the prevention of some

---

21  See Fletcher, *Rethinking Criminal Law*, supra note 2, pp. 761-762; P. Alldridge, "The Coherence of Defences" [1983] *Criminal Law Review* 665, p. 666.

22  See D. Horowitz, "Justification and Excuse in the Program of the Criminal Law" (1986) 49 *Law and Contemporary Problems* 109, p. 122.

23  6 Edw. I.c.9 (1278).

atrocious crime",[24] and excusable homicide which could be of two kinds: "either *per infortunium*, by misadventure; or *se defendendo*, upon a principle of self preservation".[25] Killing in self-defence was considered excusable when two persons became engaged in a fight in the course of which deadly violence was used by one of the parties. If the killing took place in the heat of the moment, it was called "chance-medley" and the offender was guilty of the lesser crime of manslaughter. If, however, the accused had killed the other after he had retreated as far as possible, this was excusable homicide *se defendendo*. [26]

---

[24] At p. 179.

[25] At p. 182.

[26] Francis Bacon was one of the first English writers to comment on the distinction between justification and excuse. In discussing what he called "necessity of conservation of life" Bacon used as examples the stealing of food by a person to satisfy his present hunger, the escaping of prisoners from a jail following an accidental fire, and a situation where one of two shipwrecked sailors struggling to gain control of a plank, drowns the other. Bacon regarded the first and third of these cases as examples of excusing necessity; however he treated the second case as an example of justifying necessity, a view that was to be questioned by later writers. Further, Bacon described as justifiable action one's pulling down the wall or house of another to prevent a fire from spreading and as excusable the killing of another by misfortune, *The Elements of the Common Laws of England* (1630), pp. 29 ff. And see Coke, *The Third Part of the Institutes* (1660), pp. 50 ff.; Michael Dalton,*Countrey Justice* (1619) pp. 224 ff. In his *Pleas of the Crown*, published in 1678, Hale distinguished between three kinds of homicide: "(1) Purely voluntary, viz., murder and manslaughter; (2) purely involuntary, as that other kind of homicide *per infortunium*; (3) mixed, partly voluntary and partly involuntary, or in a kind necessary; and this again of two kinds, viz., including a forfeiture as *se defendendo*, or not including a forfeiture as (1) in defence of a man's house; (2) in defence of his person against an assault in *via regia*; (3) in advancement or execution of justice", p. 472. Hale differentiated homicides which were "justifiable, and consequently including no forfeiture at all, nor needing pardon", from homicides which were "excusable and including a forfeiture", pp. 39-40. William Hawkins, in his *Treatise of the Pleas of the Crown* (1716), explained justifiable homicide as being "either of a publick or a private nature. That of a publick nature, is such as is occasioned by the due execution or advancement of publick justice. That of a private nature is such as happens in the just defence of a man's person, house, or goods", (at p. 70). Moreover, he distinguished between two kinds of excusable homicide: *per infortunium* and *se defendendo*. "[H]omicide *per infortunium*, or by misadventure...is when a man in doing a lawful act, without any intent of hurt, unfortunately chances to kill another..." (p. 73). "[H]omicide *se defendendo*... seems to be where one who has no other possible means of preserving his life from one who combats with him on a sudden quarrel, or of defending his person from one who

East, in his *Pleas of the Crown* (1803) offered a more elaborate analysis of the distinction between justifiable and excusable homicides. Three kinds of homicide *ex necessitate* were identified: 1) homicides in the advancement of justice, deemed justifiable by permission of the law, e.g. where a person having authority to arrest or imprison another kills the party who resists arrest in a fight; 2) homicides in execution of justice, regarded as justifiable by the command of the law, e.g. the lawful execution of a convicted criminal; 3) homicides "in defence of person or property under certain circumstances of necessity" which are "either justifiable by permission of the law, or only excusable".[27] In the third category East included: 1) the justifiable killing of another "who comes to commit a known felony with force against his person, his habitation, or his property";[28] 2) the excusable killing of another in self-defence upon a sudden combat, described as homicide *se defendendo* upon chance-medley, and 3) the killing of a person in circumstances of "dire necessity, which is not induced by the fault of either party, where one of two innocent men must die for the other's preservation: this has been holden by some to be justifiable; perhaps it may more properly be considered as excusable: justification is founded upon some positive duty; excuse is due to human infirmity".[29] A further kind of excusable homicide, identified by East, was homicide by misadventure which occurs "when a man doing a lawful act, without any intention of bodily harm, and using proper precaution to prevent danger, unfortunately happens to kill another person". In East's time it was recognised that in this case the "the jury under the direction of the court may acquit the party, without putting him to purchase a pardon under the statute of Gloucester, c.9". [30]

Although at first pardons were granted in special occasions, their number gradually increased until they came to be granted by the chancellor as a matter of course, without the need to consult the monarch. Until the pardon was confirmed, the excusable offender

---

attempts to beat him... kills the person by whom he is reduced to such an inevitable necessity", (pp. 74-75). See also: M. Foster, *Crown Cases* (1762), p. 273; James Fitzjames Stephen, *A History of the Criminal Law of England* III (1883); F. Pollock and F. Maitland, *The History of English Law* (2nd ed., 1898), pp. 478-481; T. A. Green, "Societal Concepts of Criminal Liability in Medieval England" (1972) 47 *Speculum* 669, pp. 675 ff; "The Jury and the English Law of Homicide, 1200-1600" (1976) 74 *Michigan Law Review* 413, p. 428; J. M. Kaye, "The Early History of Murder and Manslaughter" (1967) 83 *Law Quarterly Review* 365 and 569.

[27] At pp. 220-221.

[28] At p. 221.

[29] Ibid.

[30] At pp. 221-222.

remained in jail or, in later years, under bail. Besides the pardon, the excused offender was granted a special writ of restitution of his goods. Gradually the practice relating to the forfeiture of the accused's goods fell into abeyance, until 1828 when forfeiture was formally abolished by statute.[31] Thus, at the end, both justifications and excuses led to the same result, namely the accused's acquittal.

As the difference between the effects of pleading a justification and an excuse gradually disappeared, the significance of the distinction for the common lawyer withered away and its possible role in formulating a comprehensive system of criminal law defences was subsequently overlooked. The terms justification and excuse have often been avoided by common lawyers and, when they have been used by judges and commentators, they have often been treated as interchangeable or synonymous.[32] The view that came to prevail in English criminal law was that the absence of a justification or an excuse constitutes part of the legal definition of a criminal offence. According to this approach, when a person acts under a valid justification or excuse he cannot commit the offence charged. Some authors have subsumed the absence of such a defence under the requirement of *actus reus*, while others have treated it as an independent definitional requirement that should be distinguished from the *actus reus* and *mens rea* elements of the offence.[33] Under the latter view, a distinction should be drawn between excusing conditions negating the *actus reus* and/or *mens rea* elements of offences (e.g. automatism, mistake), and excusing conditions operating outside these elements (duress,

---

31  9 Geo. IV c. 1, s. 10 (1828).

32  As one commentator remarked: "[T]he distinction between justifiable and excusable self-defence was, at one time, one of considerable importance. Moreover, it is still occasionally referred to in the cases and the two are still separately classified in the texts. However, so far as the present day law is concerned, the distinction is one without a difference... The terms are generally used synonymously and interchangeably", J. Miller, *Handbook of Criminal Law* (1934), p. 199. And see James Fitzjames Stephen, *History of the Criminal Law of England* III (1883), p.1.

33  Glanville Williams, for example, argues that: "[the] actus reus includes not merely the whole objective situation that has to be proved by the prosecution, but also the absence of any ground of justification and excuse", *Criminal Law: The General Part* (1961), p.20. And according to H.L.A. Hart, "[The modern English lawyer] would simply consider both [excuse and justification] to be cases where some element, negative or positive, required in the full definition [of the offence] was lacking". Hart goes on to point out, however, that "...the distinction between these two different ways in which actions may fail to constitute a criminal offence is still of great moral importance". "Prolegomenon to the Principles of Punishment" in *Punishment and Responsibility* (1968), p.13.

necessity). In the latter cases the actor brings about the *actus reus* of an offence with the requisite intent, but criminal responsibility is precluded or diminished (in the case of a partial excuse) on the basis that, in the overwhelming circumstances the actor found himself in, his normal capacity to choose the course of his action was vitiated or substantially impaired. Sometimes the statutory definition of an offence includes the phrase "without lawful authority or excuse". It is suggested that the aim of this phrase is to serve as a reminder to judges and juries that the application of the provision creating the offence is not absolute but always subject to the absence of a recognised general defence. On the other hand, the use of the phrase "without reasonable excuse" instead of "lawful excuse" in the legal definition of an offence implies that, at the court's discretion, the accused may rely on an excuse not formally recognised by the criminal law, provided that such an excuse is reasonable.[34]

Professor George Fletcher has offered an important lead in re-awakening interest in the distinction between justification and excuse in Anglo-American criminal jurisprudence. Fletcher traces the decline of the distinction to the prevalence of positivistic ideas in the development of modern law. He argues that the judges' tendency to abstract the judicial decision from the individual case in order to formulate general rules of law resulted in the overlooking of the fundamental character of criminal law as "an institution of blame and punishment".[35] According to Fletcher criminal condemnation and punishment presupposes a negative moral judgment of the actor's character as reflected in his voluntary violation of a criminal prohibition. From this viewpoint, excuses are seen as introducing exceptions in the application of the rules of positive law, for their role is to block the normal inference from a wrongful act that the actor's character is, in a sense, flawed. Such moral assessment of the accused's character is essential to any theory of criminal liability that connects the application of criminal punishment with considerations of "just deserts".[36]

Fletcher argues, moreover, that the common law's reliance on the concept of reasonableness as providing a single standard for dealing with legal disputes, tends to overshadow the distinction between

---

[34]   J.C. Smith, *Justification and Excuse in the Criminal Law*, supra note 7, pp. 47 ff.

[35]   Fletcher, *Rethinking Criminal Law*, supra note 2, p.467. See also his article "The Individualization of Excusing Conditions", *Southern California Law Review* 47, (1974) 1269.

[36]   See G. Fletcher, *Rethinking Criminal Law*, supra note 2, p. 800. See also M. Bayles, "Character, Purpose and Criminal Responsibility", *Law and Philosophy* 1, (1982) 5-20. For a fuller discussion of the "character" theory of criminal responsibility see chapter 2 below.

justification and excuse. The common law approach is characteristic of what he calls a "flat" legal discourse — a system in which all the criteria pertinent to the resolution of a legal problem revolve around the application of a single norm. In Fletcher's words

> The reasonable person enables us to blur the line between justification and excuse, between wrongfulness and blameworthiness, and thus renders impossible any ordering of the dimensions of liability. The standard "what would a reasonable person do under the circumstances?" sweeps within one inquiry questions that would otherwise be distinguished as bearing on wrongfulness or blameworthiness. Criteria of both justification and excuse are amenable to the same question.[37]

Fletcher contrasts the common law approach with what he terms "structured" legal discourse, and points to the German law as an example. In this context legal disputes are resolved in two stages. The admission of an absolute norm, at the first stage of analysis, is followed by the introduction of qualifications introducing restrictions to the application of the norm, at the second. The distinction between justification and excuse is most at home in a system which adopts such a structured approach to defining and tackling legal disputes. In such a system, the question of wrongfulness of an act logically precedes the question of its attribution to the actor. Questions of justification, as pertinent to the issue of wrongdoing, take precedence over questions of excuse. This structured approach to criminal liability, Fletcher argues, is consistent with a theory of criminal responsibility that lays special emphasis on retributive punishment and the principle of just deserts. From the viewpoint of retributive theory, the question of whether the actor deserves punishment cannot be considered before determining the wrongdoing to be punished. As related to the requirement of just deserts, claims of excuse become relevant following an admission that a wrongful act has been committed.[38]

By contrast with the general trend in modern common law jurisprudence, the distinction between justification and excuse has been instrumental in the formation of criminal law doctrine in Germany and other Continental European jurisdictions. A general account of the distinction as developed in German criminal law theory is offered in the following paragraphs.

---

[37] G. Fletcher, "The Right and the Reasonable", supra note 7, pp. 962-963.

[38] Fletcher, *Rethinking Criminal Law*, supra note 2, p. 961. For an interesting account of the role of excuses from the viewpoint of retributive theories of punishment see J. Dressler, "Reflections on Excusing Wrongdoers: Moral Theory, New Excuses and the Model Penal Code", *Rutgers Law Journal* 19 (1988) 671.

## Justification and Excuse in German Criminal Law Theory

In Germany and other Continental European legal systems legal doctrine is permeated by the fundamental idea that the normative principles of law are not reducible to the body of enacted legal rules, or law in a strict sense (*Gesetz*). According to Kant, the transcendental conception of law, captured in the notion of Right (*Recht*), pertains to the conditions of freedom that allow diverse choices in society to harmonise with each other.[39] Right, or law in a broad sense, derives its binding force from its content; enacted law derives its binding force from its form - from the fact that its rules have been duly enacted by a legislative authority. The principles of the Right are perceived as pre-existing and transcending the body of enacted rules whose role is merely to lay down what is to happen when the former principles are violated. An enacted rule, which by definition pertains to a specific type of legal relationship, draws on the Right, but cannot be identified with it - it is only a *vinculum iuris,* a bond of Right.The application of a legal rule is typically strict (hence the phrase "*dura lex sed lex*"), for the act or dispute is treated under the conditions specified by the letter of the law, without taking into account the circumstances of the individual case. By contrast, the application of the Right is flexible and as such adaptable to the needs of each particular case. Unlawfulness is defined primarily in relation to the Right, for an unlawful act is taken to encroach upon the normative principles which inform the particular legal provision under which the act is subsumed.[40] The distinction between Right, or law in a normative sense and enacted, posited law is characteristic of continental jurisprudence.[41] The prevalence of positivistic views in Anglo-American jurisprudence precluded a similar distinction from being recognised at common law jurisdictions. The distinction between Right, or law in a broad normative sense, and enacted law, as elaborated by the jurist Karl Binding,[42] allowed German theory to advance a conception of unlawfulness that goes

---

39  I. Kant, *The Metaphysical Elements of Justice*; and see G. Fletcher, "The Right and the Reasonable", supra note 7, p. 965; *Rethinking Criminal Law*, supra note 2, pp. 779 ff.

40  See Jescheck, *Lehrbuch des Strafrechts, Allgemeiner Teil* (2nd ed. 1972), p.154.

41  Thus the Germans distinguish between *Gesetz* and *Recht*, the French between *Loi* and *Droit*, the Italians between *Legge* and *Dirrito*, the Russians between *Zakon* and *Pravo*, the Greeks between *Nomos* and *Dikaeon*.

42  K. Binding, 1 *Die Normen und ihre Ubertretung* 135 (1872). Binding's second important contribution to the theory of criminal liability was his analysis of guilt in terms of intention, recklessness and negligence, an approach that was widely adopted by later jurists.

beyond the statutory definition of a criminal offence. This development was, in turn, essential to distinguishing between unlawfulness and guilt and, subsequently, between justification and excuse.

In German legal thinking the theory of justification and excuse emerged from the elaboration of the fundamental distinction between wrongfulness and blameworthiness. Although initially expressed in these general moral terms, this distinction was brought closer to law through a contrast between unlawfulness (*Rechtswidrigkeit*) and guilt (*Schuld*).[43] The latter distinction was first recognised in the domain of private law and was subsequently introduced in criminal law theory.[44] This development is associated with the emergence of the so called "tripartite" system in German criminal law theory. Crime was described as an act which a) meets the statutory definition of an offence (*Tatbestandsmassigkeit*), b) is objectively unlawful (*Rechtswidrig*) and c) can be subjectively attributed to the actor (*Schuldhaft*).[45] From this viewpoint, guilt was described as the subjective or internal relationship between the actor and the prescribed harm and as such it was distinguished from the objective or external unlawfulness of the act. The subjective link between the actor and the harm captured in the notion of guilt pertains to the elements of intention, recklessness and negligence. This interpretation became known as the "*psychological*" theory of guilt.[46] In criticising the tripartite system, some authors have argued that the satisfaction of the formal requirements of a legal provision is but another condition of unlawfulness. These authors have proposed, instead, a twofold approach to criminal liability based solely on the distinction between unlawfulness and guilt.[47]

The clear-cut dichotomy between objective, i.e. pertinent to unlawfulness, and subjective, i.e. pertinent to guilt, aspects of crime

---

[43] Consider, e.g., Achenbach, *Historische und dogmatische Grundlagen der strafrechtssystematischen Schuldlehre* (1974) pp. 19 ff.; Jescheck, supra note 40, pp. 153 ff.

[44] As Jhering first explained, the negation of the subjective blameworthiness of the actor does not necessarily preclude the wrongful act from having certain legal consequences. R. Jhering, *Das Schuldmoment im Romischen Privatrecht* 4 (1867); for a fuller discussion of this matter see A. Eser, "Justification and Excuse" *American Journal of Comparative Law* 24 (1976) 625.

[45] As proposed first by E. Beling in his *Lehre vom Verbrechen* (1906) and elaborated by V. Liszt in his *Lehrbuch des Deutschen Strafrechts* (1919) p. 110 ff.; For an interesting discussion of this approach to criminal liability see G. Fletcher, "The Right Deed for the Wrong Reason: A Reply to Mr Robinson", supra note 11, p. 293.

[46] A. Eser, supra note 44, pp. 626-627.

[47] See e.g. Schmidhauser, *Strafrecht, Allgemeiner Teil*, (2nd ed. 1975), pp. 141 ff. See reference in Eser, supra note 44, p. 627.

was finally set aside in the light of subsequent developments in German criminal theory. Jurists recognised that unlawfulness cannot be adequately canvassed without reference to certain subjective requirements. Thus, knowledge on the part of the actor that his conduct met the objective conditions of lawfulness was seen as a further condition of legal justification. Moreover, it was accepted that the notion of guilt hinges not only on subjective but also on objective considerations. The introduction of an objective element in relation to guilt meant that a claim denying attribution of an unlawful act to an accused was to be assessed also by reference to the question of what could reasonably be expected of a normal person when faced with the circumstances of pressure the accused found himself in. As a result of this development the "psychological" theory of guilt was abandoned in favour of the so called "*normative*" theory of guilt.[48] According to the latter theory, the requirements of guilt are not restricted to intention, recklessness and negligence, but include, in addition, considerations of capacity and control. Lack or substantial impairment of the actor's ability to comply with the law would exclude or mitigate guilt, notwithstanding his acting intentionally, recklessly or negligently. Nevertheless, the tripartite approach to criminal liability, despite the criticisms and further refinements it was subjected to, continued to be regarded as the basis of legal doctrine in German criminal jurisprudence.

James Goldschmidt was the first jurist to offer a convincing analysis of justification and excuse in German criminal law theory. Goldschmidt's theory proceeds from the fundamental distinction between legal norm (*Rechtsnorm*) and norm of responsibility (*Pflichtnorm*).[49] According to him, a formally expressed legal norm, i.e. a statutory provision, is tacitly complemented by a norm of responsibility requiring one to regulate her internal stance so that his actions do not conflict with the legal norm. The distinction between justification and excuse is attuned to that between legal norm and norm of responsibility. Claims of justification dispute the unlawful character of a prima facie infringement of a legal norm; claims of excuse, in contrast, challenge the violation of a norm of responsibility, i.e. the required correspondence between internal attitude and external conduct according to a legal norm. In cases of justification criminal liability is excluded by virtue of what Goldschmidt calls a "*greater objective*

---

48  As elaborated by R. Frank in his *Der Aufbau des Schuldbegriffs* (1907) and *Das Strafgesetzbuch fur das Deutsche Reich* (18th ed. 1931) pp. 136 ff. and J. Goldschmidt in his "Normativer Schuldbegriff" 1 *Festgabe fur R. v. Frank* 428 (1930).

49  J. Goldschmidt, "Der Notstand, ein Schuldproblem", 4 *Osterr. Zeitschrift fur Strafrecht* (1913), pp. 144 ff.

*interest*". In cases of excuse, on the other hand, it is excluded by virtue of an "irresistible subjective motivation". The distinction between justification and excuse, as articulated by Goldschmidt, was subjected to further theoretical elaboration and refinement and is now fully recognised in German criminal law. Thus, under the new German Penal Code, enacted in 1975, self-defence is regarded as a justification.[50] The defence of necessity is treated under two separate headings: necessity as a justification,[51] and necessity as an excuse.[52]

## The Theory of Justification and Excuse as a Basis for the Classification of Criminal Law Defences

The distinction between justification and excuse offers a basic theoretical formula for understanding the way criminal law defences operate. One may seek to explain, on this basis, the demarcation of different defences as well as of different ways in which a legal defence operates or, to put it otherwise, of different pleas treated under the same label. From this viewpoint one may distinguish, for example, between self-defence as a justification and duress as an excuse, as well as between justifying and excusing necessity.[53] Although, at a

---

50 Para 32 (Self-defence) provides: "(1) Whoever commits an act in self-defence does not act unlawfully. (2) Self-defence is that defence which is required in order to prevent a present unlawful attack on oneself or another".

51 Para 34 (Necessity as justification) provides: "Whoever commits an act in order to avert an imminent and otherwise unavoidable danger to life, limb, liberty, honor, property or other legal interest of himself or of another does not act unlawfully if, taking into account all the conflicting interests, especially the legal ones, and the degree of danger involved, the interest protected by him significantly outweighs the interest which he harms. The rule applies only if the act is an appropriate means to avert the danger".

52 Para 35 (Necessity as excuse) provides: "(1) Whoever commits an unlawful act in order to avert an imminent and otherwise unavoidable danger to his own life, limb, or liberty, or to that of a relative or person close to him, acts without guilt...".

53 As Robinson notes, it is possible to recognise "two different categories of defense under the same label at the same time and in the same jurisdiction. A jurisdiction may properly provide a 'self-defense' justification and a 'self-defense' excuse. Such multiple defenses may even occur in the same provision...". He goes on to argue, however, that "when this is done, the potential for misunderstanding and confusion increases significantly", "Criminal Law Defenses: A Systematic Analysis", supra note 6, p. 240. For a further discussion of this problem see M. Gur-Ayre, "Should the Criminal Law Distinguish Between Necessity as a Justification and Necessity as an Excuse?", *Law Quarterly Review* 102 (1986) 71.

theoretical level, the distinction between justification and excuse presents few difficulties, attempts at a general classification of the criminal law defences along these lines come up against a number of problems. These problems have much to do with the fact that, in practice, elements of excuse often appear to overlap with elements of justification. According to Kent Greenawalt

> The difficulty in distinguishing rests on the conceptual fuzziness of the terms 'justification' and 'excuse' in ordinary usage and on the uneasy quality of many of the moral judgments that underlie decisions that behavior should not be treated as criminal. Beyond these conceptual difficulties, there are features of the criminal process, notably the general verdict rendered by lay jurors in criminal trials, that would impede implementation in individual cases of any system that distinguishes between justification and excuse.[54]

Greenawalt argues that there is little room for a systematic classification of criminal law defences on the basis of the justification-excuse distinction in Anglo-American law, although he does not deny the importance of the distinction in elucidating problems of moral and criminal responsibility.

Necessity offers an example of a defence whose rationale may be seen as resting upon both justificatory and excusative considerations. Necessity relates to situations where a person is forced to commit an offence in order to avoid a greater, imminent threat to himself or another. What distinguishes this defence from that of duress is that the danger which compels a person to break the law arises from the circumstances the person finds himself in, rather than from the threats of another human being.[55] Although, in Anglo-American jurisprudence, necessity is traditionally recognised as an excuse,[56] questions of justification may still arise in so far as the person is still regarded as being capable of exercising a degree of choice. Thus, in English law, when an accused pleads necessity the jury are directed to consider these two interrelated questions: a) was the accused compelled to act as he did because he had a good reason to believe that otherwise he or another person would suffer death or grievous bodily harm? and b) if so, would a reasonable person, sharing the relevant characteristics of the accused, have responded to the situation the way the accused

---

54   K. Greenawalt, "The Perplexing Borders of Justification and Excuse", 1984) 84 (*Columbia Law Review* 1897, p. 1898. Consider also "Distinguishing Justifications from Excuses" (1986) 49 *Law and Contemporary Problems* 89. And see Eric Colvin, *Principles of Criminal Law* (1991), pp. 204-205.

55   Hence the defence of necessity is sometimes referred to as "duress of circumstances".

56   See e.g. *Moore v Hussey* (1609) Hob 96.

did? [57] The first of these questions is concerned with the subjective condition of compulsion, and as such it pertains to excuse; the second is concerned with the requirement of proportionality, or the objective appropriateness of the accused's conduct in the circumstances, and as such it relates to justification. The defence may be available only if, from an objective standpoint, the accused can be said to have acted reasonably and proportionately in order to avoid the forms of harm specified, i.e. death and serious bodily injury. A similar position was adopted by the Supreme Court of Canada in *Perka v. The Queen.*[58] In that case it was held that necessity should be recognised as an excuse, as a concession to human frailty, and therefore it implies no vindication of the accused's actions. At the same time, however, it was stated that the defence requires a balancing of harms and that a plea of necessity should fail unless the harm inflicted was less than the harm prevented. According to this interpretation of the necessity defence, the success of the proposed compulsion-based excuse depends upon objective, justificatory considerations.

Similarly, the defence of self-defence, which is traditionally treated as a justification, may also be conceptualised as an excuse if the emphasis is placed on the assumption that a person whose life is under immediate threat is incapable of exercising free choice, i.e. acts morally involuntarily.[59] This interpretation of the defence may also be adopted in cases where force in self-defence is used against an excusable aggressor, e.g. an insane person or a child. In such cases the aggressor's culpability in starting the fight can no longer be said to render the aggressor's rights less worthy of protection. Further, it is recognised that when the defence of self-defence is raised, a mistaken belief as to the existence or intensity of an attack and/or the psychological pressure an accused was experiencing in the circumstances (excuses) are usually taken into account in deciding whether his response was reasonable and therefore justified.[60] What is

---

[57] *Conway* [1988] 3 All ER 1025; *Martin* [1989] 1 All ER 652.

[58] *Perka v The Queen* [1984] 2 SCR 232; 42 CR (3d) 112; (1985) 14 CCC (3d) 385.

[59] For a discussion of the rationale of self-defence see N. Omichinski, "Applying the Theories of Justifiable Homicide to Conflicts in the Doctrine of Self-Defence" (1987) 33 *Wayne Law Review* 1447; G. Fletcher, "The Right to Life" (1979) 13 *Georgia Law Review* 1371; S. Kadish, "Respect for Life and Regard for Rights in the Criminal Law" (1976) 64 *California Law Review* 871; A. Ashworth, "Self-Defence and the Right to Life" (1975) 34 *Cambridge Law Journal* 282; J. Dressler, "New Thoughts about the Concept of Justification in the Criminal Law: A Critique of Fletcher's Thinking and Rethinking", supra note 4, p. 61.

[60] See e.g. Lord Morris' judgment in *Palmer v R* [1971] AC 814.

known as "putative self-defence" offers another example of a defence whose rationale involves an overlap of justificatory and excusative considerations. In English law, when an accused is charged with an offence against the person and pleads self-defence or defence of another, he will be judged in the light of the circumstances as he believed them to be. The accused's belief need only be honest, not reasonable.[61] What this means is that, even if the accused's actions were based on a mistaken assessment of the situation, his response will be deemed justified if the force used was reasonable in the light of that mistaken belief. It is obvious that here an excusing condition, i.e. mistake of fact, becomes an element of self-defence as a justification-based defence. One may argue, however, that in such cases the accused's initial mistake converts the entire defence into an excuse. From this viewpoint it may be said that only where the use of force, as well as the amount of force used, is objectively warranted one may speak of self-defence as a justification.[62] On the other hand, it has been argued that, in moral discourse, the justification of an action is seen as depending not only on its consequences but, more importantly, on the propriety of the reasons for which the action is taken. If the emphasis is placed on this letter element, then we may speak of a person as acting justifiably irrespective of whether his actions, in view of their consequences, are objectively justified or not.[63]

Elements of justification and excuse also appear to overlap in some cases where a mitigating or partial defence is raised. A plea for mitigation may be at issue, for example, where an accused's defence of self-defence has failed on the grounds that the amount of force used was unreasonable or excessive. In such a case the accused may seek to rely on a partial excuse, claiming that under the pressure of the circumstances it was very difficult for him to assess correctly the amount of force needed to stifle the attack; or he may seek to rely on a

---

61   *Williams* (Gladstone) [1987] 3 All ER 411 (CA); *Beckford v R* [1988] AC 130. The traditional approach has been that for self-defence to be accepted in such cases the accused's mistake must be both honest and reasonable. This position was recognised in England prior to the decisions in *Williams* and *Beckford* and is still accepted in other common law jurisdictions. See e.g. the decision of the High Court of Australia in *Zecevic v DPP* (1987) 162 CLR 645; Canadian Criminal Code, ss 27, 34, 35, 37; New Zealand Crimes Act ss 48-49.

62   See, e.g., Fletcher, supra note 2, pp. 762-769; Robinson, "Criminal Law Defenses: A Systematic Analysis", supra note 6, pp. 239-240.

63   See Colvin, *Principles of Criminal Law*, supra note 54, p. 211; Dressler, "New Thoughts about the Concept of Justification in the Criminal Law: A Critique of Fletcher's Thinking and Rethinking", supra note 4, pp. 92 -95; Greenawalt, "The Perplexing Borders of Justification and Excuse", supra note 54, pp. 1922-1925.

partial justification, claiming that the fact that he was defending against an unlawful attack is sufficient to diminish the objective wrongfulness of his response.[64] A similar overlap of excusative and justificatory elements is apparent in relation to the partial defence of provocation. Provocation, when pleaded as a partial defence to murder in English law, is not aimed at complete exoneration but only at the reduction of homicide from murder to manslaughter. Conceptually, the defence is understood to hinge upon two interrelated requirements, namely the wrongful act of provocation and impaired volition or loss of self-control. If the emphasis is placed on the assumption that the accused was acting in response to the victim's wrongdoing, the defence could be regarded as a partial justification. If, on the other hand, the emphasis is placed on the fact that the accused had lost self-control at the time of the killing, the defence would appear to operate as a partial excuse. As J. Dressler comments

> Confusion surrounds the provocation defence. On the one hand, the defence is a concession to human weakness; the requirement that the defendant act in sudden heat of passion finds its roots in excuse theory. On the other hand the wrongful conduct requirement may be, and certainly some decisions based on that element are, justificatory in character. It is likely that some of the confusion surrounding the defence is inherent to the situation, but it is also probably true that English and American courts were insufficiently concerned about the justification-excuse distinctions while the law developed.[65]

The main obstacle to drawing a clear distinction between justifications and excuses is that, in moral discourse, warranted conduct ranges from that which might properly be approved and encouraged through that which might only be accepted to what might be tolerated as a regrettable but unavoidable consequence of the interplay of human nature and circumstance. Anglo-American law has attempted to circumvent these problems of moral shading by avoiding framing legal defences in terms of justification and excuse, placing the emphasis, instead, on the all-embracing requirement of reasonableness.

---

[64] For a fuller discussion of the problem of excessive self-defence see chapter 6 below.

[65] J. Dressler, "Provocation: Partial Justification or Partial Excuse?" *Modern Law Review* 51 (1988) 467, p. 480. And see Dressler, "Rethinking Heat of Passion: A Defence in Search of a Rationale", 73 *Journal of Criminal Law and Criminology* (1982) 421, p. 428.

## Excuse, Justification and the Reasonable Person

The mythical figure of the "reasonable person" maintains a tenacious hold on Anglo-American criminal law doctrine. As Fletcher points out, the law's recourse to the standard permits a continuous infusion of commonly accepted moral values into the law and, as such, constitutes an effort to go beyond the formal sources of the criminal law and to reach for "a higher, enduring, normative plane".[66] This understanding of the "reasonable person" gains support in the light of the ever-increasing tendency towards leaving questions of reasonableness to be determined by the jury, the embodiment of community values and expectations. Nonetheless, one could not easily account for those moral considerations which underpin the "reasonable person", as the basis of a generally applicable test, nor could one prescribe the nature of the disputes to be resolved on such a basis. According to Fletcher, the law's reliance on the "reasonable person" means that heterogeneous criteria of justification and excuse, of wrongfulness and blameworthiness, are subsumed under the same inquiry and this makes it difficult to demarcate between fundamentally different perspectives of liability.

Nevertheless, the role of the "reasonable person" may be interpreted in different ways, depending on the nature of the inquiry within which the relevant standard operates. With regard to inquiries of justification, the "reasonable person" indicates the course of action that should be regarded, in the circumstances, as right or legally permissible. In this respect the "reasonable person" embodies the moral principles that inform and support judgments of legal justification, recognising exceptions to the primary or prohibitory rules of the criminal law. In this context reasonableness defines the required levels of vigilance, prudence and regard for the welfare of others which need to be met for conduct to be considered justified. Thus, in a situation wherein a conflict of values or interests becomes inevitable the actor is called on to act as a reasonable person, that is to preserve the value or interest which is considered as being objectively superior. According to the lesser evil theory of justification, such an act, harmful though it may be, should nonetheless be considered legally acceptable. Further, causing harm in pursuance of a legal right, e.g. the right of self-defence, would not be legally warranted unless the actor observes certain limitations or, one might say, does not act "in abuse" of the right. In this regard the "reasonable person" is referred to as relevant to circumscribing the bounds within which a legal right is regarded as being properly exercised.

---

[66] Fletcher, "The Right and the Reasonable", supra note 7, p. 980.

With regard to inquiries of excuse, on the other hand, the central question is whether the actor is fairly expected to stand up to the pressure of the circumstances and refrain from acting wrongfully. The "reasonable person" provides a yardstick in answering this question. In this context the standard of reasonableness is based on a minimalist conception of ethics. What is excluded from criminal responsibility is conduct that meets common sense expectations as to what degree of pressure ordinary people, concerned for the welfare of others, should be able to stand up to, even though such conduct may be regrettable from an idealistic viewpoint. In the context of excuse theory, the interpretation of the standard is for the most part informed by considerations having to do with what is often referred to as the "realities" or "failings" of human nature. The slide from the notion of "reasonable" to that of "ordinary" or "average" or "normal" person is sometimes suggestive of a shift from justification to excuse, as the latter notions seem more apposite to accommodate the element of human frailty.[67]

Although legal excuses are said to constitute concessions to the failings of human nature because it is assumed that these failings are common to all people, the combination of factors that occasion a person's surrender to pressure, as a manifestation of human frailty, could only be determined by reference to the idiosyncrasies of the particular case. Thus it becomes necessary to endow the "reasonable person" with certain individual characteristics of the accused, i.e. those that are deemed relevant to determining, in an objective way, the degree of pressure to which the actor was subjected. Only on such a basis may it properly be asked whether the accused should fairly be expected to resist the pressure and abstain from breaking the law. Of the characteristics that may bear upon the actor's capacity to withstand the compelling situation, only those for which he cannot be blamed may be taken into account in describing the ambit of the applicable test. The singling out of those individual characteristics that are material to the assessment of the proposed excuse can itself be perceived as a involving an objective moral judgment. In this respect, it seems correct to say that incorporating certain personal characteristics of the actor into the "reasonable person" standard does not in reality undermine the basically objective character of the relevant test.[68] A clear distinction should be drawn, however, between individual peculiarities that may be attributed to the "reasonable person" and peculiarities whose

---

[67] See K. Greenawalt, "The Perplexing Borders of Justification and Excuse", *supra* note 54, pp. 1904-1905.

[68] For a further discussion of the standard of reasonableness see H. Allen, "One Law for All Reasonable Persons?" (1988) 16 *International Journal of Sociology of Law* 419.

presence would render the standard inapplicable. The latter pertain to conditions which are taken to remove the actor from the category of "reasonable" or "normal" people. As was indicated before, these conditions provide the basis for a different class of legal defences revolving around the notion of *abnormality of mind* rather than a general assumption of human frailty.[69]

## Concluding Note

At the heart of the theory of justification and excuse lie questions that have been the focus of moral philosophy for centuries. And the difficulties in categorising legal defences have largely to do with the confusion surrounding the choice of the moral theory upon which the role of legal defences is to be explained and justified. From the viewpoint of consequentialism, conduct is evaluated by reference to its effects. In this respect defences such as necessity and duress bear closer to justifications, for the emphasis is on whether the harm prevented by the relevant conduct outweighs the harm caused. On the other hand, the classification of the same defences as excuses reflects a nonconsequentialist, deontological approach which stresses a person's duty to abstain from performing certain actions that constitute violations of moral standards. For a deontologist, such actions remain wrongful, irrespective of their consequences, and the only way for exculpating the actor would be on the basis of an excuse. As this suggests, the same defence could be regarded as a justification or as an excuse, depending upon the moral viewpoint which one adopts.

Despite the apparent difficulties in formulating a comprehensive system of criminal defences on the basis of the justification-excuse distinction in Anglo-American law, the increased emphasis on the distinction in recent years has enabled courts and legislatures to achieve a greater measure of consistency in the criminal law.[70] The distinction has provided judges with a valuable tool in elucidating problems of criminal responsibility and in interpreting and declaring the law in a way that reflects more accurately community values and expectations.[71] In the work of codification of the criminal law,

---

69  In *Ward* [1956] 1 QB 351 at p. 356 the 'reasonable person' was described as "a person who cannot set up a plea of insanity".

70  For a reply to the critics of the theory of justification and excuse see J. Dressler, "Justifications and Excuses: A Brief Review of the Concepts and the Literature" (1987) 33 *Wayne Law Review* 1155, pp. 1168-1169. And see Stanley M.H. Yeo, *Compulsion in the Criminal Law* (1990), pp. 5 ff.

71  "The theory of justification and excuse provides a jurisprudential thread which runs through all the defences. Subscription to the theory by judges enables

legislatures rely on the distinction as a useful guide towards achieving and maintaining coherence and clarity of definition. The analysis of existing and future defence categories in terms of the justification-excuse distinction is important in bringing the criminal law closer to the community's moral standards and expectations and ensuring a greater degree of comprehension and acceptance of the law.

them to analyse the roots of the defences being compared and thereby to effect a far greater measure of consistency in the law than might be accomplished without the theory", M. Bennun, "Necessity - Yet Another Analysis" (1986) *Irish Jurist* 186, p. 196.

# 2 Excusing Conditions and Criminal Liability

## Introductory

We saw in chapter 1 that an act which meets the external requirements of a criminal offence is deemed nonetheless not unlawful if it falls under a norm of justification. Justifications complement or modify the primary or prohibitory norms of the criminal law by allowing for exceptions in prescribed circumstances. To plead a justification-based defence is to claim both that the act took place in the prescribed situation and that it satisfied the requirements of the related justificatory provision. When an accused pleads self-defence, for example, he claims both that he was confronted with an unjustified attack (the prescribed circumstance), and that his use of force in self-defence was reasonable, i.e. proportionate to the attack (as required by the relevant provision). Excuses, by contrast, do not dispute the wrongfulness and unlawfulness of the act, but call in question the attribution of an unlawful act to the actor. As has been suggested before, one may distinguish between excusing conditions negating a mental state as a prescribed element of an offence definition, and excusing conditions denying or diminishing moral blame as a necessary prerequisite of criminal liability, despite the presence of the requisite state of mind. Cases where breaking the law results from the extraordinary psychological pressure to which the actor was subjected are treated under the latter category of excuses. In such cases the wrongful and unlawful act may be committed with both knowledge of its unlawful character and intention, but culpability is precluded or diminished on the assumption that, in the overwhelming circumstances the actor found himself in, he could not have acted otherwise. In these cases the actor is said to act morally involuntarily. On the other hand, conditions falling under the former category of excuses are understood to negate the necessary volitional or cognitive elements required by offence definitions. In such cases the actor is either unable to exercise control over his bodily movements, i.e. he acts involuntarily, or is unaware of or mistaken about some material fact relating to the nature of his

33

conduct. The defences of automatism and mistake of fact belong to this group of excuses.[1]

The question of excusing in law and morals has been the subject of different philosophical theories of responsibility. These theories attempt to shed light on the nature and function of legal excuses and to justify their role in a criminal justice system. To gain some insight into the rationale of excuse-based defences it is necessary to consider how the role of excuses has been explained from different theoretical standpoints. It is to the most important of these theories that this discussion now turns.

## Criminal Responsibility and Moral Character

Writers in criminal law often emphasise the important relationship between criminal law and what is described as social or common morality. The main difference, it is pointed out, between criminal law and other branches of the law is that criminal law seeks to punish conduct which threatens the system of values upon which society is based. The criminal law, as an institution of blame and punishment, aims not only at protecting individual or collective interests but also at reinforcing society's values by denouncing certain activity as immoral.[2] Criminal sanction expresses society's disapproval of a wrongful act not in the abstract but as reflecting the actor's moral stance with regard to commonly shared moral values and expectations and, as such, it constitutes the strongest formal condemnation that society can inflict on wrongdoers. It is the element of moral stigma that marks out the social significance of criminal liability and punishment and it is precisely this element that requires a clear justification.[3]

The principal claim of the theory under consideration is that when a person is convicted of a crime, society expresses a negative judgment on that person's moral worth. This means that only when the wrongful act reveals a flaw in the actor's character the imposition of criminal

---

1    For a discussion of the legal use of the term "voluntariness" see A. R. White, *Grounds of Liability*, (1985), pp. 57 ff.

2    For an elaborate defence of this view of the criminal law see P. Devlin's *The Enforcement of Morals* (1965). Devlin argues that there is a common or shared morality which ensures the cohesion of society. Any deviation from this common morality poses a threat to society by undermining its cohesion. For this reason, he argues, it may be justifiable and necessary to penalise immoral behaviour.

3    See J. Feinberg, "The Expressive Function of Punishment", in H. Gross and A. von Hirsch (eds), *Sentencing* (1981), pp. 23-36.

punishment may be morally justified.[4] The assumption here is that moral and legal responsibility is primarily concerned with those enduring and interrelated features which make up what we call a person's character, his emotions, values, desires, aversions, ambitions etc. These attributes of character as well as the way they manifest themselves in conduct are the result of a person's prior experience, moral education and critical self-reflection. Actions, the object of praise or blame, are seen as expressions of particular character traits in their authors.[5] But judgments of blame or praise ultimately pertain not to actions as such but to the character traits or attitudes that bring them about. Such an approach to moral and legal responsibility presupposes that persons are in some way responsible for their characters.[6] It is assumed that persons are capable of being aware of and exercising a degree of control over those character traits and dispositions that motivate their rational choices in acting. It is precisely this assumption that makes the attribution of moral and legal responsibility possible. As Arenella points out

A character-based conception of moral agency could be used to explain why moral agents possess the capacity to think, feel, interpret and behave like a

---

4   As N. Lacey remarks "it is unfair to hold people responsible for actions which are out of character...[and] fair to hold them so for actions in which their settled dispositions are centrally expressed", *State Punishment* (1988), p. 68.

5   The character theory of responsibility is often associated with the Scottish philosopher David Hume and his doctrine of the moral sense. According to this doctrine, a form of intuitionism prevalent in eighteenth century British philosophy, the perception of certain actions gives rise to special feelings of pleasure or pain in the observer. These feelings enable him to distinguish right from wrong actions and, at the same time, provide motives to moral conduct. But the object of the moral sense is not so much actions as such but the character reflected in them. As Hume remarked "actions are objects of our moral sentiment, so far only as they are indications of the internal character", *An Inquiry Concerning Human Understanding*, p. 108. And see his *Treatise of Human Nature*, pp. 477, 575. See also A. Smith, *Theory of Moral Sentiments*, p. 153. Smith, like Hume, claimed that people are praised and blaimed for their characters as manifested by their external conduct. For an account of Hume's theory see Michael Bayles, "Hume on Blame and Excuse", *Hume Studies* 2, 1 (1976) 17-35.

6   Aristotle believed that we are responsible for our characters because we are in a way capable of choosing to be the persons we are (*Nichomachean Ethics*, III, 1111b31 - 1112a17). According to a weaker version of this approach, although initially we have no control over the processes through which our characters are formed, we later on develop an ability to maintain or shape our characters through our choices. For a fuller account of this view as it relates to criminal responsibility see Edmund L. Pincoffs, "Legal Responsibility and Moral Character", *Wayne Law Review* 19 (1973) 905-923.

reasonable person...[T]his character model would locate [a person's] moral culpability in his earlier failure to do something about a character defect that clearly could impair his ability to make the right moral choice in certain circumstances. We blame him for not acting like a reasonable person because we believe he is morally responsible for not doing something about those defective aspects of his character that prevent him from acting like one.[7]

As this suggests, the ultimate basis for holding people culpable lies in their failure to do something about those character traits or attitudes that prompt them to engage in morally and legally objectionable conduct.

The various states of mind, such as intention, recklessness or negligence, which the law requires to be proved before an accused is convicted of an offence, are seen as indicating differing attitudes towards societal values or interests. Although attitudes may be short-lived or changing the law relies upon a general hypothesis that certain conduct accompanied by the requisite state of mind manifests a socially undesirable character trait or attitude. Thus, a person who commits an offence intentionally is taken to manifest a clear desire to cause the prescribed harm and, consequently, a strong attitude towards the occurrence of that harm. A person who brings about the prohibited state of affairs recklessly, i.e. with the knowledge that his conduct involves a substantial risk that such state of affairs may occur, displays a less undesirable disposition toward the prescribed harm. He does not desire the harm to occur, but is indifferent as to whether it occurs or not. Depending on the degree to which the relevant harm is likely to eventuate, the person may be said to manifest a more or less undesirable attitude. And the more undesirable the attitude the more blame and, consequently, punishment the person deserves.

From the point of view of the character theory of responsibility, criminal liability and punishment turns on two interrelated requirements, namely just deserts and voluntariness. The requirement of just deserts relates to the assumption that the distinctive feature of criminal punishment is that it expresses moral blame. And, as was said above, moral blame involves something more than the formal disapproval of the wrongful act: it involves also the moral disapproval of the wrongdoer's character as manifested by his commission of an offence. In the words of Professor Fletcher, one of the chief contemporary advocates of this approach to criminal responsibility,

An inference from the wrongful act to the actor's character is· essential to a retributive theory of punishment. A fuller statement of the argument would go like this: (1) punishing wrongful conduct is just only if punishment is measured

---

7    P. Arenella, "Character, Choice and Moral Agency: The Relevance of Character to Our Moral Culpability Judgments", 7 *Social Philosophy and Policy* 59 (1990), reprinted in *Justification and Excuse in the Criminal Law*, M.L. Corrado (ed.), (1994) 241, p. 257.

by the desert of the offender, (2) the desert of an offender is gauged by his character - i.e., the kind of person he is, (3) and therefore, a judgment about character is essential to the just distribution of punishment.[8]

According to Fletcher, we blame a person who committed a wrongful act only if the act reveals what sort of person the actor is, that is, only if we can infer from the commission of a wrongful act that the actor's character is flawed.[9] From this point of view the chief aim of criminal punishment is retribution: inflicting pain on offenders who are morally blameworthy.[10] Some retributivists offer purely deontological justifications for requiring a connection between just deserts and punishment. By adopting Kant's categorical imperative that a moral agent must be treated as an end in himself, not as a means to an end, they argue that it is "right" to give people what they deserve, irrespective of the desirable or otherwise consequences for society that such a practice may entail, because this is what justice demands.[11] Others have adopted a comparative notion of desert, which links punishment with justice in the distribution of benefits and burdens in society.[12] But if, according to the character theory, it is character traits rather than acts that are the focus of just deserts, what is wrong with punishing people directly for bad character? As Fletcher explains

[T]he limitation of the inquiry to a single wrongful act follows not from the theory of desert, but from the principle of legality. We accept the artificiality of inferring character from a single deed as the price of maintaining the suspect's

---

8    G. Fletcher, *Rethinking Criminal Law* (1978), p. 800.

9    A similar approach is adopted by Joel Feinberg, *Doing and Deserving* (1970), p. 126. See also J. Glover, *Responsibility* (1974); M. Bayles, "Character, Purpose and Criminal Responsibility", *Law and Philosophy* 1 (1982) pp. 5-20.

10   For a discussion of contemporary approaches to retributive punishment and the notion of just deserts see Ted Honderich, *Punishment, The Supposed Justifications* (1984), Postscript; and see C. L. Ten, *Crime, Guilt and Punishment* (1987), pp. 38 ff.; H. A. Bedau, "Retribution and the Theory of Punishment", *The Journal of Philosophy* 75 (1978), 601-20; J. Cottingham, "Varieties of Retribution", *The Philosophical Quarterly* 29 (1979), 238-46; J. Finnis, "The Restoration of Retribution", *Analysis* 32 (1971-72), 131-5; D.J. Galligan, "The Return to Retribution in Penal Theory" in C. Tapper (ed.), *Crime, Proof and Punishment* (London 1981), pp.144-71.

11   See, e.g., John Kleining, *Punishment and Desert* (The Hague 1973), p. 67. See also L.H. Davies, "They Deserve to Suffer", *Analysis* 32 (1971-72), pp. 136-40.

12   See, e.g., Herbert Morris, "Persons and Punishment" in Jeffrie G. Murphy (ed.) *Punishment and Rehabilitation* (Belmont, 1973); D.J. Galligan, "The Return to Retribution in Penal Theory", supra note 10, esp. pp. 154-7.

privacy...Disciplining the inquiry in this way...secures the individual against a free-ranging enquiry of the state into his moral worth.[13]

The character theory of criminal responsibility makes just deserts dependent upon the requirement of voluntariness. In this context the notion of voluntariness is understood as being wide enough to encompass all cases in which a person is said to be in control of and therefore morally responsible for his or her actions. As has been indicated before, the concept of voluntariness may be interpreted to denote either the actor's ability to control his external conduct — i.e. to act in a strict sense — or the actor's capacity to determine freely the course of his action — i.e. to give effect to his choice of action. In the former sense voluntariness refers to intentional action as a necessary prerequisite for ascribing what may be called *authorship-responsibility*; in the latter sense voluntariness pertains to action which is both intentional and free as required for the attribution of moral responsibility. It is moral responsibility as presupposing *authorship-responsibility* that the notion of voluntariness should be understood as being referring to here.

Criminal responsibility, as involving just deserts, hinges on the requirement of voluntariness simply because only voluntary action can warrant the inference from a wrongful act that the actor's character is flawed. The requirement of voluntariness indicates that a person cannot be convicted and punished of an offence unless he was capable of exercising control of his conduct. In this respect excusing conditions, by negating voluntariness, block the normal inference from a wrongful act to a flawed or defective character and hence preclude the attribution of moral blame as a necessary prerequisite of criminal responsibility. Excuses, in other words, negate moral and legal responsibility for prima facie wrongful actions which are not expressive of undesirable character traits. For example, an accused who, acting under a reasonable mistake of fact, brought about a prohibited harm cannot be said to have manifested, through his action, an undesirable character trait and therefore he cannot be held morally and legally responsible for the harm caused.[14] If, however, the accused's mistake was

---

13   Supra note 8, pp. 800-801. And as Dworkin notes "The government may restrain a man  for his own or the general good, but it may do so only on the basis of his behaviour, and it must strive to judge his behaviour from the same standpoint  as he judges himself, that is, from the standpoint of his intentions, motives, and capacities", *Taking Rights Seriously* (1977), p. 11.

14   As Fletcher remarks, "mistaken beliefs are relevant to what the actor is trying to do if they affect his incentive in acting. They affect his incentive if knowing of the mistake would give him a good reason for changing his course of conduct", Supra note 8, p. 161.

unreasonable, he may be found guilty of a negligence-based offence. In such a case, the accused's failure to realise that his conduct involved a substantial and unjustifiable risk of harm in a situation where he should have realised it can be said to indicate an undesirable character trait and therefore a degree of blame is appropriate. Here the accused's failure to conform to a prescribed standard of care reflects a socially undesirable attitude, namely indifference to the welfare of others. A person who commits an offence intentionally, but only because he is compelled to do so by threats or other forms of coercion which he cannot reasonably be expected to avoid or resist, does not display a defect of character as required for the attribution of moral and legal responsibility (such a person, as indicated earlier, acts morally involuntarily). However, if the person is found to have caused, through his own fault, the conditions of coercion or lack of self-control under which the offence was committed, his excuse might perhaps reduce but will not negate culpability for the offence. In such a case, the person's causing or failing to prevent the incapacitating condition is seen as reflecting an defect in that person's character.

The character theory of criminal responsibility also provides a basis for understanding the role of partial excuses in the criminal law. A person who kills another under provocation does not deserve to be branded as a murderer, for the fact that he had lost his normal self-control capacities, as any reasonable person would when faced with similar provocation, precludes the normal inference from the act of killing of a character flaw grave enough to justify a conviction of murder. Nevertheless, the accused is still culpable to a lesser degree for allowing his anger at the provoker to fester to the point that it unduly interfered with his capacity to exercise self-control. The accused's criminal liability for manslaughter, in such cases, is based on the assumption that, by allowing himself to be carried away by passion and kill, the accused has displayed a defect of character .

The character theory of criminal responsibility has been criticised on the grounds that it builds upon an incomplete view of the criminal law.[15] Modern criminal law, it is argued, is not concerned only with what is seen as immoral conduct expressive of bad character. There is an increasing number of criminal offences in which the element of moral stigma is absent or hardly distinguishable. With regard to these

---

[15] For a fuller account of the criticisms against the character theory see e.g. Hyman Gross, *A Theory of Criminal Justice* (1979), esp. pp. 340, 386; Michael Moore, "Choice, Character and Excuse", 7 *Social Philosophy and Policy* 59 (1990), reprinted in *Justification and Excuse in the Criminal Law*, M. L. Corrado (ed), (1994), p. 197; Alan Brudner, "A Theory of Necessity" 7 *OJLS* (1987) 339, pp. 344 - 52; And see J. Horder *Provocation and Responsibility* (1992), pp. 131-134.

offences criminal liability is imposed merely as a practical means of regulating or controlling certain social activity. The moral blame, which normally accompanies the more serious crimes (*mala in se*) is almost absent in what is referred to as "regulatory" offences (*mala prohibita*).[16] As far as the latter offences are concerned, moral blame — the inference from a wrongful act to a flawed character — cannot provide the test for criminal liability. These offences therefore fall outside the scope of the present theory of criminal responsibility.

Another problem which the theory faces, according to some critics, is that the bounds of what is referred to as common or social morality, in the light of which conduct is assessed as immoral and hence as possibly illegal (for, of course, not all rules of social morality are subject to enforcement by the criminal law), is sometimes very difficult to circumscribe. It has been argued that common morality can be defined and measured according to the strength of the feelings of ordinary people. So, if certain conduct gives rise to feelings of intolerance or indignation among ordinary members of society, this would be a sufficient indication that the conduct in question threatens common morality — and as such it may be criminalized. According to Devlin common morality could be discovered by assembling a group of ordinary citizens — in the form of a jury — and asking them to consider how certain forms of conduct should be classified.[17] But, as Devlin's critics have remarked, the feelings of ordinary people may not be moral in nature but, rather, an expression of prejudice. Devlin's proposed method of discovering common morality — resorting to a jury made up of ordinary members of the community — besides the fact that it does not preclude prejudice, it may also fail to lead to agreement on a number of morally disputed issues in society such as, for example, abortion or euthanasia.[18] With regard to criminal offences based on conduct whose moral basis remains in question, it seems difficult to say that criminal liability is imposed only because the relevant conduct reflects a flaw in the actor's character, or because we

---

16   Merely regulatory offences are considered, for example, the illegal parking of a motor vehicle, or the riding of a bicycle without lights. In common law jurisdictions the large majority of these offences fall in the categories of strict and absolute liability offences, i.e. offences requiring a minimal only degree of fault or even no fault at all on the person's part.

17   P. Devlin, *The Enforcement of Morals* (1965), pp. 22-23.

18   For an evaluation of Devlin's views see e.g.: Williams "Authoritarian Morals and Criminal Law" [1966] *Criminal Law Review* 132; R. Dworkin "Lord Devlin and the Enforcement of Morals" (1966) 75 *Yale Law Journal* 986; G.B. Hughes "Morals and the Criminal Law" (1962) 71 *Yale Law Journal* 662. See also R. E. Sartorius "The Enforcement of Morality" (1972) 81 *Yale Law Journal* 891.

disapprove of the actor as an unworthy person. Indeed, the opposite may be the case if most members of society agree that certain conduct should no longer be considered immoral and must therefore be decriminalised. On the other hand, even where there is agreement as to the immorality of certain conduct, one cannot infer from a single instance of such conduct that the actor's character is flawed. Legal blame is sometimes imposed on persons with good characters who, at a moment of weakness, have made a conscious but uncharacteristic choice to break the law. Although the commission of a criminal offence may be "out of character" for the offender, this does not preclude criminal liability and punishment from being imposed. And, conversely, even though an act may be expressive of a bad character, this does not necessary entail that the actor should be punished.

It may be true that legal punishment, as a particular type of social response, is not always imposed for morally blameworthy conduct. But criminalisation rests upon the application of the harm principle. According to that principle, only conduct that causes or is likely to cause societal harm should be criminalised.[19] It is on the basis of the harm principle that certain forms of conduct are prescribed as criminal offences. But the character theory is not concerned with the issue of criminalisation (or decriminalisation) as such. Rather, the character theory is concerned with the quite separate question of whether a person who has caused one of the prescribed harms should be punished as a criminal or not. Its primary aim is to provide a basis for dealing with the question of culpability in the application of the criminal law in a way that accords with our common conceptions of justice and fairness. In dealing with this question, the character theory relies on the assumption that every harmful action is expressive of an undesirable character trait, irrespective of whether such action is "in" or "out" of character for the offender.[20] Thus, if a person of previously impeccable character suddenly and unexpectedly gives in to an impulse to steal someone else's umbrella, his generally good

---

19   For a fuller discussion of the harm principle see J. Raz, *The Morality of Freedom* (Oxford 1986), esp. Ch. 15.

20   As Joel Feinberg explains, "When we say that a man is at fault, we usually mean only to refer to occurrent defects of acts or omissions, and only derivatively to the actor's flaw as the doer of the defective deed. Such judgments are at best presumptive evidence about the man's general character. An act can be faulty even when not characteristic of the actor, and the actor may be properly "to blame" for it anyway; for if the action is faulty and it is also *his* action ( characteristic or not ), then he must answer for it. The faultiness of an action always reflects some discredit upon its doer, providing the doing is voluntary", "Sua Culpa" in *Doing and Deserving*, supra note 9, p. 192.

character will be irrelevant as far as that person's criminal liability for stealing is concerned.[21] As the character theory is concerned with bad character only to the extent that it is reflected in harmful actions, it is a mistake to think that, from this point of view, criminal punishment is imposed for bad character as such.[22] No matter our differences as to what constitutes immoral and therefore socially undesirable behaviour, as regards the majority of criminal offences, moral blameworthiness remains a necessary (although not sufficient) condition for justifiable punishment. With regard to these offences, therefore, the character-based theory is both plausible and compatible with current criminal law doctrine.

## The Motivational Theory: a Utilitarian Approach to the Character Conception of Criminal Responsibility

Contemporary utilitarian philosophers have proposed an approach to legal responsibility that has attracted considerable attention in recent years.[23] An essential feature of the utilitarian theory is its consequentialism, the idea that human institutions are to be evaluated in the light of the beneficial or otherwise consequences they produce or are likely to produce in the future for society. The theory is a version of what is known as "rule utilitarianism" which focuses upon the consequences of observing certain rules or of maintaining certain social institutions, rather than on the consequences of particular acts.[24]

---

21  Nevertheless, depending on the seriousness of the offence committed, previously good character is usually considered as a factor in mitigation of the sentence imposed for the offence.

22  As Horder points out, "the character conception of culpability is parasitic on (a version of ) the harm principle. It is therefore also focused on actions, the harmful actions proscribed under the harm principle. This naturally and properly limits the aspects of character that will be relevant to culpability", supra note 15, p. 133.

23  See e.g. R. Brandt, "A Motivational Theory of Excuses in the Criminal Law", *Criminal Justice* Nomos XXVII (1985), reprinted in *Justification and Excuse in the Criminal Law*, M. L. Corrado (ed.), (1994), p.95.; "A Utilitarian Theory of Excuses", *Philosophical Review* 78 (1969) 337; *Ethical Theory* (1959); P. H. Nowell- Smith, "On Sanctioning Excuses", *The Journal of Philosophy* 67 (1970) 609.

24  In general, the theory referred to as "Act Utilitarianism" is based on the idea that the rightness or wrongness of an action is to be assessed by reference to the bad or good consequences of the action itself. "Rule Utilitarianism", on the other hand, claims that the rightness or wrongness of an action must be determined by reference to the goodness or badness of the consequences of the

Drawing upon the concept of general welfare, utilitarians call for the design and evaluation of social institutions in general, and the criminal law and justice systems in particular, on the basis of the principle of maximum efficiency. The principle postulates that when it comes to choosing between different policies or institutional arrangements preference should be given to those which are likely to promote higher levels of net aggregate benefits for society.[25] From this point of view, the utilitarians argue that the design and evaluation of the criminal justice system should be guided by the purpose which this institution serves in society, namely the reduction of the incidence of socially harmful conduct.

By contrast with the character theory of responsibility, the utilitarian theory does not view moral culpability as a necessary prerequisite for criminal liability and punishment. After all not all criminal offences involve the doing of a morally objectionable act. Many utilitarians regard the retributivists' idea of just deserts as nothing more than a social utility requirement in disguise.[26] From this point of view, the so called "moral stigma" which a conviction for a criminal offence entails is considered relevant to promoting general deterrence, the main objective of the system, and therefore is seen as serving an important purpose. Moreover, limiting criminal responsibility only to those who are morally to blame for their conduct reassures the law-abiding citizens that their choices are respected. Imposing criminal punishment to persons who, in the eyes of the public, do not deserve to be branded as criminals undermines people's trust in the system and consequently the system's deterrent efficacy.

According to utilitarians, the criminal law and justice systems would be open to criticism if they accomplish their objective — the prevention of socially harmful behaviour — at too great a cost. Criminal punishment, as involving harm, detracts from general welfare and, as such, its imposition may be justified only if the benefits it produces outweigh its costs and only if there are no other methods or institutional arrangements that could produce the same results at a

---

rule which requires that everyone should perform that action under similar circumstances.

25  As Brandt remarks, "[informed rational persons] would prefer a legal/moral system the currency of which in the society would maximize general benefit - general happiness, if you like. In other words, a rule-utilitarian system", "A Motivational Theory of Excuses in the Criminal Law", supra note 23, p. 100.

26  See, e.g., Louis M. Seidman, "Soldiers, Martyrs, and Criminals: Utilitarian Theory and the Problem of Crime Control", 94 *Yale Law Journal* 2 (Dec. 1984) 315-49.

lesser cost.[27] One way to ensure that the criminal law system meets this requirement is to recognise, as part of the system, a set of legal excuses because "a correct system of excuses would tend to exempt from punishment those cases in which the usefulness of punishment is likely to be outweighed by the advantages of not punishing".[28] Thus, for the utilitarian, recognising legal excuses is another requirement of a criminal law system concerned with the maximisation of general welfare, not with the punishment of wrongdoers as such. But how do utilitarians explain the role of excuses in such a system?

For the utilitarian the criminal law is, above anything else, an instrument of social education. And the chief aim of social education is the cultivation of motivation in people to avoid being engaged in conduct that causes or is likely to cause societal harm. As to the level of motivation required, this need not be higher than that which would allow a reasonable person of ordinary firmness to subdue every possible contrary motivation or impulse in given circumstances. From this viewpoint it is argued that when a person commits an offence this is an indication that person's motivation is in a sense defective. When speaking of defects in motivation here we mean "those stated or implied by the prohibitions (in statutes or precedents) of a given legal system...".[29] Only where a failure in motivation can be inferred from the commission of an offence the imposition of criminal punishment can be justified. As Brandt notes

a rational and informed person, if he were to be given a choice among possible systems of criminal justice for the society in which he expects to live, would

---

27 According to Bentham, the imposition of punishment is inappropriate in the following cases: a) when it is unfounded, i.e. when the act for which it is imposed caused no harm, or when the harm it caused was less than the harm it prevented; b) when it is ineffective, i.e. when it will contribute nothing to the prevention of harm; c) when it is unprofitable, i.e. when the harm which the punishment entails is greater than the harm which it aims at preventing; d) when it is unnecessary, i.e. when it is not the most economical way of preventing the relevant harm-causing conduct, *Introduction to the Principles of Morals and Legislation*, J. H. Burns and H.L.A. Hart (eds) (London 1982) 173-175. For a general account of the utilitarian theory of punishment see C.L. Ten, *Crime, Guilt , and Punishment*, supra note 9, pp.7 ff.; D. Lyons, *Forms and Limits of Utilitarianism* (Oxford 1965); M. Bayles (ed.),*Contemporary Utilitarianism* (New York 1968).

28 P.H. Nowell-Smith, supra note 23, p.611.

29 Brandt, "A Motivational Theory of Excuses in the Criminal Law", supra note 23 , p. 104. Brandt notes, further, that "the law may be bad law, in which case the 'defects' will not really be defects from any point of view other than that of bad law. The law is always subject to improvement from the standpoint of reflective morality" (idem).

opt for a system exempting from punishment those persons who have committed an unjustified unlawful act, but did not thereby manifest any defect of standing motivation or character.[30]

The theory is supplemented by the principle of proportionality which requires that the severity of punishment for a offence should be proportionate to the gravity of the motivational flaw manifested by the criminal act. Thus, if a person causes harm intentionally, his act reflects a defect of motivation that is more grave than that manifested by one who causes the same harm recklessly or negligently.[31] As this suggests, the law's reliance on the concept of *mens rea* — as expressing the different mental states required by offence definitions — strengthens the warrant for inferring from an unlawful act a defect of standing motivation or character.[32]

According to the motivational theory, criminal liability and punishment rest upon the requirement of voluntariness. A person acting involuntarily is exempted from criminal liability and punishment because such a person manifests no failure of motivation and therefore criminal punishment is no longer needed to bring that person's motivation up to standard. The normal inference from a prima facie unlawful act that the actor's motivation is faulty is blocked when the actor, due to the presence of an excusing condition, cannot be said to have acted voluntarily. From this point of view, criminal liability presupposes answering these two questions: (1) did the accused cause a legally prescribed harm by failing to act as any reasonable person with normal capacities would, in the circumstances, have acted? (2) could the accused, given his state of mind and physical capacities have avoided causing such harm? Answering these questions presupposes commonsense familiarity with the way ordinary people are expected to act in certain situations, although some reference to the accused's individual characteristics and state of mind is necessary.

Thus, from the point of view of the motivational theory, a person who commits an offence acting under a reasonable mistake of fact, i.e. a mistake that could not, in the circumstances, have been avoided, is legally excused because, in such a case, no defect of motivation can be inferred. On the other hand, if the person's mistaken belief is unreasonable, i.e. avoidable, he or she may be found guilty of a

---

30  Ibid, p. 124-125.

31  According to Brandt, "[T]he movement of the law from motive to intent may be more verbal than real, since a person's intent reflects his motivation", ibid, p. 98.

32  On the issue of character and character traits see Brandt, "Traits of Character: A Conceptual Analysis", 7 *American Philosophical Quarterly*, No 1 (Jan. 1970) 23-37.

negligence-based offence, for such a mistake can be said to manifest a defect of motivation, i.e. indifference to a legally warranted societal value or interest. When an accused raises the defence of duress, he admits that he brought about the *actus reus* of an offence with the requisite intent, but claims that he did so only because his will had been overcome by the wrongful threats of another. The success of the accused's excuse depends on both the nature of the offence he was forced to commit and the seriousness of the harm threatened. It is on the basis of these considerations that the question of whether the accused's act manifests a defective level of motivation is answered. In the light of the present definition of duress in English law, only where the actor is faced with an immediate and unavoidable threat of death or grievous bodily harm, i.e. a threat that any person of reasonable firmness would be unable to resist, and only if the offence committed does not involve the taking of human life, the unlawful act cannot be said to manifest  a defect of motivation or fault on the actor's part.[33] Further, it is recognised that if the accused, through his own fault, exposed himself to the risk of coercion, he cannot rely on the defence. A plea of excuse on these grounds will not be accepted, for example, if the accused had voluntarily joined a group of criminals engaged in violent acts being aware of the risk that they might bring pressure on him to commit an offence. In this situation, an inference of defective motivation at the time of joining the criminal organisation would justify the imposition of criminal liability and punishment.[34] The partial defence of provocation may also be explained on this basis. As was mentioned earlier, provocation, when pleaded as a partial defence, is aimed at reducing the level of the offence from murder to manslaughter. The basis of the defence is that at the time of the killing, the accused, as a result of the provocation, was so disturbed by anger, that he was unable to exercise self-control. If the provocation was such that could have had the same effect on any ordinary person, the accused is liable to lesser punishment, for the degree of fault inferred from the act of killing in such a case is substantially less than that usually required for murder.[35]

---

[33]   See, e.g., *Howe* [1987] 1 AC 417; *Graham* (1982) 74 Cr App R 235; *Abbott v The Queen*  [1976] 3 All ER 140; *Lynch* [1975] AC 653; *Hudson and Taylor* [1971] 2 QB 202. See also the American Model Penal Code (2.09).

[34]   See, e.g., *Sharp* [1987] 1 QB 853; *Shepherd*  (1988) 86 Cr App R 47. And see New Zealand Crimes Act 1961, s. 24.

[35]   According to Brandt, "[The law of provocation] is best read as suggesting that the standing motivation of the provoked man is not so very far from that of the ordinary man (but surely he is a difficult person with a hot temper!), and hence, combined with a theory of proportionality, that his punishment should be

The utilitarian theory of criminal responsibility has been subjected to the general criticism that it does not preclude, in principle, the punishment of excusable offenders. In so far as the emphasis is placed on general deterrence, as the chief aim of criminal punishment, it does not follow from the fact that the *threatened* punishment of excusable offenders cannot deter *them* from breaking the law that the *actual* punishment of these offenders will not deter *others*. As Hart and other critics have pointed out, it is possible that, in some cases at least, the benefits to be gained for general deterrence from the punishment of excusable offenders may outweigh its costs.[36] In defending their position against this criticism some utilitarians have argued that speaking of punishing an excusable and therefore innocent person involves a logical contradiction because, by its very definition, punishment presupposes guilt.[37] But their main argument has been that, on balance, the costs of punishing excusable offenders could outweigh any increase in general deterrence that is likely to result for such a practice, when it becomes known, will undermine people's confidence in the legal system as a whole.[38]

It is submitted that although the utilitarian theory of excuses reaches the right conclusion it does so for the wrong reasons. For if it is wrong to punish excusable persons, it is not merely because it would be counterproductive to do so but because of the injustice done to an innocent person. A person is not a cog within a social machine, whose conduct is subject to manipulation by others, but is capable of self-control. And someone capable of self-control is held to be responsible for his choices, as a manifestation of his character, and therefore subject to blame or praise for his actions. Criminal liability and punishment cannot be justified only on the basis of a utilitarian "cost-benefit analysis", that is without any reference to just deserts and the other principles of retributive justice.[39]

---

less", "A Motivational Theory of Excuses in the Criminal Law", supra note 23, p. 114.

[36] See Hart, *Punishment and Responsibility* (1968) esp. pp. 72-83; G. Fletcher, supra note 8, p. 813.; H. J. McCloskey, "A Non-Utilitarian Approach to Punishment" in M. Bayles (ed.) *Contemporary Utilitarianism* (1968).

[37] See, e.g., Antony Quinton "On Punishment" in H. B. Acton (ed.) *The Philosophy of Punishment* (1969).

[38] See R. Brandt, *Ethical Theory* (1959), p. 492. And see T.L.S. Sprigge, "A Utilitarian Reply to Dr McCloskey" in Michael (ed.), *Contemporary Utilitarianism* (1968), pp. 278-82.

[39] For an illuminating analysis of the interconnection between desert and social utility see Joel Feinberg, "Justice and Personal Desert" in *Doing and Deserving*, supra note 9, pp. 55 ff.

## Choice, Fairness and Criminal Responsibility: H.L.A. Hart's Theory

In his writings on criminal law Professor Hart has elaborated a theory of criminal responsibility that has received wide recognition in common law jurisdictions.[40]   The starting-point of Hart's theory (sometimes referred to as the "choice" theory) is the position that the general justifying aim of the institution of punishment is the utilitarian one of general deterrence — the prevention of socially harmful conduct. This should be distinguished, however, from the principles of justice applying to the distribution of punishment.[41] Justice in the distribution of punishment requires that the application of punishment should be restricted to those who could have avoided  breaking the law.[42] Although Hart rejects retribution as the general aim of punishment, he considers it to be relevant to the distribution of punishment (hence he often speaks of "retribution in the distribution" of punishment).[43]

According to Hart, the principles applying to the distribution of punishment represent values that are, to some extent, independent of general deterrence as the justifying aim of the institution of punishment. The chief function of these principles is to ensure that justice or fairness to the individual citizen is not sacrificed in the pursuit of utilitarian aims — such as general deterrence. And it is against justice to use individuals as a mere means for achieving certain social aims, no matter how important the latter may be, unless they

---

40   Hart's theory of criminal responsibility and punishment is contained in a series of essays published together under the title *Punishment and Responsibility: Essays in the Philosophy of Law* (1968). And see R. Wasserstrom, "H.L.A. Hart and the Doctrines of *Mens Rea* and Criminal Responsibility", *The University of Chicago Law Review*, 35 (1967) 92.

41   Hart distinguishes between the following three questions: a) What is the justification of the institution of punishment? b) Who may be subjected to criminal punishment? c) How severe should the punishment of an offender be? Only the first of these questions has to do with the general justifying aim of punishment - according to Hart, this is general deterrence, or the prevention of socially harmful conduct. The second and third questions pertain to the distribution of punishment.

42   A similar position  is reflected in Kant's famous dictum "ought implies can", although, unlike Hart, Kant places the  emphasis on retribution rather than deterrence as the general justification of punishment.

43   For a discussion of Hart's theory of punishment see J. Finnis, "Old and New in Hart's Philosophy of Punishment", *The Oxford Review* 8 (1968), 73-80.

have the capacity and fair opportunity to comply with the law.[44] From Hart's point of view, just punishment presupposes striking a balance between the pursuit of general deterrence and the need to protect the individual from being used as a means to achieving general social goals.[45] He recognises, however, that in certain exceptional cases the principle of fairness to the individual may be overridden by the need to promote or safeguard an important societal interest. He points out, nonetheless, that when we think it right to set aside the constraints laid down by the requirement of fairness to the individual "we should do so with the sense of sacrificing an important principle. We should be conscious of choosing the lesser of two evils, and this would be inexplicable if the principle sacrificed to utility were itself only a requirement of utility."[46]

Hart views criminal responsibility as being dependent upon two interrelated requirements, namely fairness to the individual and voluntariness. The basis of his understanding of fairness to the individual is a conception of society as a form of voluntary co-operation for mutual advantage among free and equal individuals. All members of society have a right to mutual forbearance from certain kinds of harmful behaviour. Society warrants that right by offering individuals

> the protection of the laws on terms which are fair, because they not only consist of a framework of reciprocal rights and duties, but because within this framework each individual is given a fair opportunity to choose between keeping the law required for society's protection or paying the penalty. From this point of view the actual punishment of a criminal appears not merely as something useful to society (General Aim) but as justly extracted from the criminal who has voluntarily done harm; from the second it appears as a price justly extracted because the criminal had a fair opportunity beforehand to avoid liability to pay.[47]

Within such a framework, Hart maintains, individual freedom is guaranteed and the citizen's life is protected from excessive interference on the part of state officials, for punishment may be imposed only for failures to comply with the fair demands of society.

---

[44] *Punishment and Responsibility*, pp. 22-23, 181-83, 201. A similar position is adopted by Hyman Gross in *A Theory of Criminal Justice* (1979), p. 137.

[45] It is precisely the application of these principles of justice, especially the one requiring that only those who break the law voluntarily should be punished, that distinguishes punishment from other measures, e.g. the compulsory isolation of people infected with certain contagious diseases, in which these principles do not apply.

[46] *Punishment and Responsibility*, p.12.

[47] Ibid at pp. 22-23.

And only failures to conform to the demands of the law that are the outcome of a free choice warrant society's interference into a person's life. As Hart puts it, society needs a "moral licence" to punish, and this presupposes that those charged with offences have had the capacity and fair opportunity to comply with the law. In Hart's words

> One necessary condition of the just application of a punishment is normally expressed by saying that the agent "could have helped" doing what he did, and hence the need to inquire into the "inner facts" is dictated not by the moral principle that only the doing of an immoral act may be legally punished, but by the moral principle that no one should be punished who could not help doing what he did. This is a necessary condition...for the moral propriety of legal punishment and no doubt also for moral censure; in this respect law and morals are similar. But this similarity as to the one essential condition that there must be a "voluntary" action if legal punishment or moral censure is to be morally permissible does not mean that legal punishment is morally permissible only where the agent has done something morally wrong.[48]

As this suggests, the moral principles of justice that apply to the distribution of punishment are independent of the moral or not character of the unlawful act at stake or the morality or immorality of the particular legal provision under which punishment is imposed.[49] If a morally evil law is applied even to those who have not broken it voluntarily, this is seen as an added wrong inflicted by the law.

According to Hart, it is the moral principle of fairness to the individual that requires making criminal liability and punishment conditional on the requirement of voluntariness (as a prerequisite of a free choice).[50] The chief claim of the theory is that an accused should be excused for committing an offence if, at the time he did so, he did not have the capacity or opportunity to choose to do otherwise. Where, under the circumstances, the exercise of choice was very difficult, even though not impossible, an accused may be able to rely on a mitigating excuse, i.e. an excuse that will only reduce, although not totally negate, culpability. But this is as far as the theory goes. For Hart one does not need to go beyond the issue of choice and into the question of whether one's choices manifest a fault in the actor's character. It is

---

48   Ibid, pp. 39-40; see also Hart, *The Concept of Law* (Oxford 1961), p. 173.

49   See also Hart, *The Concept of Law*, p. 173; H. Morris, "Persons and Punishment" in J.G. Murphy (ed.), *Punishment and Rehabilitation* (Belmont 1973), pp. 40-64.

50   For, as Hart explains, "...even if things go wrong, as they do when mistakes are made or accidents occur, a man whose choices are right and who has done his best to keep the law will not suffer", *Punishment and Responsibility*, p.182. Note, however, that here "right choice" means choosing to act in accordance with the law.

argued that, while a choice always evidences the possession of a will, it is not necessarily representative of the actor's character as a whole. Thus, a wrongful act may render the actor morally and legally responsible if it is the result of a free choice, even though such an act may be "out of character" for the offender.

Under the choice theory, a person can rely on an excuse where his conduct has not been caused, wholly or partly, by his choice but by factors over which he has had no control.[51] In Hart's words

> What is crucial is that those whom we punish should have had, when they acted, the normal capacities, physical and mental, for abstaining from what it [the law] forbids, and a fair opportunity to exercise these capacities. Where these capacities and opportunities are absent, as they are in different ways in the varied cases of accident, mistake, paralysis, reflex action, coercion, insanity, etc., the moral protest is that it is morally wrong to punish because 'he could not have helped it', or 'he could not have done otherwise' or 'he had no real choice'.[52]

Consider the defence of necessity, for example. Necessity, as currently defined in English law, pertains to situations in which a person commits an offence in order to avoid an imminent threat of death or serious bodily harm.[53] Unlike duress, in which the danger to one's life comes from another human being, in necessity the danger arises from the circumstances in which the person or persons are placed. When the defence of necessity is raised the jury are required to consider the following questions: (a) was the accused compelled to act as he did because he had a good reason to fear (in view of the circumstances as he believed them to be) that otherwise death or serious injury would result? (b) if so, would a reasonable person of ordinary firmness, sharing the characteristics of the accused, have responded to the situation as the accused did?[54] From the point of view of the choice theory of responsibility a plea of necessity may be interpreted in two interrelated ways. Firstly, it may be said that, being faced with an imminent threat to his life or limb, the accused was so overwhelmed by

---

51  A similar approach was adopted by William Blackstone in his *Commentaries on the Laws of England* (1769). Blackstone remarked that "[A]ll the several pleas and excuses, which protect the committer of a forbidden act from the punishment which is otherwise annexed thereto, may be reduced to this single consideration, the want or defect of *will*. An involuntary act, as it has no claim to merit, so neither can it induce any guilt: the concurrence of the will, when it has its choice either to do or to avoid the fact in question, being the only thing that renders human actions either praiseworthy or culpable" (pp. 20-21).

52  *Punishment and Responsibility*, p.152.

53  See, e.g., *Howe* [1987] AC 417;*Conway* [1988] 3 All ER 1025; *Martin* [1989] 1 All ER 652.

54  See also *Perka v The Queen* (1985) 14 CCC (3d) 385, 13 DLR (4th) 1.

fear that it was impossible for him to have acted in a different, i.e. non-unlawful, way. The emphasis in this reading of the excuse is on the psychological pressure the accused found himself under in the circumstances. The second interpretation of the excuse places the emphasis on how unfair the threat on his life or limb made the accused's situation of choice as compared to that of other ordinary people normally placed. The first interpretation focuses on the person's defective capacity ; the second on his diminished opportunity to comply with the law.

Choice theorists have had some difficulties in explaining the attribution of responsibility in cases involving negligence. The problem is that the negligent actor cannot be said to have chosen to do the prohibited act. Hart's answer to this problem is that the negligent actor is morally and legally responsible not for choosing to do a wrongful act, but for not exercising his capacity to choose not to do it, when he had a fair opportunity to do so.[55] In so far as the standard by which the actor's conduct is assessed is also a subjective one, it can be said that the negligent actor "could have done otherwise, given [his] capacities",[56] and therefore he is morally and legally responsible for his actions.[57] Responsibility for negligently bringing about the conditions of one's own defence can also be explained on this basis. But how, from this point of view, could one explain the difference in blameworthiness and, correspondingly, culpability, between negligent and intentional wrongdoings? The assumption here is that a person who chooses to do a wrongful act is more to blame than one who simply fails to exercise his capacity to choose not to do it. But why is this so? The choice theory, by abstracting choice, or the capacity to choose, from the agent's character, cannot offer a satisfactory answer to this question. By contrast, the character theory, by viewing choice, or a failure to exercise a capacity to choose, as manifestations of more or less reprehensible character traits, provides a better basis for understanding why intentional wrongdoings entail a higher degree of blame  than negligent ones.[58]

---

55  *Punishment and Responsibility*, pp. 136 ff.

56  Ibid, pp. 152-157.

57  Some have argued, however, that moral culpability presupposes some degree of awareness of at least the risk of harm which one's conduct entails. In this respect the negligent actor cannot be held morally culpable, for his lack of awareness of the risk precludes him from choosing to engage in conduct that involves a risk of bringing about the prohibited harm. See G. Williams, *Criminal Law: The General Part* (2nd ed. 1961) pp. 122-123.

58  As Arenella remarks, "By suppressing the link between character and choice, rational choice theorists offer an impoverished account of moral blame that does not accurately reflect the meaning of moral culpability embedded in our actual

From the point of view of the choice theory, a person may be precluded from exercising a free choice either by an incapacitating condition in the person, or by the lack of a fair opportunity to use a normal, i.e. non-defective, capacity. In other words, a person's inability to act voluntarily might be attributed either to an internal defect (e.g., an abnormality of mind), or to a situation in which the person cannot use his normal choosing capacity effectively.[59] But how is the choosing agent to be described here? Is the choosing agent to be identified solely with the conscious will, the rational aspect of the choosing self, or should our description include emotional states, such as feelings, desires, aversions and the like? Are these largely unconscious factors part of the choosing self or should they be viewed as potential obstacles to reasoned deliberation which the choosing self must endeavour to overcome? It is submitted that the choosing agent should be described as including both, for emotions play a part in the choosing process as both products and causes of the judgments that determine our decisions.[60] Thus, when a person gets angry in the face of an act of injustice, such as the infliction of undeserved punishment, his anger need not be an obstacle to reasoned deliberation and choice. As Moore remarks, "internal factors, like emotions, cannot be said to

---

blaming practices", "Character, Choice and Moral Agency", supra note 7, p. 244.

[59] According to Blackstone, "there are three cases, in which the will does not join the act: 1. Where there is a defect of understanding. For where there is no discernment, there is no choice; and where there is no choice, there can be no act of the will, which is nothing else but a determination of one's choice, to do or abstain from a particular action: he therefore, that has no understanding, can have no will to guide his conduct. 2. Where there is understanding and will sufficient, residing in the party; but not called forth and exerted at the time of the action done: which is the case of all offences committed by chance or ignorance... 3. Where the action is constrained by some outward force and violence. Here the will counteracts the deed; and in so far from concurring with, that it loathes and disagrees to what the man is obliged to perform....[The] several species of defect in will fall under one or other of these three general heads: ...infancy, idiocy, lunacy, and intoxication, which fall under the first class; misfortune and ignorance, which may be referred to the second; and compulsion or necessity, which may properly rank in the third." supra note 51, pp. 21-22.

[60] See John Sabini and Mauri Silver, "Emotions, Responsibility, and Character", in *Responsibility, Character, and the Emotions*, F. Schoeman (ed.) (Cambridge1987), pp. 164-75, p. 168.

incapacitate our choices, except by an impermissibly narrow view either of who we are or of what our choosing agency consists".[61]

Furthermore, it is recognised that some emotions, such as fear or anger, when they get out of hand, are capable of incapacitating choice, rendering the actor excusable. For emotions to have such an incapacitating effect on choice they must be "blind", i.e. not caused by judgments, and intense enough to cause action directly, that is without the mediation of rational judgment and choice. The rationale of the excuse in provocation may be explained on this basis.[62] But when the ability to choose is overcome by powerful emotions, how could the choice theorist explain the fact that the agent is still, to some degree, morally and legally to blame? By shifting the emphasis from choice to capacity, the answer, again, seems to be that although the agent does not choose to do the wrongful act, he had the capacity and a fair opportunity to have chosen not to do it — and this implies that the agent was capable of choosing to keep his emotions in check. But the choice theorist maintains that the agent's moral culpability in such cases does not rest on a prior assumption about those aspects of his character that precluded him from exercising his capacity to control his emotions. By leaving outside the scope of the inquiry character-related considerations the choice theorist fails to account for what really justifies our actual blaming judgments in such cases. When we hold a person morally responsible for a wrongful act that was motivated by e.g. anger, it is because we blame him for not doing something about those aspects of his character that made it so difficult for him to control his anger and avoid engaging in morally and legally wrongful conduct.

Hart defends the role of legal excuses on the grounds that their presence within the legal system maximises individual liberty as it increases our powers of predicting and controlling the law's interference with our lives. For if we were to be punished for harm we cause accidentally, or involuntarily, this would mean that we could no longer determine, by our free choices, whether or not the law will interfere with our lives. Even if it was true that our actions are causally pre-determined by factors which are beyond our control, as determinists argue, this, Hart claims, would not remove the satisfaction which we experience from the exercise of choice, no matter what the intended consequences of our choices may be.[63] Hart's theory is a version of rule-utilitarianism, for it views the system of excuses as a factor contributing to the maximisation of "the efficacy of the

---

61  M. Moore, "Choice, Character and Excuse", 7 *Social Philosophy and Policy* 59 (1990), reprinted in *Justification and Excuse in the Criminal Law*, M. L. Corrado (ed.), (1994), p. 209.

62  See chapter 4 below.

63  *Punishment and Responsibility*, p. 49.

individual's informed and considered choice".[64] The role of legal excuses is justified on the grounds that a system of excuses operates as a balancing factor between the maximisation of general welfare, as pertinent to crime prevention, on the one hand, and the maximisation of that other common good, individual liberty and freedom of choice, on the other. As Hart points out, however, there can be no comparison between the two social goods — crime prevention and freedom of choice — in an all-inclusive calculation of the general good, for each occupies its own, distinct area or appropriate domain. It is from this point of view that Hart argues that the principles pertaining to the maximisation of the good that is freedom of choice operate as a constraint on the maximisation of the other good, that is, the reduction of socially harmful conduct.

Hart maintains that the recognition of legal excuses, as connected with the requirement of fairness to the individual, reflects deeply rooted moral distinctions that pervade social life. As he explains,

> Human society is a society of persons; and persons do not view themselves or each other merely as so many bodies moving in ways which are sometimes harmful and have to be prevented or altered. Instead persons interpret each other's movements as manifestations of intentions and choices, and these subjective factors are often more important to their social relations than the movements by which they are manifested or their effects...This is how human nature in human society actually is and as yet we have no power to alter it.[65]

It is a fact of life that people respond in different ways to harm caused by others, depending on their judgments about whether the harm inflicted was deliberate, i.e. the result of a free choice, or accidental. In this respect it is important for the law to take into account and reflect those moral distinctions by reference to which the character of human relations in society is determined. According to Ronald Dworkin, "the government should treat its citizens with the respect and dignity that adult members of the community claim from each other".[66]

Hart's interpretation of the role of excuses in law departs from the traditional utilitarian understanding of excuses, as expressed by Jeremy Bentham and other representatives of the utilitarian tradition. As was indicated in the previous section, utilitarians view criminal punishment as a form of harm and, as such, as detracting from general welfare. From this point of view they argue that punishment should not be imposed for harmless or justified conduct or when it is ineffective, i.e. when its application contributes nothing to the prevention of socially

---

64  Ibid at p. 46.
65  Ibid at pp. 182-183.
66  Ronald Dworkin, *Taking Rights Seriously* (1977, 4th ed. 1984), p. 11.

harmful conduct. Furthermore, punishment should be avoided when it is unprofitable, i.e. when the harm which it entails is greater than the harm which is prevented by it, and when it is needless, i.e. when it is not the most economical way of preventing harmful conduct. From this viewpoint, utilitarians assert, punishing a person who has a valid excuse would be pointless for, among other things, it would have no good effect on the conduct of the excusable offender.[67] Hart, in criticising the traditional utilitarian approach to the role of legal excuses, argues that although the threat of punishment may be ineffective against the excusable offender, it does not follow that the punishment of excusable offenders would not have a general deterrent effect.[68] For that reason the role of legal excuses cannot be justified simply on the basis of a utilitarian balancing of costs and benefits. For Hart, as was pointed out before, the recognition of legal excuses as part of our legal system draws its justification from the principle of fairness to the individual citizen. It is only the general aim of punishment that is justified on purely utilitarian grounds.[69]

Hart's theory of criminal responsibility, with its emphasis on the requirement that the law should be applied so as to respect the choices of individual citizens, is built upon the modern liberal conception of a social order. Within this order, the law both sets constraints upon the pursuance of individual preferences and, at the same time, guarantees the individual's freedom to express and, within limits, to implement his choices. In a liberal and individualist society compliance with the law is regarded as a means to achieving a balance between different and often conflicting individual choices. The effectiveness of individual choices is seen as depending upon the legal rules being observed.[70] In this respect, moral blame, as a basis of criminal

---

67  Jeremy Bentham, *An Introduction to the Principles of Morals and Legislation*, Burns and Hart (eds) (1970). (First published in 1789.)

68  *Punishment and Responsibility*, pp. 19, 43, 48, 77.

69  From this point of view Hart argues against the introduction of a system of strict liability and the resulting elimination of legal excuses. According to him such a system will undermine fairness for it will result in the individual's being punished as a direct means to the promotion of social goals. He acknowledges, however, that with regard to certain types of offences, strict liability may be given priority over the requirement of fairness to the individual. Ibid, esp. Ch. 7.

70  From the liberal's standpoint, the realisation of individual or social choices presupposes an ability to engage in a certain kind of practical reasoning. This reasoning consists, firstly, in the ordering of one's choices according to their significance, secondly, in the soundness of the methods by which choices are translated into decisions and actions and, thirdly, in the ability to act so as to maximise the satisfaction of those choices according to their ordering. The third

responsibility and punishment, pertains to the violation of the law as a condition for securing social cooperation rather than to the doing of an immoral act as such. Indeed within the liberal order no particular moral standpoint can be given priority, for different moral standpoints are interpreted merely as expressions of individual preferences. This explains the shift in emphasis in Hart's theory from the concept of just deserts to that of fairness to the individual. As was said, at the centre of Hart's conception of fairness lies the idea that criminal punishment is morally unacceptable, unless the accused chose to subject himself to the risk of punishment by voluntarily breaking the law. It is the preponderance of liberal ideas in today's social and political life that seems to account for the importance and continuing influence of Hart's theory on criminal law doctrine.

The choice theory has been subjected to the general criticism that it offers little practical guidance for a criminal justice system faced with a much less ideal world than the one Hart appears to presume. As one critic has remarked, the fairness theory is built upon a "gentlemen's club" understanding of justice.[71] The theory rests on a conception of society in which people live together sharing the same values and being subject to rules of conduct that work to everyone's advantage. Within this framework, anyone who breaks the rules gains an unfair advantage over the other members of society and so he violates the reciprocal bonds that warrant the well-being of all society members, including the offender himself. Criminal punishment cancels out that advantage and, at the same time, reaffirms the values which the criminal justice system is designed to protect. Although this picture may be accurate enough with regard to a certain categories of offenders (e.g. those who commit "white collar crimes"),[72] it appears too far off base when it comes to the large majority of criminals who come from the poorer classes of society. Although even the least advantaged members of society may be said to enjoy some benefits from living under the law, e.g. a certain degree of personal protection, these do not usually regard themselves as sharing fairly in the benefits of social cooperation that are distributed under law's protection. From this point of view, therefore, the claim that each person in society is given a *fair* opportunity to choose between keeping the law or paying the penalty — the basis of Hart's theory of responsibility — has been called into question.

Furthermore, the choice theory, by placing the emphasis on the concept of rational choice capacity as the sole basis of moral and legal

---

condition reflects the central role of utilitarian principles in the liberal social and political theory.

[71] See Jeffrey Murphy, *Retribution, Justice and Therapy* (1979), p. 107.

[72] E.g. the corporate executive who commits fraud to avoid paying taxes.

blame misrepresents the meaning of moral responsibility as reflected in our actual moral judgements. Choice theorists focus on a person's ability to make rational choices — choices that are logically linked with the person's attaining certain identifiable objectives. Their concern is primarily with the person's reasoning ability as a means to achieving certain ends, not with what shapes the person's desires that motivate his choice of action. This way of looking at the choosing agent has allowed choice theorists to treat the agent's ability for rational choice as a matter separate from those aspects of the agent's character, his desires, values, feelings, perceptions and goals, that are the source of his rational choices. In this respect they offer an unacceptably narrow description of the object of our moral judgments that leaves outside those important attributes of the moral character that give meaning to the agent's choices and provide the basis for holding people morally blameworthy (or praiseworthy) for their actions. When we blame someone for choosing to do a wrongful act, or for not exercising his capacity to choose to act according to the norm, it is because we hold him morally responsible for failing to do something about those aspects of his character that impair his ability to make the right moral choice in the circumstances. Similarly, when we excuse a person accused of a wrongful act, it is because we acknowledge that the wrongful conduct does not reflect a fault in that person's character as required for holding the person morally blameworthy. It is submitted that the character theory of responsibility, by drawing attention to what lies behind and motivates actual choices, offers a better basis for interpreting the moral significance of human actions and for explaining our actual blaming judgments with regard to those actions. If we place the emphasis on the necessary connection between choosing agency and character, then the difference between responsibility for choice and responsibility for character would tend to disappear.

## Concluding Note

All three theories examined in this chapter proceed from the assumption that criminal responsibility is a defeasible concept: an accused cannot be held criminally liable if he or she successfully raises a legal excuse.[73] Much of the discussion about criminal responsibility

---

[73]   One may contrast the three theories discussed with the so called 'objective' theory of criminal responsibility. The 'objective' theory does not regard voluntariness as a necessary condition of criminal liability . It holds, instead, that criminal liability should not be imposed if the accused has acted as a reasonable person with ordinary intelligence and reasonable prudence would have acted in the circumstances. The theory rejects the requirement of

revolves therefore around the notion of involuntariness as a prerequisite for excusing. The theories give different answers to the question of how involuntariness, as the basis of excusing, negates criminal liability — answers that reflect broader philosophical differences regarding the character and objectives of a criminal justice system. Under the character theory, excuses preclude the attribution of moral and legal blame by denying that a wrongful act reflects a flaw in the actor's character. According to the utilitarian variant of the character theory, when an excuse is successfully pleaded, the wrongful act cannot be said to manifest a socially undesirable attitude or defect of motivation. The choice theorist's position is that excusing conditions preclude criminal liability because, when these conditions are present, the actor does not have sufficient capacity or a fair opportunity to choose to act as the relevant legal norm requires. What the first two theories have in common is the assumption that criminal responsibility is concerned not with wrongful actions as such but with those undesirable character traits or faults in motivation that bring such acts about. The two theories differ, however, on their approach to the interrelationship between moral culpability and criminal responsibility. For the character theorist, moral blame is a necessary condition of criminal liability and punishment. Utilitarians, by contrast, do not view judgments of moral culpability as a necessary prerequisite for criminal liability, although most of them regard just deserts as a disguised social utility requirement. The choice theory, by treating moral culpability requirements only as a useful side-constraint on the pursuance of general deterrence as the chief aim of criminal liability and punishment, adopts a similar approach. The two theories differ, however, on the kinds of causes of action they each find to provide the basis for holding people responsible. The utilitarian theory, like the character theory, focuses on character, the choice theory on choice and the capacity to choose. Although all three theoretical approaches have exerted, and continue to exert, an important influence on the development of criminal law doctrine in Anglo-American jurisdictions,

---

voluntariness as well as the individualisation of the criteria of criminal liability, on the basis that we cannot have a full picture of a person's capacities and limitations that may affect his ability to act according to the law in the circumstances (the problem of proof). The individualisation of the criteria of liability, it is argued, is incompatible with a system, such as the criminal law, whose aim is the utilitarian one of inducing people's external conformity to the rules. See O. Holmes, *The Common Law*, Lecture II (1881), 42, 43, 87. For a critical view of this theory see Hart, *Punishment and Responsibility*, pp. 242-244; G. Fletcher, *Rethinking Criminal Law*, pp. 504 ff. For a defence of the theory see J.R. Lindgren, "Criminal Responsibility Reconsidered", *Law and Philosophy* 6 (1987) 89.

none seems capable of offering generally acceptable or conclusive answers to all the questions that may arise. This means that when it comes to dealing with important doctrinal issues or to deciding on matters of criminal policy, elements of all three theories enter the discussion. It is submitted that the character theory, with its emphasis on moral blameworthiness, provides a better basis for understanding the attribution of criminal responsibility and the role of legal excuses in relation to criminal offences which also constitute moral wrongs (i.e. those offences known as *mala in se*). The choice theory, on the other hand, may be given priority when considering the question of criminal responsibility in relation to criminal offences in which the element of moral stigma is absent or minimal (*mala prohibita*), or whose moral basis remains in question.

# 3 Homicide, Provocation and Culpability

## Introductory

In England and other common law jurisdictions, provocation operates, together with diminished responsibility and the rule relating to suicide pacts, as an independent partial defence to murder, aimed at the reduction of that offence to voluntary or intentional manslaughter. Moreover, provocation is usually taken into account as a factor in mitigation at the sentencing level with respect to offences other than murder. Professor Hart has proposed a distinction between "informal" and "formal" mitigation. He speaks of informal mitigation in those cases where it is left to the sentencer to impose a penalty below the maximum level provided by the law, by taking into account certain mitigating factors. Formal mitigation, on the other hand, pertains to those cases where, according to law, the presence of certain mitigating factors should always remove the crime into a lower offence category. Provocation, when pleaded as a partial defence to murder, offers the typical example of formal mitigation.[1] The defence operates on the assumption that a provoked killing, even though intentional, is less culpable than an unprovoked one, provided that certain conditions are met: the acts or words relied upon as provocation must have been serious enough to provoke an ordinary person (the "objective" condition) and, at the same time, they must have actually caused the accused to lose his self-control and kill (the "subjective" condition). The emergence of provocation as a partial defence to murder in the 17th century had much to do with the fact that, in English law, a conviction of murder entailed a mandatory death penalty. Indeed, some modern commentators have argued that the category of partial defences would be superfluous if the fixed penalty for murder — presently life

---

[1]  H.L.A. Hart, "Prolegomenon to the Principles of Punishment", in *Punishment and Responsibility* (1968), p. 15.

61

imprisonment — was abolished.[2] A reply to this argument has been
that what justifies the role of partial defences in the criminal law is not
the mandatory penalty as such but the special gravity of the crime of
murder and the moral stigma which a conviction of that crime entails.[3]
To understand the function of provocation as a partial defence it is
necessary to consider, briefly, the history and theoretical basis of the
distinction between murder and manslaughter.

## Murder, Manslaughter and the Origins of the Provocation Defence

At the earliest stages of English law a distinction was drawn between
the worst kinds of killing, such as killing by stealth, which were
punishable by death, and other forms of homicide, not subject to state
punishment, such as killing resulting from an open fight, which were
considered remediable through compensation to the victim's family.[4]
But the distinction between killings in open fight and hidden or
concealed killings had disappeared in the 13th century and almost all
killings were subsumed under a single capital offence of culpable
homicide. The term murder (*murdrum*) was used to denote the special
fine imposed on the hundred for the killing of a Norman by one of its
members when the killer could not be found.[5] In popular usage,
however, the term "murder" signified those most reprehensible
killings, thought of as deserving the ultimate punishment, especially
secret killings. For a conviction of culpable homicide it was required
that the accused had an intention to kill, or to cause serious bodily harm
to the person killed. The typical example of culpable homicide was the
killing of another "upon a sudden occasion". During this period, the
term "premeditated malice", as a legal term, did not mean anything
more than "deliberately" or "wickedly". In 1278 the Statute of

---

2   See, e.g., G. Williams, *Textbook of Criminal Law* (1978), pp. 477 and 501;
    Thomas, "Form and Function in Criminal Law", in *Reshaping the Criminal
    Law*, Glazebrook (ed.) (1978), p. 21 and pp. 28-29.

3   For a defence of the role of partial defences see M. Wasik, "Partial Excuses in
    the Criminal Law", *The Modern Law Review* 45 (1982) 516.

4   See T. Green, "The Jury and the English Law of Homicide", 74 *Michigan Law
    Review* 413, p. 420.

5   The term *Hundreds* referred to the larger administrative units in which local
    communities were organised under the Normans for purposes of local
    government and judicial administration. This fine was abolished by statute in
    the 14th century (14 Edward III, st. 1, ch. 4). See J.M. Kaye, "The Early
    History of Murder and Manslaughter", *The Law Quarterly Review* 83 (1967)
    365 and 569.

Gloucester was enacted, which provided that if the accused had killed in self-preservation (*se defendendo*), or by misadventure (*per infortunium*), the trial judge was to report the matter to the king who could grant pardon, "if he pleased". But the excused killer still incurred a forfeiture of his chattels, for his act was regarded as tort depriving the king of a subject.[6] Later, when the king's pardon became a matter of course, the juries were allowed to find the accused not guilty in such cases.[7]

Towards the end of the 14th century the term "murder" began to be used by justices commissions in reference to killings committed by stealth or from ambush. In 1390 a statute was enacted which sought to restrict the granting of pardons in such cases. Under this statute, a pardon could not be granted for "murder, killing by lying in wait, assault or malice aforethought".[8] After the introduction of this statute the jury's task became more complex, for they now had to determine whether or not the accused had killed with malice aforethought. Thus, for a first time, a distinction was recognised between premeditated killings (killings "par malice devant pourpense" or with malice aforethought) and hot-blooded killings on the spur of the moment (killings "par chaude melle" or by sudden chance). In the 15th century, however, the judges returned to treating felonious homicide as a single, undivided offence, in much the same way as it was treated in the 13th and early 14th centuries. At the same time the distinction was maintained between culpable homicide and those killings deemed excusable on the grounds of self-defence and misadventure. By the early 16th century the law had also recognised felonious homicides based on wanton negligence.

The distinction between murder and manslaughter began to emerge in the early years of the 16th century. At first, the distinction was introduced to deal with problems resulting from the practice known as "the benefit of clergy". This related to the right of all clerks in holy orders accused of crimes before lay courts to seek to be tried by ecclesiastical courts. If the accused's claim of clergy was successful, the case came under the jurisdiction of the ecclesiastical courts where the accused had a much better chance of avoiding conviction and punishment. However, frequent resort to the benefit of clergy by

---

6    6 Edward I, c.9. For a fuller discussion see T.A. Green, "Societal Concepts of Criminal Liability for Homicide in Medieval England" 47 *Speculum* (1972) 669 at pp. 675 ff.; *Verdict According to Conscience* (Chicago1985), pp. 86-93, 123-125.

7    See J. F. Stephen, *A History of the Criminal Law of England*, III (London 1883), pp. 76-77.

8    Stat. 13 Ric. II, stat. 2, c. 1. And see T.A. Green, "The Jury and the English Law of Homicide, 1200-1600", 74 *Michigan Law Review* (1976) 413, p. 432.

persons accused of serious crimes tended to undermine the credibility of the secular criminal law and, in the early 16th century, a number of statutes were enacted which removed benefit of clergy from those charged with "murder of malice prepensed".[9] Through these statutes a tripartite classification of homicide was introduced: homicides committed with malice aforethought, punishable by death; homicides committed without prior malice, known by 1510 as "chance medley manslaughters"; and excusable homicides, i.e. homicides *per infortunium* or *se defendendo*, which were subject to royal pardon. To these one may add, as a fourth category, those homicides considered justifiable and entitling the accused to full acquittal. Manslaughter, or chance medley, at first referred to an accidental killing which occurred in the course of a fight involving acts of violence not directed at the person killed or anyone close to him. The only difference between chance medley manslaughter and homicide *per infortunium*, or by accident, was that the former took place in the course of an unlawful act. The distinction between murder and manslaughter was redefined, however, following the enactment of a statute in 1547, which clearly excluded the benefit of clergy from those found guilty of "wilful murder of malice prepensed", but not from those found guilty of manslaughter.[10] After the passing of that statute, murder was distinguished from manslaughter on the basis of the presence or absence of premeditation.[11] From that time the term manslaughter came to mean a deliberate killing on the spur of the moment, as understood by Coke and other commentators of the 16th and 17th centuries.[12] Basis of the distinction was the assumption that a premeditated killing,

---

9   4 Hen. VIII, c.2; 23 Hen. VIII, c.1, s.3.

10   1 Edw. 6, c. 12. And see Green, "The Jury and the English Law of Homicide", supra note 9, 483 n. 251.

11   See *Salisbury's Case* (1553) Plowd Comm 100.

12   See William Lambarde, *Eirenarcha* (1607), pp. 235-236, 245-248; Coke, *The Third Part of the Institutes* (1660), pp. 47, 55-56. According to Coke, "Murder is when a man of sound memory, and of the age of discretion, unlawfully killeth within any county of the realm any reasonable creature in *rerum natura* under the king's peace, with malice aforethought, either expressed by the party or implied by law, so as the party wounded, or hurt, etc. die of the wound or hurt, etc. within a year and a day after the same" (p. 47). Coke defined malice aforethought as follows: "Malice prepensed is, when one compasseth to kill, wound, or beat another, and doth it sedato animo. This is said in law to be malice forethought, prepensed, malitia praecogitata" (p. 51). On this basis, Coke defined manslaughter as a voluntary killing "not of malice forethought, [but] upon some sudden falling out...There is no difference between murder and manslaughter, but that the one is upon malice forethought, and the other upon a sudden occasion: and therefore is called chance medley" (p. 55). And see Michael Dalton, *Countrey Justice* (1619), p. 217.

or a killing in cold blood, was more reprehensible than a killing which, although deliberate, took place in the course of a sudden fight at a time when the accused had been overwhelmed by anger.[13] The punishment for manslaughter was forfeiture of goods, burning in the hand and one year imprisonment. But the distinction between killing with malice aforethought and chance medley manslaughter proved unsatisfactory, for malice was difficult to define precisely and even more difficult to prove. So, in many cases, malice had to be implied from the circumstances surrounding the killing. For example, malice was presumed or implied in those cases where the accused killed the victim without apparent provocation on the victim's part, or where the accused killed an officer of justice in execution of his duty, or where the accused killed another while doing an unlawful act involving violence.[14] In all these cases the accused was found guilty of murder, despite the absence of evidence or premeditation of his part.[15] Gradually, the doctrine of chance medley was abandoned and the test of manslaughter came to be the presence or absence of provocation rather than the absence of premeditation as such. This development was facilitated by the enactment, in 1604, of the Statute of Stabbing,

---

[13]  It is important to note that only if the fight in the course of which the killing took place was a sudden one a finding of manslaughter was justified. As Coke pointed out: "if two men fall out upon a sudden occasion, and agree to fight in such a field, and each of them go and fetch their weapon, and go in the field, and therein fight, the one killeth the other: here is no malice prepensed, for the fetching of the weapon and going into the field, is but a continuance of the sudden falling out, and the blood was never cooled. But if they appoint to fight the next day, that is malice prepensed", *Third Institute*, p. 51.

[14]  Thus, according to Coke, malice aforethought "is implied in three cases (1) If one kills another without any provocation on the part of him that is slain. (2) If a magistrate, or known officer, or any other that hath lawful warrant, and in doing or offering to do his office, or to execute his warrant, is slain, this is murder by malice implied by law. (3) In respect of the person killing. If A assault B to rob him, and in resisting A killeth B, this is murder by malice implied, albeit he (A) never saw or knew him (B) before. If a prisoner by the duress of the gaoler cometh to an untimely death, this is murder in the gaoler, and the law implieth malice in respect of the cruelty..." (3rd Inst. pp. 50-51). And see *Young's Case* (1586) 4 Co Rep 40a.

[15]  According to Lambarde, "Many times the law doth by the sequel judge of that malice which lurked before within the party, and doth accordingly make imputation of it. And therefore if one (suddenly and without any outward show of present quarrel or offence) draw his weapon and therewith kill another that standeth by him, the law judgeth it to have proceeded of former malice, meditated within his own mind, however it be kept secret from the fight of other men...", *Eirenarcha*, p. 205. And see Crompton *L'Office et Auctority de Justices de Peace*, (1606: fo. 21a, e.g. 2).

which removed the benefit of clergy from those who killed another by stabbing, where the victim had not drawn his weapon, even though the killing was committed without premeditation.[16]

The narrow scope of the Statute of Stabbing made its application problematic in certain cases, however, as, for example, in the case where the accused stabbed and killed another caught in the act of adultery with his wife. To deal with these cases, judges of the late 17th and 18th centuries began to lay down criteria for determining what sorts of conduct could amount to provocation in law. At the same time, it was re-confirmed that provocation could provide no defence to those who killed in cold blood out of revenge.[17] It is at that time that provocation, as a distinct defence reducing murder to manslaughter, clearly emerged.[18] Forms of conduct amounting to provocation included grave assaults,[19] attacking one's relative, friend or master,[20]

---

[16] Stat. 2 Jac. VI, c.8 (1604). The Statute stated: "Every person...which shall stab or thrust any person or persons that hath not then any weapon drawn, or that hath not then first stricken the party, which shall so stab or thrust so as the person so stabbed or thrust shall thereof die within the space of six months then following, although it cannot be proved that the same was done of malice forethought, ...shall be excluded from the benefit of his clergy, and suffer death as in case of wilful murder". And see Stephen, *A History of the Criminal Law of England*, III, pp. 47-48.

[17] As Hawkins noted: "It also seems, that he who upon a sudden provocation executeth his revenge in such a cruel manner, as shews a cool and deliberate intent to do mischief, is guilty of murder, if death ensue", *A Treatise of the Pleas of the Crown*, I (1716) p. 83.

[18] See Hale, Pleas of the Crown (1678), p. 43, pp. 48-50, p. 56. In his *Commentaries on the Laws of England* IV (1769) Blackstone says: "Manslaughter is ...the unlawful killing of another, without malice either express or implied: which may be either voluntarily, upon a sudden heat; or involuntarily, but in the commission of some unlawful act. As to the first, or *voluntary* branch: ...if a man be greatly provoked, as by pulling his nose, or other great indignity, and immediately kills the aggressor, though this is not excusable *se defendendo*, since there is no absolute necessity for doing it to preserve himself; yet neither is it murder, for there is no previous malice; but it is manslaughter. But in this, and in every other case of homicide upon provocation, if there be a sufficient cooling-time for passion to subside and reason to interpose, and the person so provoked afterwards kills the other, this is deliberate revenge and not heat of blood, and accordingly amounts to murder" (p. 191).

[19] See *Lanure's Case* (1642), described by Hale, 1 Pleas of the Crown (1678), 455; *Mawgridge* (1707) Kel 119; *Lord Morley's Case* (1666) 6 St Tr 770.

[20] See *Royley's Case* (1612) 12 Co Rep 87 and (1612) Cro Jac 296; *Cary's Case* (1616) mentioned by Stephen, *A History of the Criminal Law of England*, p. 221.

unlawfully depriving a man of his liberty[21] and seeing a man in the act of adultery with one's wife.[22] The emphasis on the wrongfulness of the provocative conduct exercised a considerable influence on the subsequent development of the provocation defence. However, the real basis of the defence, as many commentators observed, was the law's compassion to human frailty.[23] It was believed that, as a result of provocation, the accused becomes so subject to passion that his ability to reason and exercise judgment is temporarily suspended. At the same time, it was recognised that if the accused's response was out of all proportion to the provocation received, the presumption of malice would not be negated.[24] This approach to provocation is reflected in a number of cases decided in the 18th and 19th centuries.[25] During this period, there appears to be a gradual shift in emphasis from the wrongfulness of the provocative conduct to the requirement of loss of self-control, although the courts continued to recognise and apply the categories of legal provocation as laid down by 17th and early 18th century authorities.[26]

An important step towards the formation of the modern doctrine of provocation was the emergence, in the late 19th century, of the concept of the reasonable person, as providing a universal standard of self-control by which the accused's response to provocation was to be assessed. One of the earliest cases in which the reasonable person was

---

21 *Hopkin Huggett* (1666) Kel 59; *Tooley* (1709) Holt KB 485; and see *Mawgridge* (1707) Kel 119, 136-7.

22 *Manning's Case* (1617) 1 Vent 158 and 83 Eng Rep 112 (KB 1683-84); *Mawgridge* (1707) Kel 119, 137. And see Blackstone, *Commentaries on the Laws of England* (1769), IV, pp. 191-192; Hawkins, *A Treatise of the Pleas of the Crown*, I (1716), pp. 82-83.

23 According to East, "[T]o have received such provocation as the law presumes might in human frailty heat the blood to a proportionate degree of resentment, and keep it boiling to the moment of the fact: so that the part may rather be considered as having acted under a temporary suspension of reason, than from any deliberate malicious motive", p. 238. And see Hawkins, I *Pleas of the Crown* (1716) 97, s. 28; Foster, *Crown Cases* (1762) 296.

24 In East's words, where the accused's retaliation "is outrageous in its nature, either in the manner or the continuance of it, and beyond all proportion to the offence, it is rather to be considered as the effect of a brutal and diabolical malignity than of human frailty", 1 *Pleas of the Crown*, 234.

25 See, e.g., *Ayes* (1810) R & R 166; *Lynch* (1832) 5 C & P 324, 325; *Hayward* (1833) 6 C & P 157, 159; *Fisher* (1837) 8 C & P 182; *Kelly* (1848) 2 C & K 814.

26 For a thorough and illuminating account of the early history of provocation see J. Horder, *Provocation and Responsibility* (1992), chapters 1-5. And see A. Ashworth, "The Doctrine of Provocation", *Cambridge Law Journal* 35 (1976) 292, pp. 292-297.

referred to was *Welsh*,[27] a case which many modern commentators regard as the starting-point in the development of the modern law of provocation.[28] There was no immediate recognition of the role of the "reasonable person" in the law of provocation, however, as manifested by the fact that the objective standard is not mentioned by Sir James Fitzjames Stephen in his influential works *Digest of the Criminal Law* (1877) and *A History of the Criminal Law of England* (1883). Stephen simply lays down the different forms of conduct that were taken to amount to provocation in law, pointing out that the success of the accused's plea in such cases depended, firstly, on whether the victim's conduct came under one of the established categories of legal provocation and, secondly, on whether the accused actually lost his self-control as a result. [29] Only where these conditions were met the offence of murder was reduced to manslaughter.[30]

---

[27]   *Welsh*  (1869) 2 Cox CC 336.

[28]   In that case  Keating J. stated: "...in law it is necessary that there should be a serious provocation in order to reduce the crime to manslaughter, as, for instance,  a  blow, and a severe blow - something which might naturally cause an ordinary and reasonable-minded person to lose his self-control" (at p. 338).

[29]   Articles  224-226 of Stephen's *Digest*  reflect the common law position on the defence   of   provocation   as   it   was   in   the   late   19th   century. "224. Homicide,  which  would  otherwise  be  murder,  is  not  murder but manslaughter  if the act by which death is caused is done in the heat of passion caused  by  provocation  as  hereinafter  defined,  unless  the  provocation  was sought or voluntarily provoked by the offender as an excuse for killing or doing bodily harm. The following acts, subject to the provisions contained in Article 225,  amount  to  provocation:  (a)  An assault and battery of such nature as to inflict  actual  bodily  harm  or  great  insult  is  a  provocation  to the person assaulted.  (b)  If  two persons quarrel and fight upon equal terms, and upon the spot, whether with deadly weapons or otherwise, each gives provocation to the other, whichever is right in the quarrel and whichever strikes the first blow. (c) An  unlawful  imprisonment  is  a provocation to the person imprisoned, but not to  the  bystanders,  though  an  unlawful  imprisonment  may  amount  to such a breach  of  the  peace  as  to entitle a bystander to prevent it by the use of force sufficient for that purpose. An arrest made by officers of justice whose character as  such  is known, but who are acting under a warrant so irregular  as to make the  arrest  illegal,  is  provocation  to  the  person illegally arrested, but not to bystanders. (d) The  sight  of  the  act  of  adultery committed with his wife is provocation  to  the  husband  of the adulteress on the part of both the adulterer and  of the adulteress. (e) The sight of the act of sodomy committed on a man's son is provocation to the father on the   part  of  the  person  committing   the offence.   (f) Neither words, nor gestures, nor injuries to property, nor breaches of contract,  amount  to  provocation  within this article, except (perhaps) words expressing an intention to inflict actual bodily injury, accompanied by some act which  shows  that  such  injury  is  intended; but words used at the time of an assault - slight  in itself- may be taken into account in estimating the degree of

It was not until the early 20th century that the role of the reasonable person in the law of provocation received full recognition. In *Lesbini*[31] the court rejected the argument that a lower standard of provocation should apply with regard to those suffering from some form of mental disability, pointing out that in all cases the provocation must be serious enough to affect the mind of a reasonable person. In those and subsequent cases it was confirmed that for the defence of provocation to succeed two conditions must be satisfied, namely (a) the accused must have actually been deprived of his self-control at the time of the killing and (b) the victim's provocation, which caused the accused to lose his self-control, must have been such as to be likely to have the same effect on any reasonable or ordinary person. However, until the passing of the Homicide Act 1957, the question of whether the victim's conduct amounted to provocation or not was a question of law and, as such, it was for the judge, not for the jury, to decide.

There have been cases in early law in which provocation was accepted as a defence to the charge of attempted murder.[32] This does not represent the present law, however, which recognises provocation

---

provocation given by a blow. (g) The employment of lawful force against the person of another is not a provocation to the person against whom it is employed. 225. Provocation does not extenuate guilt of homicide unless the person provoked is, at the time when he does the act, deprived of the power of self-control by the provocation which he has received, and in deciding the question whether this was or was not the case regard must be had to the nature of the act by which the offender causes death, to the time which elapsed between the provocation and the act which caused death, to the offender's conduct during the interval, and all the circumstances tending to show the state of his mind. 226. Provocation to a person by an actual assault, or by a mutual combat, or by a false imprisonment, is, in some cases, provocation to those who are with that person at the time, and to his friends who, in the case of a mutual combat, take part in the fight for his defence. But it is uncertain how far this principle extends."

30   In *Welsh* provocation was said to negate the malice element of murder which, according to law, is implied when a killing is committed intentionally. In the court's words: "*Malice aforethought* means intention to kill. Whenever one person kills another intentionally, he does it with *malice aforethought*. In point of law, the intention signifies the malice. It is for him to show that it was not so by showing sufficient provocation, which only reduces the crime to manslaughter, because it tends to negative the malice. But when that provocation does not appear, the malice aforethought implied in the intention remains".

31   [1914] 3 KB 1116. The same position was adopted in *Alexander* (1913) 109 LT 745.

32   See, e.g., *Thompson* (1825) 1 Mood 80, 168 ER 1193; *Bourne* (1831) 5 C & P 129, 172 ER 903; *Beeson* (1835) 7 C & P 142, 173 ER 63; *Hagan* (1837) 8 C & P 167, 173 ER 445.

as a defence to murder only.[33] The present approach to the defence has been criticised on the grounds that, in so far as murder and attempted murder share the same internal elements, provocation should have the same mitigating effect, at the verdict level, on both. It has been argued that a person who attempted to kill in response to grave provocation does not deserve to be stigmatised as someone who was in fact disposed to commit murder.[34]

## Provocation as a Partial Defence to Murder

The traditional common law division of culpable homicide into murder and manslaughter reflects the different degrees of culpability which these offences entail. Whereas both types of homicide share the same external elements — in England, the unlawful killing of a human being within the Queen's Peace and where the death occurs within a year and a day of the last act done by the accused to the victim — they differ significantly as regards the accused's state of mind at the time of his death-causing act. However, identifying the relevant states of mind has been a matter of dispute both in practice and in theory; in practice because the requisite states of mind often appear to be inaccessible to traditional methods of proof; in theory a major problem has been how to articulate a comprehensive basis upon which to conceptualise those states of mind as they relate to different categories of homicide. In dealing with the latter question the notion of *malice aforethought* has traditionally played the decisive part. An unlawful homicide is to be categorised as murder only if it is accompanied by malice aforethought. An unlawful homicide committed without malice aforethought is to be treated under the wider category of manslaughter.[35] Further, manslaughter is subdivided into voluntary and involuntary manslaughter. Only as regards involuntary manslaughter the accused does not have malice aforethought. Voluntary manslaughter, by contrast, is committed with the malice aforethought of murder, but homicide is reduced to a lower offence category due to the presence of certain legally prescribed mitigating circumstances, namely provocation

---

33  See, e.g., *Cunningham* [1959] 1 QB 288, [1958] 3 All ER 711; *Bruzas* [1972] Crim LR 367; *Peck* (1975) *Times*, 5 Dec; *Campbell* (1977) 38 CCC (2d) 6 (Can); *Jack* (1970) 17 CRNS 38 (Br Col). But see CLRC/OAP/R, para. 98.

34  For a discussion of provocation as a possible defence to crimes other than murder see P. English, "Provocation and Attempted Murder", *Criminal Law Review* [1973] 727; P. Fairall, "Provocation, Attempted Murder and Wounding with Intent to Murder", *Criminal Law Journal* 7 (1983) 44.

35  As stated in *Doherty* (1887) 16 Cox CC 306 at 307.

and, after the introduction of the Homicide Act 1957, diminished responsibility and suicide pacts.

But what does "malice aforethought" mean? As we saw in the previous section, at an earlier stage in the development of common law the term was used to denote deliberate and premeditated killings. This interpretation of the term is no longer accepted, however. According to the modern view, malice aforethought does not necessarily involve premeditation.[36] As was stated in *Vickers* [37]

> Murder is, of course, killing with malice aforethought, but 'malice aforethought' is a term of art. It has always been defined in English law as either an *express* intention to kill, as could be inferred when a person, having uttered threats against another, produced a lethal weapon and used it on a victim, or *implied*, where, by a voluntary act, the accused intended to cause grievous bodily harm to the victim, and the victim died as a result.

Thus, according to the current approach, to establish the requisite *mens rea* or malice aforethought for murder, the prosecution must prove that the accused intended to kill or cause serious bodily injury knowing that the killing was unlawful.

However, in order to include within the category of murder homicides involving gross recklessness, attempts have been made to expand the meaning of malice aforethought. These attempts have been a source of controversy in English law. Briefly, in *Smith*,[38] the House of Lords interpreted the requirement of malice aforethought for murder

---

36 J. T. Lowe, "Murder and the Reasonable Man", *Criminal Law Review* [1958] 289, p. 298. And see *Kenny's Outlines of Criminal Law*, 19th ed., (Cambridge 1966), p. 172. See also R. Perkins, *Criminal Law* (1957), p. 40: "Malice aforethought is an unjustifiable, inexcusable and unmitigated man-endangering-state-of-mind"; *Russell on Crime*, 12th ed. (1964), Vol.1, p. 466: "If, as has been suggested, mens rea is now a realisation of the consequences which one's conduct may bring about, then we can say that the malice aforethought is the realisation that one's conduct may cause the death of a human being". For a fuller account of the development and meaning of the notion of malice aforethought see: Stephen, *A History of the Criminal Law of England* (1883), III, pp. 41-46; J.M. Kaye, "The Early History of Murder and Manslaughter", *Law Quarterly Review* 83 (1967), 365-395 (part 1), 569-601 (part 2); T.A. Green, "The Jury and the English Law of Homicide", *Michigan Law Review* 74 (1976) 414; R. Perkins, "A Re-examination of Malice Aforethought", 43 *Yale Law Journal* (1934) 537; G. Fletcher, *Rethinking Criminal Law* (1978), p. 253 ff.; R. Goff, "The Mental Element in Murder", *Law Quarterly Review* 104 (1988), 30.

37 *Vickers* (1957) 2 All ER 741 and [1957] 2 QB 664; and see *Cunningham* [1957] 2 QB 396.

38 *DPP v Smith* [1961] AC 290.

in terms broad enough to encompass homicides involving gross recklessness. In *Hyam*,[39] the majority of the House of Lords adopted the view that malice aforethought should be deemed present where the accused foresaw death or serious bodily harm as a highly probable consequence of her action. However, in *Moloney*,[40] the House of Lords reinstated the position that malice aforethought requires proof either of an intention to kill or of an intention to cause grievous bodily harm. Recklessness was therefore excluded as a basis for establishing the mens rea of murder. Further, as was recognised in the subsequent case of *Hancock and Shankland*,[41] the question of whether the accused foresaw death or serious bodily harm as a probable result of his action is relevant to proving an intent to cause such a result on his part. In clarifying this point, the Court of Appeal in *Nedrick* [42] pointed out that only where death or serious bodily harm was virtually certain to occur, the jury should be entitled to infer the necessary intention.[43] As R. Goff has noted[44]

> After the journey through Smith, Hyam, Moloney and Hancock, the law is really back where it was in Vickers. The mental element in the crime of murder is either (1) an intent to kill or (2) an intent to cause grievous bodily harm. Foresight of the consequences is not the same as intent, but is material from which the jury may, having regard to all the circumstances of the case, infer that the defendant actually had the relevant intent.

---

[39]  *Hyam v DPP* [1975] AC 55.

[40]  *Moloney* [1985] AC 905. In this case Lord Bridge of Harwich stated: "...so far as I know, no one has yet suggested that recklessness can furnish the necessary element in the crime of murder...Foresight of consequences, as an element bearing on the issue of intention in murder, belongs, not to the substantive law, but to the law of evidence" (at pp. 927-928).

[41]  *Hancock and Shankland* [1986] AC 455.

[42]  *Nedrick* (1986) 3 All ER 1; [1986] 1 WLR 1025.

[43]  But see *Walker and Hayles* (1990) 90 Cr App R 226, where it was accepted that, as there was very little difference between "highly probable" and "virtually certain", the judge's use of the phrase "a very high degree of probability" did not amount to a misdirection.

[44]  "The Mental Element in Murder", *Law Quarterly Review* 104 (1988) 30, p. 48. And see Clause 54 of the Law Commission's Draft Criminal Code - Law Comm. No. 177, which states that the mens rea of murder must be "(a) intending to cause death; or (b) intending to cause serious personal harm and being aware that it may cause death". As to the meaning of intention, Clause 18(b) of the Draft Criminal Code states: "...a person acts intentionally with respect to a result when he acts either in order to bring it about or being aware that it will occur in the ordinary course of events".

Provocation operates as a partial defence to murder, reducing murder to voluntary manslaughter.[45] Considering that, in modern law, malice aforethought is defined as an intention to kill or to cause grievous bodily harm, provocation does not negative the required malice element of murder.[46] Indeed, pleading provocation presupposes that the prosecution has provided sufficient evidence to justify the jury's returning a verdict of guilty of murder. If the jury are not satisfied beyond reasonable doubt that the accused had the *mens rea* of murder - i.e. an intention to kill or to cause grievous bodily harm - they must find the accused not guilty of murder and, necessarily, of voluntary manslaughter.[47] But if the jury conclude that the accused had the requisite intention for murder, they must convict him of manslaughter if they find that he was provoked.[48] One might envisage a case in which the accused is provoked to lose his self-control to such a degree that he is no longer aware of what he is doing. In such a case

---

45    Jurisdictions which do not belong to the common law family also recognise provocation as a partial or mitigating defence to homicide. For example, Para 213 of the German Criminal Code creates a less serious offence of manslaughter for killings committed under provocation: "If the person committing manslaughter, through no fault of his own, had been aroused to anger by the abuse of his own person or of a relative of his by the grossly insulting conduct of the victim, and committed the homicide under the influence of passion, or the circumstances otherwise indicate the existence of a less serious case, the imprisonment to be imposed shall be from six months to five years". See also Article 321 of the French Penal Code (under this article provocation is treated as a mitigating defence to murder as well as to offences involving the application of physical violence); Articles 62 (applying to all offences) and 587 (Homicide or Personal Injury for Reasons of Honour) of the Italian Penal Code; Article 299 (2) of the Greek Penal Code (covering all cases of homicide committed in the heat of passion).

46    See, e.g., *Kenny's Outlines of Criminal Law*, J.W.C. Turner ed. (Cambridge 1966), at p. 172: "...it was only in the ancient period, when *malice aforethought* was an expression used to denote a calmly premeditated killing, that it would be true to say that provocation negatived malice aforethought". According to Robinson, "Provocation was traditionally drafted as negativing the malice required for murder. In this form it is a failure of proof defense. The same concept may be formulated as an offense modification, an independent defense to murder - independent in the sense that it does not negate any element of the offense. Usually, this formulation is slightly broader in scope and is called 'extreme emotional disturbance'", "Criminal Law Defenses: A Systematic Analysis", *Columbia Law Review* 82 (1982)199, pp. 205-6.

47    Although this does not preclude the accused being convicted of involuntary manslaughter.

48    Similarly, in Scots law it is accepted that, where a killing has been committed with intent or wicked recklessness, provocation may be pleaded to reduce the offence from murder to the lesser offence of culpable homicide.

the accused may be able to rely on a lack of *mens rea* defence, but not on provocation.[49]

The definition of provocation offered by Devlin J. in *Duffy*, although now somewhat out of date, is still taken to provide a useful starting-point in the discussion of the defence. According to Devlin J.

> Provocation is some act, or series of acts, done by the dead man to the accused, which would cause in any reasonable person, and actually causes in the accused, a sudden and temporary loss of self-control, rendering the accused so subject to passion as to make him or her for the moment not master of his mind.[50]

Lord Devlin's definition admits the application of an objective test relied upon to determine whether the provocation offered was serious enough to overcome the capacity for self-control of a reasonable person. In addition to this, for the defence of provocation to succeed, what is referred to as the "subjective test" must also be met: it must be established that the accused himself did in fact lose his self-control as a result of the provocation he received.

The common law definition of the provocation defence has been amended by s. 3 of the Homicide Act 1957. According to this section

> Where on a charge of murder there is evidence on which the jury can find that the person charged was provoked (whether by things done or by things said or both together) to lose his self-control, the question whether the provocation was enough to make a reasonable man do as he did shall be left to be determined by the jury; and in determining that question the jury shall take into account everything both done and said according to the effect which, in their opinion, it would have on a reasonable man.

As regards its effect on criminal liability, this provision is similar to those found in other common law jurisdictions.[51] The provision affirms the application of a dual test in provocation, comprising the

---

49  See on this A. Ashworth, "Reason, Logic and Criminal Liability", *Law Quarterly Review* 91 (1975) 102 at pp. 128-9. See also T. Archibald, "The Interrelationship Between Provocation and Mens Rea: A Defence of Loss of Self-Control", *Criminal Law Quarterly* 28 (1985-1986) 454 esp. pp. 456-7.

50  *Duffy* (1949) 1 All E.R. 932n.

51  E.g. s. 169 of the New Zealand Crimes Act 1961 provides: "(1) Culpable homicide that would otherwise be murder may be reduced to manslaughter if the person who caused the death did so under provocation. (2) Anything done or said may be provocation if - (a) In the circumstances of the case it was sufficient to deprive a person having the power of self-control of an ordinary person, but otherwise having the characteristics of the offender, of the power of self-control; and (b) It did in fact deprive the offender of the power of self-control and thereby induced him to commit the act of homicide."

subjective question of whether the accused was in fact provoked to lose his self control, and the objective one of whether the provocation was serious enough to make a reasonable person do as the accused did. At the same time, however, it adopts an approach broader than had previously been accepted to the question of what may constitute provocation in law, for it includes not only "things done" but also

---

In Canada, s. 232 of the Criminal Code provides: "(1) Culpable homicide that would otherwise be murder may be reduced to manslaughter if the person who committed it did so in the heat of passion caused by sudden provocation. (2) A wrongful act or insult that is of such nature as to be sufficient to deprive an ordinary person of the power of self-control is provocation enough for the purposes of this section if the accused acted upon it on the sudden and before there was time for his passion to cool. (3) For the purposes of this section the questions (a) whether a particular wrongful act or insult amounted to provocation, and (b) whether the accused was deprived of the power of self-control by the provocation he alleges he received, are questions of fact, but no one shall be deemed to have given provocation to another by doing anything that he had a legal right to do, or by doing anything that the accused incited him to do in order to provide the accused with an excuse for causing death or bodily harm to any human being. (4) Culpable homicide that otherwise would be murder is not necessarily manslaughter by reason only that it was committed by a person who was being arrested illegally, but the fact that the illegality of the arrest was known to the accused may be evidence of provocation for the purpose of this section". And see *LeFrancois* 47 CR 54 [1965] 4 CCC 255 (Man CA); *LeBlanc* (1985) 22 CCC (3d) 126, 11 OAC 315. Similar provisions have been introduced in Australian jurisdictions; see e.g. s. 23 of the New South Wales Crimes Act 1900, s. 304 of the Queensland Criminal Code, ss. 281 and 245 of the Criminal Code of Western Australia, s. 13 of the Australian Capital Territory Crimes Act 1900, s. 160 of the Tasmanian Criminal Code 1924. These statutory provisions are largely based on the traditional common definition of the provocation defence. According to s. 304 of the Queensland Criminal Code, for example, "When a person who unlawfully kills another under circumstances which, but for the provisions of this section, would constitute murder does the act which causes death in the heat of passion caused by sudden provocation, and before there is time for his passion to cool, he is guilty of manslaughter only". In Queensland and Western Australia, as well as reducing murder to manslaughter, provocation operates as a complete defence with respect to certain offences which have assault as an element (see ss. 269 and s. 268 of the Queensland Criminal Code, and s. 246 of the Criminal Code of Western Australia). In South Africa, provocation, besides its role in reducing murder to culpable homicide, is also relied upon as a defence aimed at reducing the level of seriousness of assault (see, e.g., *Attwood* (1946) AD 331; *Lushozi* (1968) (1) PH, H 21 (T), *Masondo* (1968) (2) PH, H 191 (N)). A number of provisions relating to provocation are also found in the criminal codes of many American jurisdictions. See, e.g., California Penal Code paras 188, 192; New York Penal Code, paras 125.25, 125.20; and see Model Penal Code, Article 210.3.

"things said" into its definition of provocation. As we saw in the previous section, at common law the traditional position was that verbal insults did not amount to provocation sufficient to reduce murder to manslaughter.[52] Some form of physical aggression, either against the accused himself or someone close to him, was necessary, with one notable exception, namely, seeing a man in the act of adultery with one's wife. With regard to this latter case, the authorities provide no clear answer to the question of whether a lawful marriage had to be proved before the accused could rely on the provocation defence. [53] Further, it was recognised that an unexpected confession of adultery may constitute sufficient provocation in law.[54] Under s. 3 of the Homicide Act 1957, there is no restriction as to what may constitute provocation in law other than that the alleged provocation must have been serious enough to provoke a reasonable or ordinary person. As Lord Diplock stated in *Camplin*:

> [s.3] abolishes all previous rules of law as to what can or cannot amount to provocation...The judge is entitled, if he thinks it helpful, to suggest considerations which may influence the jury in forming their own opinion as to whether the test [of provocation] is satisfied; but he should make it clear that these are not instructions which they are required to follow; it is for them and no one else to decide what weight, if any, ought to be given to them.[55]

---

52   As Fletcher has remarked: "Though it is generally recognized that proof of a serious physical blow is sufficient to submit the issue of provocation to the jury, the general rule [at common law] is that insults and abusive language are insufficient. The premise obviously is that though 'sticks and stones may break our bones', we are all expected to maintain a stiff upper lip in the face of verbal aggression", *Rethinking Criminal Law* (1978), p. 244. See eg. *Rothwell* (1871) 12 Cox CC 145; *Ellor* (1920) 15 Cr App R 41. And see Viscount Simon's position in *Holmes v DPP* [1946] AC 588. This view still prevails in Scotland, although it is recognised that there may be cases where verbal provocation could, exceptionally, be accepted. See e.g. *Thomson v HM Adv* (1986) SLT 281; *Cosgrove v HM Adv* (1991) SLT 25; *Berry v HM Adv* (1976) SCCR Supp 156; *Stobbs v HM Adv* (1983) SCCR 190.

53   See, e.g., the cases of *Palmer* [1913] 2 KB 29; *Greening* [1913] 3 KB 846, where it was accepted that a plea of provocation involving an allegation of adultery presupposes the existence of a lawful marriage. In other cases, however, the courts adopted the view that adultery may be admitted as provocation notwithstanding the absence of a lawful marriage. See, e.g., *Kelly* (1848) 2 C & K 814; *Alexander* (1913) 9 Cr App R 139; *Gauthier* (1943) 29 Cr App R 113; *Larkin* [1943] KB 174.

54   But this approach was rejected in *Holmes v DPP* [1946] AC 588.

55   *Camplin* (1978) AC 705 at 716.

As this suggests, it is social convention, rather than law, that now determines the standard of adequate provocation. From this point of view, it is accepted that an accused may be able to rely on provocation, even if the victim's conduct by which he was provoked was not in any way unlawful.[56] But mere circumstances or naturally occurring events cannot amount to provocation for, under s.3, only human conduct could constitute provocation. However, if the circumstances have been brought about by a human being, then they might be treated as potential provocation.[57]

Further, at common law it was required that the provocation must come from the victim,[58] and that it must be directed at the accused,[59] as Lord Devlin's definition in *Duffy* has indicated. However, under s.3 no such limitation as to the author or the addressee of the offensive conduct is imposed, the only question being whether the accused was provoked to lose his self-control. Thus, an accused may be entitled to the defence, even if the provocation came from a person other than the victim, or it was directed at a party other than the accused. As was stated by Lord Widgery in *Davies*[60] "whatever the position at common

---

56    As G. Williams has noted, "[T]he Homicide Act, in allowing insults as provocation, inevitably alters the position, because an insult uttered in private is neither a crime nor even a tort. Section 3 contains no restriction to unlawful acts, and the courts seem to be ready to allow any provocative conduct to be taken into consideration, even though that conduct was itself provoked by the defendant", *Textbook of Criminal Law* (1983), pp. 534-535. As stated by Lowry LCJ in *Browne* [1973] NI 96: "I should prefer to say that provocation is something unwarranted which is likely to make a reasonable person angry or indignant" ( at 108 ). And see *Doughty* (1986) 83 Cr App R 319, where it was held that the crying of a baby may constitute adequate provocation for purposes of mitigation. See on this J. Horder, "The Problem of Provocative Children" [1987] *Criminal Law Review* 655. But other common law jurisdictions have adopted a different approach to the question of what may constitute provocation in law - one closer to the traditional common law position - excluding acts that a person has a legal right to do from the scope of legal provocation. See e.g. s. 215 (3) of the Canadian Criminal Code. And see Howard, *Australian Criminal Law* (2nd ed.) 93.

57    For example, finding one's house damaged by a landslide could not be relied upon as provocation, if the accused lost his self-control and killed as a result. On the other hand, finding one's house damaged by thieves might amount to provocation in law.

58    As was held, e.g., in *Simpson* (1915) 84 LJKB 1893, CCA

59    *Duffy* [1949] 1 All ER 932. But there have been cases in which it was accepted that provocation directed at a near relative was sufficient. See, e.g., *Harrington* (1866) 10 Cox CC 370.

60    [1975] QB 691, [1975] 1 All ER 890, [1975] 2 WLR 586.

law, the situation since 1957 has been that acts or words otherwise to be treated as provocative for present purposes are not excluded from such consideration merely because they emanate from someone other than the victim".[61] Moreover, if the accused, acting in response to provocation, killed an innocent person by accident, he may still be able to rely on the defence (an implication of the application of the doctrine of transferred malice).[62] Similarly, if an accused's losing his self-control and killing was the result of a mistake as to the facts which constituted provocation, his offence may still be reduced to manslaughter. In such a case the accused's conduct is assessed in the light of the facts as he mistakenly believed them to be.[63] In the past the dominant view was that the accused could not rely on a defence in such cases, unless his mistake was reasonable. However, recent developments in the English law of mistake suggest that the accused's mistake need only be an honest one.[64]

If there is some evidence raising the possibility that the accused was provoked, the judge must put the defence to the jury.[65] It is for

---

61   See also *Pearson* [1992] Crim LR 193; *Twine* [1967] Crim LR 710. And see O'Regan, "Indirect Provocation and Misdirected Retaliation" [1968] *Criminal Law Review* 319.

62   The same position was accepted under common law. See e.g. *Gross* (1913) 23 Cox CC 455; *Porritt* [1961] 3 All ER 463, [1961] 1 WLR 1372. And see G. Williams, *Textbook of Criminal Law* (2nd ed, 1983), p. 533 at n9: "[I]t has long been recognized that in cases of transferred intention provocation is transferred with the intention".

63   See, e.g., *Brown* (1776) 1 Leach 148;*Letenock* [1917] 12 Cr App Rep 221.

64   See *Beckford v The Queen* [1988] AC 130.

65   See *Acott* [1997] 1 All ER 706, where it was held that, for the defence of provocation to be put to the jury, there must be evidence of some identifiable words or actions of another likely to have provoked the accused into losing his self-control. It is not sufficient that the accused's loss of self-control may possibly have been caused by some unidentified conduct of another. And see relevant comment in *The Independent,* Tuesday, 11 March 1997. In *Clarke* [1991] Crim LR 383, the accused lost his self-control and killed his girlfriend when she told him that she was pregnant and that she was planning to have an abortion; the defence was left to the jury and was rejected. In *Cocker* [1989] Crim LR 740 the accused killed his wife, who was suffering from a painful and incurable disease, after she had repeatedly begged him to kill her. The trial judge refused to put the issue of provocation to the jury as there was no evidence that the accused was provoked. See also *Wellington* [1993] Crim LR 616. In some cases evidence given by a pathologist relating to the nature of the victim's injuries may be crucial, as such evidence may suggest that the victim was subjected to a frenzied attack - an indication that the accused had lost his self-control. See, e.g., *Rossiter* (1992) 95 Cr App R 326.

the judge to decide, as a matter of law, whether there is any such evidence, even though the accused himself may not wish to raise the issue e.g. because raising provocation may be inconsistent with another defence relied upon by the accused.[66] If no evidence of provocation appears in the case, as presented by the prosecution, then the accused will bear the burden of introducing some evidence of provocation.[67] It is not required, as it was the case in the past, that the judge should first be satisfied that the alleged provocation was serious enough to provoke a reasonable person, or that the accused had lost his self-control as a result.[68] Once the defence is put to the jury, it is for them to decide whether, as a matter of fact, the accused was provoked to lose his self-control (this is often referred to as "the factual question" in provocation). And it is upon the prosecution to prove, beyond reasonable doubt, that the accused was not in fact provoked or did not lose his self-control at the time of the killing.[69] However, after the defence has been introduced, the judge may still seek to advise the jury on the question of whether the alleged provocation should be considered serious, or on whether a reasonable person may have responded to the provocation offered the way the accused did. The judge's opinion may still affect the final outcome of the case, although not as decisively as before the introduction of the 1957 legislation.[70] If the jury are left with a reasonable doubt as to

---

[66] See *Mancini v DPP* [1942] AC 1, [1941] 3 All ER 272. Where an accused charged with murder pleads self-defence - a defence leading to full acquittal - he may be unwilling to raise the issue of provocation, for evidence of provocation might be detrimental to his plea of self-defence. In such cases the courts have recognised that the accused has a tactical reason for not raising provocation, notwithstanding the fact that such a defence may be supported by existing evidence. See *Bullard v R* [1957] AC 635, [1961] 3 All ER 470n; *Rolle v R* [1965] 3 All ER 582; *Lee Chun-Chuen v R* [1963] AC 220, [1963] 1 All ER 73; *Johnson* [1989] 1 WLR 740.

[67] Similarly, in Canada it is accepted that, with regard to the provocation defence, the accused bears an evidentiary burden and that the judge should not put the defence to the jury unless this burden is discharged. See, e.g., *Parnerkar* [1974] SCR 449, 21 CRNS 129.

[68] But this rule has been challenged by the Criminal Law Revision Committee (see CLRC/OAP/R, para. 88).

[69] See, e.g., *Cascoe* [1970] 2 All ER 833.

[70] But leaving the issue of provocation to be determined by the jury, as is currently required, does not necessarily give an advantage to the accused. As A. Samuels has remarked, " ...although in principle it is preferable that all substantive issues of fact and opinion in a criminal case should be determined by the jury, the accused is in one respect in a worse position than before 1957, for now the judge cannot direct the jury that on evidence, if accepted, a reasonable man would have been provoked, although there is no appeal for the

whether all the conditions of the defence were met, they must find the accused guilty of manslaughter only.

## The Requirement of Loss of Self-Control

In dealing with a plea of provocation the jury have to consider, first, the subjective or factual question of whether the accused was actually provoked to lose his or her self control.[71] If they are not satisfied, beyond reasonable doubt, that the accused was in fact deprived of his self-control at the time of the killing they will have to find the accused guilty of murder, without considering how a reasonable person would have reacted to the provocation received. Thus, if the accused has an unusually phlegmatic temperament and he did not lose his self-control his defence will fail, even though the provocation may have been serious enough to provoke a reasonable person to lose his self-control. In dealing with the subjective question the jury are entitled to consider the immediate act that caused death as well as all the relevant circumstances preceding or surrounding that act. The nature of the alleged provocation, the manner in which the accused reacted, the time which elapsed between the provocation and the accused's response, previous relations between the parties, the sensitivity or otherwise of the accused are considerations relevant to answering the subjective question in provocation. As Widgery CJ said in *Davies*, considering the relevant background "is material to the provocation as the setting in which the state of mind of the defendant must be judged".[72]

In a number of cases the courts have confirmed the position, expressed in *Duffy*, that for the defence of provocation to be accepted there must be "a sudden and temporary loss of self-control, rendering the accused so subject to passion as to make him or her for the moment not master of his mind".[73] According to the current formulation of the

---

prosecution agains a judge who is over-indulgent towards the defence", "Excusable Loss of Self-Control in Homicide", *Modern Law Review* 34 (1971), 163.

71  See *Brown* [1972] 2 All ER 1328 at 1333; *Cocker* [1989] Crim LR 740.

72  *Davies* [1975] QB 691 at 702. Similarly in *McGregor* [1962] NZLR 1069 was held that background circumstances, such as earlier provocations, "could be taken into account in determining whether a subsequent comparatively trivial act of provocation...could cause slumbering fires of passion to burst into flame" (at 1080).

73  *Duffy* [1949] 1 All ER 932n. In *McGregor* [1962] NZLR 1069 North J pointed out: "[I]t is of the essence of the defence of provocation that the acts or words of the dead man have caused the accused a sudden and temporary loss of

provocation defence, a killing that has been planned, or over which the actor has had control, cannot be reduced to manslaughter, for planning or premeditation is inconsistent with the requirement of loss of self-control. In provocation the intention to kill is expected to have been formed immediately after the provocation was received. If the provocation was received some time before the time of killing, it is assumed that the accused had enough time to regain his self-control. A clear distinction is thus drawn between a person who loses his self-control and kills, immediately upon receiving provocation, and one who retaliates after brooding over past wrongs he suffered at the victim's hands. As was stated in *Duffy*

> Severe exasperation or a long course of conduct causing suffering and anxiety are not by themselves sufficient to constitute provocation in law. Indeed, the further removed an incident is from the crime the less it counts. ...It does not matter how cruel [the victim] was, how much or how little he was to blame, except in so far as it resulted in the final act of the appellant.[74]

As this statement suggests, despite the evidence of grave provocation, the accused could not shelter under the provocation defence if he had not lost his self-control, or if he has regained it before his killing of the provoker. In *Ibrams*[75] the defendants, who had been terrorised by the victim over a period of time, killed the victim following an agreement between them to do so. There was no evidence that, on the day of the killing, the victim had done anything to provoke them, the last provocation on his part having been offered a few days earlier. The Court of Appeal adopted the view that the formulation of a plan to kill as well as the lapse of time between the last act of provocation and the killing negated the accuseds' claims of loss of self-control. The Court of Appeal approved the statement of Devlin J in *Duffy* that

> [C]ircumstances which induce a desire for revenge are inconsistent with provocation, since the conscious formulation of a desire for revenge means that the person has had time to think, to reflect, and that would negative a sudden and temporary loss of self-control, which is of the essence of provocation.[76]

The same position was adopted in the subsequent cases of *Thornton* and *Ahluwalia*.

---

self-control, rendering him so subject to passion as to make him for the moment not master of his mind" (at p. 1078).

[74]  Ibid.

[75]  (1981) 74 Cr. App. Rep. 154.

[76]  Ibid.

In *Thornton*,[77] the accused killed her husband who was an alcoholic and had been violent towards her on several occasions. Evidence suggested that the accused had expressed an intention to kill her husband a few days before the killing took place. On the night of the killing, the accused found her husband asleep on the couch. When she asked him to come to bed, he called her a prostitute and said that he would kill her if she had been out with other men. She went into the kitchen, looking for a truncheon which she planned to use for her own protection, but found a long carving knife instead. She sharpened the knife and returned to the sitting room, where her husband was lying, and again asked him to come up to bed with her. He refused and told her that he would kill her while she was asleep. At that point the accused stabbed him once in the stomach, causing his death. At her trial the accused pleaded diminished responsibility, but, as provocation was raised by the evidence, the trial judge put the issue to the jury. In doing so, the judge pointed out that the accused herself had denied losing self-control and added that, even if she did, it was questionable whether her response had been reasonable in the light of the provocation she had received.[78] The accused's appeal was based on the argument that requiring a sudden and temporary loss of self-control was inappropriate, particularly in a case where the accused was "subjected to a long course of provocative conduct, including domestic violence, which may sap the resilience and resolve to retain self-control when the final confrontation erupts".[79] The Court of Appeal, however, took the view that the requirement of loss of self-control has so long been an essential part of the provocation defence, that it could only by removed by legislative enactment. The Court held that the distinction between acting while in control of oneself and acting under a sudden and temporary loss of self-control, as drawn in *Duffy*, remained an important element of the provocation defence. It was stated that

> The distinction...is just as, if not more, important in [this] kind of case...It is within the experience of each member of the court that in cases of domestic violence which culminate in the death of a partner there is frequently evidence given of provocative acts committed by the deceased in the past, for it is in that context that the jury have to consider the accused's reaction. In every such case the question for the jury is whether at the moment the fatal blow was struck the accused had been deprived for that moment of the self-control which previously

---

77  [1992] 1 All ER 306, [1992] Crim LR 54.

78  As the judge told the jury, in circumstances such as these, "it is hardly reasonable...to stab fatally when there are other alternatives available, like walking out or going upstairs", ibid at 312.

79  Ibid at 313.

he or she had been able to exercise...We reject the suggestion that in using the phrase 'sudden and temporary loss of control' there was any misdirection of the jury.[80]

The same approach was adopted by the Court of Appeal in *Ahluwalia*.[81] The accused was found guilty for murdering her husband who had subjected her to a long period of mistreatment and violence. The accused had tried to do something about her husband's violent conduct — she secured court injunctions against him on two occasions — but she did not try to obtain a divorce. Instead, it was the victim who was trying to terminate the marriage and, in fact, had left their house on at least one prior occasion. At the time of the killing, the victim told the accused that he was having an affair with a work colleague and taunted her with this. On an earlier occasion, however, he had denied having an affair, but had expressed an intention to put an end to their marriage. The accused made an attempt to discuss their relationship, but the victim refused and threatened to burn her with an iron if she did not leave him alone. He also threatened to beat her if she did not give him money. The accused left the room and, after brooding for some time over her husband's conduct, she filled a bin full of petrol and threw it into her husband's bedroom. She then lit a stick she was holding and threw it into the room. The husband suffered severe burns and died a few days later. The fact that the accused did not act immediately after the last provocation offered by the victim, as well as her purchasing of the petrol several days before the killing, indicated deliberation and premeditation on the accused's part. The defence, once more, challenged the applicability of the loss of self-control requirement in such cases, and drew the Court's attention to a long period of mistreatment the accused had suffered in the victim's hands and the threats he made on the night of the killing. The Court of Appeal, however, approved the trial judge's insistence on the requirement of loss of self-control. The Court held that loss of self-control is an essential element of the provocation defence serving "to underline that the defence is concerned with the actions of an individual who is not, at the moment when she or she acts violently, master of his or her own mind".[82] It was recognised, moreover, that the words "sudden and temporary loss of self-control" did not imply that the accused's reaction to the provocation received had to be immediate; they imply only that the accused's act of killing must not be

---

[80]  Ibid at 314.
[81]  [1992] 4 All ER 889, [1993] Crim LR 63.
[82]  Ibid at 895.

premeditated.[83] From this point of view, it was pointed out, a delay between the acts or words of provocation and the accused's response could be fatal the accused's plea, because

> Time for reflection may show that after the provocative conduct made its impact on the mind of the defendant, he or she kept or regained self-control. The passage of time following the provocation may also show that the subsequent attack was planned or based on motives, such as revenge or punishment, inconsistent with the loss of self-control and therefore with the defence of provocation.[84]

In both cases, the Court of Appeal rejected the accuseds' appeals in connection with the defence of provocation although, in *Ahluwalia*, a new trial was ordered to consider evidence relating to the defence of diminished responsibility — a defence that had not been raised at the trial despite evidence that the accused suffered from endogenous depression at the time of the killing.

As the above cases show, loss of self-control remains a necessary condition of the provocation defence.[85] Nevertheless, judges will usually leave the defence to the jury if there is some evidence suggesting that the accused may have been provoked to lose self-control, despite evidence of premeditation, and even if the defence has not been raised by the accused.[86] For example, in *Burke*,[87] the defence of provocation was put to the jury, although the accused, following an argument at a nightclub, left the premises, fetched a knife

---

83   As the court explained, "We accept that the subjective element in the defence of provocation would not as a matter of law be negatived simply because of the delayed reaction in such cases, provided that there was at the time of the killing a 'sudden and temporary loss of self-control' caused by the alleged provocation. However, the longer the delay and the stronger the evidence of deliberation on the part of the defendant, the more likely it will be that the prosecution will negative provocation".

84   Ibid at 895-896.

85   The same position has been adopted by the CLRC (OAP/R, para. 84). According to their proposal, "...the defence applies only where the defendant's act is caused by the provocation and is committed suddenly upon the provoking event, not to cases where the defendant's violent reaction has been delayed; but the jury should continue to take into consideration previous provocations before the one which produced the fatal reaction".

86   See, e.g,. *Pearson* [1992] Crim LR 193; *Baille* [1995] Crim LR 739. And see the Court of Appeal decisions in *Cambridge* [1994] 2 All ER 760, [1994] Crim LR 690; *Burgess and McLean* [1995] Crim LR 425; *Cox* [1995] Crim LR 741.

87   *Burke* [1987] Crim LR 336.

and returned to the club where he stabbed the victim. As Lord Morris stated in *Camplin*[88]

> It will be for the court to decide whether, on a charge of murder, there is evidence on which the jury can find that the person charged was provoked to lose his self-control; thereafter...all the questions are for the jury.

Moreover, these cases show that what needs to be sudden is loss of self-control, not the provocation. Thus a long history of provocation may be relied upon to explain why the accused lost his self-control and killed as a response to an act of provocation which, considered in the abstract, would not seem to warrant such a response. The idea here is that individual incidents might be trivial but that they might become serious provocation because of the cumulative effect which a long period of provocative conduct may have had on the accused.[89]

## The Objective Test in Provocation

After the question of loss of self-control has been considered, the next question the jury has to answer is whether the accused's judgment of the actions or words that caused him to lose self-control and kill as gravely provocative was, objectively, a warranted one (this is sometimes referred to as the "evaluative question" in provocation). In the past, what was capable of amounting to provocation was limited to certain forms of conduct which, as a matter of law, were deemed sufficiently offensive. These included grossly insulting assaults, seeing a friend, relative or kinsman being attacked, seeing an Englishman unlawfully deprived of his liberty, discovering a man in the act of adultery with one's wife and finding a man committing sodomy with one's son.[90] In *Holmes*,[91] the House of Lords pointed out that "in no case could words alone, save in circumstances of a most extreme and exceptional character", amount to provocation in law. The House held, moreover, that an accused could not rely on a confession of adultery as provocation sufficient to reduce his offence to manslaughter. The modern approach is to leave open the forms of conduct capable of amounting to provocation in law, but to limit the

---

[88] *Camplin* [1978] AC 705, 67 Cr App Rep 14.
[89] See, e.g., *Humphreys* [1995] 4 All ER 1008. For a further discussion of the problem of cumulative provocation see Ch. 6 below.
[90] See, e.g., Hawkins 1 *Pleas of the Crown* c. 13, s. 36; East, 1 *Pleas of the Crown* 233; Stephen, *A Digest of the Criminal Law*, Article 224. And see *Fisher* (1837) 8 C & P 182.
[91] *Holmes v DPP* [1946] AC 588, [1946] 2 All ER 124.

class by asking whether the relevant conduct was likely to provoke a hypothetical reasonable or ordinary person. Only if the jury feel that the provocation offered was likely to provoke a reasonable person to lose his or her self-control and do as the accused did, the accused's plea of provocation could be accepted. The introduction of the objective test in provocation has been justified on public policy grounds. As stated in *Camplin*, "The public policy...was to reduce the incidence of fatal violence by preventing a person relying upon his own exceptional pugnacity or excitability as an excuse for loss of self-control".[92]

Before the introduction of the Homicide Act 1957, it rested upon the judge to instruct the jury as to the attributes of the reasonable person and the way in which a reasonable person should be expected to react when provoked. The reasonable person was defined as an adult person with normal mental and physical attributes. This way of looking at the matter has caused problems, however, for often what renders certain conduct provocative was precisely the fact that the accused is not, in some crucial respect, an "ordinary person". And yet, for a number of years, the courts refused to modify the standard to allow for certain individual characteristics of the accused to be taken into account on the grounds that such an approach would undermine the purported objectivity of the standard.[93] In *Bedder*[94] the accused, a young man who was suffering from sexual impotence, attempted to have intercourse with a prostitute to see whether he could overcome his condition. He failed, and the woman taunted him about his impotence and prepared to leave. When he tried to hold her, she slapped him, punched him and kicked him in the genitals. At this point the accused lost his self-control and stabbed her to death. Charged with murder, the accused claimed that, because the insults were directed at his impotence, about which he was particularly sensitive, such insults constituted provocation sufficient to reduce his offence to manslaughter. However, the jury was directed to ignore the fact that the accused was impotent in deciding whether the victim's conduct amounted to provocation in law. The House of Lords held that this was a correct direction, pointing out that considerations regarding any physical or mental peculiarities of the accused lie outside the scope of the objective test in provocation. Lord Simonds, in dismissing the accused's appeal, said

---

92  *Camplin* [1978] AC 705 at 716.
93  See, e.g., *Alexander* (1913) 9 Cr App Rep 139; *Smith* (1915) 11 Cr App Rep 81.
94  *Bedder v DPP* [1954] 2 All ER 801, [1954] 1 WLR 1119.

It was urged on your Lordships that the hypothetical reasonable man must be confronted with all the same circumstances as the accused, and that this could not be fairly done unless he was also invested with the peculiar characteristics of the accused. But this makes nonsense of the test. Its purpose is to invite the jury to consider the act of the accused by reference to a certain standard or norm of conduct and with this object the 'reasonable' or the 'average' or the 'normal' man is invoked. If the reasonable man is then deprived in the whole or in part of his reason, or the normal man endowed with abnormal characteristics, the term ceases to have any value. ...It would be plainly illogical not to recognise an unusually excitable or pugnacious temperament in the accused as a matter to be taken into account but yet to recognise for that purpose some unusual physical characteristic, be it impotence or another. ...It is too subtle a refinement for my mind or, I think, for that of a jury to grasp that the temper may be ignored but the physical defect taken into account.[95]

The House of Lords, in this case, drew no distinction between physical and mental characteristics when explaining the operation of the objective test in provocation.

*Bedder* shows the difficulty common law courts have had in recognising criteria for distinguishing between those individual characteristics of the accused that are morally relevant to mitigation and those that are not. One should be able to distinguish, in other words, between those individual characteristics that are relevant to determining the gravity of the provocation, which should be taken into account, and those that have to do with the actor's level of self-control, which should not. As Ashworth has noted, "To be meaningful, the 'gravity' of provocation must be expressed in relation to persons in a particular situation or group".[96] Losing sight of this distinction is liable to lead to morally contestable decisions, as the criticisms that followed the decision in *Bedder* make clear. The position adopted in this case is largely the result of a misunderstanding regarding the role of the reasonable person in provocation. The reasonable person was viewed as providing a basis upon which the judicial decision could be abstracted from the individual case to formulate rules of law of general application, an approach that tends to overlook the possible effect of certain individual characteristics of the accused on the question of culpability. As Fletcher, in criticising this approach to the objective standard in provocation, has remarked

Once we forget that the problem is the analysis of those impulses that we are fairly expected to control, it follows that judges would have difficulty distinguishing between a head injury and a bad temper. Once the moral

---

95   Ibid at 803, 804.
96   "The Doctrine of Provocation", *Cambridge Law Journal* 35 (1976) 292, p. 300.

perspective on provocation is lost, the concern develops that the individuation of the [reasonable person] standard might lead to its total collapse. Not knowing where to draw the line, judges would prefer not to include any unusual physical feature of the defendant.[97]

The decision in *Bedder* was reversed, following the introduction of s.3 the Homicide Act 1957, under which the judge cannot direct the jury as to which characteristics the reasonable person should be endowed with. However, it was not until the decision of the House of Lords in *Camplin*,[98] a case decided more than 20 years after the Act, that the effect of s.3 on the issue of characteristics was fully recognised.

In *Camplin* the accused, a fifteen-year-old boy, went to the victim's house after having a few drinks. The accused was blackmailing the victim over a homosexual relationship the latter had with one of the accused's friends. The accused claimed that, while he was at the house, the victim beat him and sexually assaulted him. Overpowered by shame and remorse when he heard the victim laughing over his sexual triumph, the accused lost his self-control and hit him twice over the head with a heavy object (a kitchen utensil known as a chapatti pan), thereby killing him. The accused was charged with murder and pleaded provocation, thus seeking to reduce the homicide to manslaughter. The chief issue in dispute in this case was whether the jury should have been directed to take into account the fact that at the time of the killing the accused was only 15 years old. The trial judge, following the *Bedder* principle, declined to draw the jury's attention to the accused's age, as proposed by the accused's counsel, and directed the jury to consider whether a reasonable man of full age would have responded to the provocation offered the way the accused did. As a result of this direction the defence of provocation was rejected and the accused was convicted of murder. The accused's conviction of murder was quashed by the Court of Appeal, however, which reduced the offence to manslaughter. The Court of Appeal adopted the view that this case should be distinguished from *Bedder*, for young age and the immaturity by which youth is usually

---

97  *Rethinking Criminal Law*, p. 249.
   And according to Ashworth, "[*Bedder*] made bad law, for it is surely impossible to assess the gravity of provocation without reference to the characteristic of the accused at which the taunts were directed. Indeed, this point is so self-evident that it must have entered Lord Simonds' mind. The tone of his speech suggests a fear that, if personal characteristics were considered even for this limited purpose, the objective standard would evaporate", supra note 96, at 301.

98  *Camplin* [1978] AC 705, [1978] 2 All ER 168.

accompanied pertain to a normal stage in every person's life; they are
not peculiar characteristics or idiosyncrasies, like the sexual impotence
of the accused in *Bedder*. The House of Lords, to which the case was
referred following an appeal by the Crown, confirmed the decision of
the Court of Appeal. In dismissing the Crown's appeal the House
adopted the broader view that *Bedder* has been overruled by s. 3 of the
Homicide Act 1957. The House took the view that as, under s. 3,
words as well as acts may constitute provocation in law, mental or
physical peculiarities cannot be ignored, for it is by reference to those
peculiarities that the gravity of verbal provocation will in most cases
depend. From this point of view, it was pointed out that "[t]he effect
of an insult will often depend entirely on a characteristic of the person
to whom the insult is directed. 'Dirty nigger' would probably mean
little if said to a white man or even if said by one coloured man to
another; but it is obviously more insulting when said by a white man to
a coloured man".[99] Lord Diplock, in explaining how the jury should
be directed in provocation cases, stated

> The judge should state what the question is, using the terms of the section. He
> should then explain to them that the reasonable man referred to in the question
> is a person having the power of self-control to be expected of an ordinary person
> of the sex and age of the accused, but in other respects sharing such of the
> accused's characteristics as they think would affect the gravity of the provocation
> to him; and that the question is not merely whether such a person in like
> circumstances would be provoked to lose his self-control but also whether he
> would react to the provocation as the accused did.[100]

But, notwithstanding the importance of the accused's age as a factor to
be taken into account in determining the gravity of the provocation, the
judge may draw the jury's attention to the accused's age only if, in his
opinion, such a consideration is relevant to explaining the accused's
response to the provocation. Thus in *Ali*,[101] the Court of Appeal held
that the trial judge was right in deciding not to draw the attention of the
jury to the fact that the accused was 20 years of age since the gravity of
the provocation would have been the same no matter what the
accused's age may have been.[102]

The position adopted in *Camplin*, which is taken to express the
common law as modified by the Homicide Act 1957, is consonant

---

[99]  [1978] AC 705 at 726.
[100]  [1978] AC 705 at 718.
[101]  [1989] Crim LR 736.
[102]  Contrast with *Roberts* [1990] Crim LR, where the fact that the accused was
23 years of age was held to be relevant, together with other factors, in
determining the gravity of the provocation offered.

with s. 169 of the New Zealand Crimes Act 1961. The New Zealand provision was intended to give some relief from the rigidity of the reasonable person test as interpreted in *Bedder*. According to s. 169 (2):

> Anything done or said may be provocation if — (a) In the circumstances of the case it was sufficient to deprive a person having the power of self-control of an ordinary person, but otherwise having the characteristics of the offender, of the power of self-control; and (b) It did in fact deprive the offender of the power of self-control and thereby induced him to commit the act of homicide.

The opening up of the objective test in provocation to some degree of individualisation was deemed necessary in order to avoid the morally controversial decisions to which the rigid application of the test has led in the past. Nonetheless, this more liberal interpretation of the objective test, although a significant improvement over the previous position, has not been without difficulties. Problems have arisen, for example, about how to distinguish those individual characteristics bearing upon the gravity of the provocation from those character traits relating, rather, to the accused's capacity for self-control. Although, in theory, it is admitted that the second are not relevant to the defence (except, perhaps, with regard to proving loss of self-control), drawing the line between the two has been a matter of dispute. On the assumption that the defence of provocation pertains to "normal" people, it has been questioned whether certain characteristics should be seen as modifying the applicable test or, rather, as rendering the test inapplicable by removing the accused from the category of normal or ordinary persons. In the latter case, however, the accused should be able to rely on diminished responsibility, or some other defence based on the concept of abnormality of mind, rather than on provocation.

In *Newell*,[103] the accused, who was a chronic alcoholic, became enraged when the victim, with whom he was drinking at a pub, began making insulting remarks about the accused's former girlfriend. The accused lost his self-control and hit the victim several times over the head with a heavy ashtray, thereby causing his death. The accused was found guilty of murder and appealed. The Court of Appeal held that the accused's being a chronic alcoholic, as a permanent characteristic, could be relevant to the assessment of the provocation, whereas his being drunk at the time of the killing or bad temper was not. As the provocation in this case was not directed at the accused's chronic alcoholism, his appeal was dismissed. The Court adopted the traditional view that, in so far as drunkenness does not negative the

---

[103]  (1980) 71 Cr App R 331, [1980] Crim LR 576.

requisite intent, an accused cannot rely on the claim that he reacted as violently as he did only because he was drunk. It was held that drunkenness lacks a sufficient degree of permanence to be regarded as a characteristic for the purposes of the provocation defence. In explaining what characteristics may be taken into account in deciding whether the provocation offered was enough to make a reasonable person do as the accused did, the Court referred with approval to a passage from *McGregor*,[104] a case decided by the New Zealand Court of Appeal. In *McGregor*, North J stated:

> It is not every trait or disposition of the offender that can be invoked to modify the concept of the ordinary man. The characteristic must be something definite and of sufficient significance to make the offender a different person from the ordinary run of mankind, and have also a sufficient degree of permanence to warrant its being regarded as something constituting part of the individual's character or personality...[It includes] not only...physical qualities but also...mental qualities and such more indeterminate attributes as colour, race and creed. ...Moreover...there must be some real connection between the nature of the provocation and the particular characteristic of the offender by which it is sought to modify the ordinary man test. The words or conduct must have been exclusively or particularly provocative to the individual because, and only because, of the characteristic.[105]

According to the approach adopted in *McGregor*, the word "characteristics" is wide enough to encompass not only to physical qualities, e.g. sexual impotence, but also mental qualities, e.g. phobias. For example A, suffering from arachnophobia, finds in his bed a large spider put there by V as a joke. If A loses his self-control and kills V, A's arachnophobia would be taken into account, as a relevant characteristic, in the application of the objective test. Here it is A's very arachnophobia, a characteristic personal to him, that converts V's conduct into provocation sufficient to reduce his offence to manslaughter. Similarly, for the impotent client of the prostitute, it is the impotence that converts the prostitute's taunts into provocation. However, North J's statement that the provocation must have been directed at the particular characteristic of the accused overlooks the fact that not all characteristics are of the type mentioned in the above examples, i.e. capable of being the direct target of the provocation. There is a class of possible characteristics which might be taken into consideration as relevant to determining the gravity of the provocation offered, even though the provocation was not aimed directly at them. For example, in *Camplin*, the fact that the accused was only 15 years old was taken to be a relevant characteristic, although the provocation

---

104  *McGregor* [1962] NZLR 1069.
105  Ibid at 1081-82.

was not aimed at the accused's age as such. An accused's sex or the fact that he or she was suffering from an illness are examples of general dispositions that may be relevant as characteristics that could be taken into account to explain the accused's reaction to the provocation.

In *Morhall*,[106] the accused, a drug addict, was taunted by the victim for his addiction to glue sniffing. In the fight that ensued, the accused stabbed the victim several times, killing him. The Court of Appeal referred with approval to the above passage from *McGregor*, but adopted the view that the accused's drug addiction could not be taken into account, for such a characteristic is inconsistent with the concept of the reasonable person. In the Court's view "a self-induced addiction to glue sniffing brought on by voluntary and persistent abuse of solvents is wholly inconsistent with the concept of a reasonable man. [If such a characteristic is taken into account] it would result in the so-called reasonable man being a reincarnation of the appellant with his peculiar characteristics whether capable of being possessed by a reasonable man or not and whether acquired by nature or by his own abuse".[107] The main question that arose from the Court of Appeal's approach was whether it is for the judge to decide whether a particular characteristic is consistent with the concept of the reasonable person and, as such, it should be taken into account by the jury. The House of Lords, in allowing the accused's appeal, held that the accused's addiction should have been taken into consideration, for "it was a characteristic of particular relevance, since the words of the deceased which were said to constitute provocation were directed towards the appellant's shameful addiction to glue sniffing and his inability to break himself of it". It was pointed out that "there is nothing in the speeches in *D.P.P. v. Camplin* to suggest that a characteristic of this kind should be excluded from consideration".[108] Moreover, the House noted that North J's judgment in *McGregor* must be treated with caution, especially in the light of the reservations expressed in relation to that judgment by the New Zealand Court of Appeal in *McCarthy*.[109]

In *McCarthy*, North J' position that there must be a direct connection between the provocation and the characteristic the accused seeks to rely upon to modify the objective standard was called into question. In that case the accused had suffered brain damage and this had affected his personality. Although the provocation offered was not

---

106 *Morhall* [1996] 1 AC 90, [1995] 3 All ER 659, [1995] 3 WLR 330, [1993] 4 All ER 888.
107 [1993] 4 All ER 888 at 894.
108 [1995] 3 All ER 659, at 661 (per Lord Goff of Chieveley).
109 *McCarthy* (1992) 8 CRNZ 58, [1992] 2 NZLR 550.

aimed directly at this characteristic, the Court held the accused was entitled to have this characteristic taken into account. The Court adopted the view that

> A racial characteristic of the accused, his or her age or sex, mental deficiency or a tendency to excessive emotionalism as a result of brain injury are ... examples of characteristics to be attributed to the hypothetical person. In a case where any of them apply, the ordinary power of self-control falls to be assessed on the assumption that the person has the same characteristics. The question is ... whether a person with ordinary power of self-control would have retained self-control notwithstanding such characteristics.[110]

But this cannot mean that any attribute of an accused's character or personality can be regarded as a relevant characteristic. A particular attribute may be treated as a characteristic for the purposes of the provocation defence only if it is capable of converting a relatively harmless conduct into grave provocation, either because the relevant conduct is aimed at the characteristic or because the accused has a tendency to interpret certain conduct differently from a "reasonable" or "ordinary" person. In either case, however, the accused is expected to have exercised ordinary powers of self-control. As was stated by the High Court of Australia in *Stingel* [111]

> In a case where it is necessary to take some such characteristic or attribute into account for the purpose of identifying the content or gravity of the wrongful act or insult (eg a case of a grave insult centred upon that characteristic or attribute), the objective test will, nonetheless, require that the provocative effect of the wrongful act or insult, with its content and gravity so identified, be assessed by reference to the powers of self-control of a hypothetical 'ordinary person' who is unaffected by that extraordinary attribute or characteristic. In other words, the fact that the particular accused lacks the power of self-control by reason of some attribute or characteristic which must be taken into account in identifying the content or gravity of the particular wrongful act or insult will not affect the reference point of the objective test, namely, the power of self-control of a hypothetical 'ordinary person'.[112]

---

110 *McCarthy* (1992) 8 CRNZ 58 at 67. The Court of Appeal held, moreover, that a temporary state of drunkenness is not a characteristic for the purposes of the provocation defence.

111 *Stingel* (1990) 171 CLR 312.

112 At 320. A similar position was adopted by the High Court of Australia in *Masciantonio* (1995) 183 CLR 58. As was stated in that case "the gravity of the conduct said to constitute provocation must be assessed by reference to relevant characteristics of the accused. Conduct which might not be insulting or hurtful to one person might be extremely so to another because of the person's age, sex, race, ethnicity, physical features, personal attributes, personal relationships or past history. The provocation must be put into

In *Luc Thiet Thuan*[113] the Privy Council referred with approval to Ashworth's view that "[t]he proper distinction is that individual peculiarities which bear on the gravity of the provocation should be taken into account, whereas individual peculiarities bearing on the accused's level of self-control should not".[114] In this case the accused, who was charged with murder in Hong Kong, pleaded both diminished responsibility and provocation. Medical evidence suggested that he had sustained a form of brain damage that often results in excessive emotionalism and a difficulty to control emotional impulses.The jury was directed to consider this evidence as relevant to the defence of diminished responsibility; but the judge made no reference to it when he directed the jury on provocation. The accused's appeal was dismissed by the Court of Appeal of Hong Kong on the grounds that the accused's mental abnormality could not be relied upon to modify the objective test, unless the provocation was directly aimed at that condition. The Privy Council also dismissed the accused's appeal. It was held that in *Newell*,[115] the Court of Appeal went too far in adopting fully and without analysis North J's dictum in *McGregor* — a dictum relating primarily to the application of s. 169 of the New Zealand Crimes Act 1961. The Privy Council took the view that treating "purely mental peculiarities" as characteristics relevant to provocation did not consort with the interpretation of the objective test under s.3 of the Homicide Act 1957. It was noted that in New Zealand law, where diminished responsibility is not recognised as an independent defence, it is possible that cases involving mental abnormality may be treated under the provocation defence. In England, however, such cases should be dealt with under the defence of diminished responsibility. The Privy Council confirmed that mental abnormality, in so far as it can provide a basis for raising diminished responsibility, cannot be a characteristic for the purposes of the provocation defence, unless the provocation bore a direct connection to that condition. This approach calls into question the position adopted in a number of cases, including *Ahluwalia*,[116] where it was suggested

---

context and it is only by having regard to the attributes or characteristics of the accused that this can be done. But having assessed the gravity of the provocation in this way, it is then necessary to ask the question whether provocation of that degree of gravity could cause an ordinary person to lose self-control and act in a manner which would encompass the accused's actions", (at p. 67).

113 [1996] 2 All ER 1033, [1996] Crim LR 433.
114 A. Ashworth, "The Doctrine of Provocation" supra note 96, p. 300. See also the commentary on *Morhall* [1995] Crim LR 891.
115 (1980) 71 Cr App Rep 331.
116 [1992] 4 All ER 889.

that mental conditions, such as that relating to post-traumatic stress disorder, cannot be excluded as characteristics relevant to the application of the objective test in provocation.[117]

The role of the reasonable person in the context of the provocation defence, it is submitted, is best understood as relating to the norms of attribution.[118] From this viewpoint the issue is not how a reasonable person would have reacted to the provocation, but whether the accused, given his personal characteristics and history, could fairly be expected to have retained his self-control in the face of the provocation received. As Fletcher points out

> The basic moral question in the law of homicide is distinguishing between those impulses to kill as to which we as a society demand self-control, and those as to which we relax our inhibitions.[119]

But what is it about some characteristics that make certain behaviour provocative when they would not be provocative to a person who does not possess the characteristic, and how is the gravity of the provocation to be determined by reference to different kinds of characteristics? As Horder notes, "[i]n a sense, having a big nose or thinning hair are characteristics, just like being of a particular colour or ethnic origin. Yet it seems obviously so much more provocative for a coloured person to be addressed as 'dirty nigger' than it does for them to be addressed as 'big nose' or 'baldy'; but why?".[120] Horder goes on to explain why it is that insulting conduct provokes. He argues that the feeling of being wronged that accompanies provoked anger pertains to a judgment that "a threat or challenge has been wrongly made to one's conception of self-worth...or to the entitlement or respect and regard from others for one's interests and concerns that the presumed intrinsic value of this conception gives one".[121] From this point of view, he argues that the gravity of the provocation depends upon at least three considerations. The first has to do with "the importance or significance to the provoked person of the aspect of self-

---

117 See also *Raven* [1982] Crim LR 51, *Dryden* [1995] 4 All ER 987, *Humphreys* [1995] 4 All ER 1008. But note that English courts are not bound by the decisions of the Privy Council. The Council's decisions may be influential but this would depend upon the degree to which the Privy Council may be said to be representative, considering its composition, of the House of Lords — something that does not appear to have been the case in *Luc Thiet Thuan*. See Smith and Hogan, *Criminal Law* (1996), pp. 371-72.

118 See ch. 1, pp. 5-6.

119 *Rethinking Criminal Law*, p. 247.

120 *Provocation and Responsibility* (1992), p. 138.

121 Ibid at p.142.

worth challenged by the provoker. Clearly, the more cherished the attribute or quality attacked, or the more fundamental it is to the fabric of one's character, the greater the provocation".[122] Secondly, the gravity of the provocation is proportionate to the degree of threat to the aspect of self-worth targeted by the provocative conduct. For example, the gravity of a provocative comment is significantly reduced where the provoked person knows that such comment is made in jest. By contrast, the provocation would be more grave where it involves an actual attack on the provoked person's sense of self-worth. Thirdly, the gravity of provocation depends upon the kind of threat that it presents (or is perceived to present) to an aspect of a person's conception of self-worth. Thus an insult that treats a person "as excluded from one's moral, cultural, intellectual, or political community, arguably involves the most deeply wounding threats or challenges to a conception of self-worth".[123] Considering the relationship between the provoked person and the provoker is also important: it is much more painful to be insulted by someone close to you than by a total stranger.

The issue of characteristics is most relevant to the first of these considerations upon which the gravity of the provocation depends. When the jury is directed to imagine themselves in the place of the provoked person, they are asked to consider what it would be like for a person with the particular qualities or attributes of the accused, central to his sense of self-worth, to have been the target of this insulting behaviour or comment. If no connection between the relevant attributes of the accused and the provocation can be established, then these attributes are not relevant to the gravity of the provocation offered. But how far is a jury to go in taking into consideration the cultural values of an accused — values which may, on occasion, be repugnant to them? An accused might claim that his or her cultural values were so different from those of the majority that the gravity of a provocation to which he or she was subjected should be assessed in the light of those values. Horder's answer is that "It must be made clear that jurors need not invest themselves with the defendant's characteristics where to do so would entail a morally or politically unacceptable compromise of liberal values such as freedom of expression and racial or religious tolerance".[124] Others have argued, however, that such characteristics should be taken into consideration in assessing the gravity of the provocation. Taking into account cultural characteristics should be viewed as a vindication of the

---

[122]   Ibid.

[123]   Ibid at 142-3.

[124]   Ibid at 145.

principles of individualised justice in a society characterised by cultural pluralism.[125]

A question that has arisen in a number of provocation cases is whether the accused's suffering from a mental condition, such as the one associated with post-traumatic stress disorder, should be regarded as a characteristic. In *Ahluwalia*,[126] the Court of Appeal said, obiter, that such a condition might be treated as a characteristic for the purpose of the objective test in provocation. In that case, however, there was no medical evidence to suggest that the accused suffered from post-traumatic stress disorder or a similar condition and so there was no basis for directing the jury on such a characteristic.[127] Similarly in *Dryden*[128] and in *Humphreys*,[129] where the defence of provocation was raised, the courts adopted the position that eccentric and obsessional personality traits, as well as abnormal immaturity are mental characteristics on which the jury should have been specifically directed. The approach taken in these cases has been thought by some commentators to suggest that "given the right sort of evidence, reasonableness ought to be judged from the perspective of a syndrome sufferer. ...[ in *Ahluwalia* ] given the finding on the evidence, and the fact that the issue of the required link between the defendant's characteristics and the provocation had not been raised, this aspect of the judgment was only obiter. Nevertheless, it may come to mark an important step in the liberalisation of the reasonable person test by allowing consideration of any characteristic affecting the defendant's power of self control".[130] This way of looking at the issue tends to minimise the value of the objective test in provocation, especially the requirement that for a characteristic to be considered relevant it must affect the gravity of the provocation, not the accused's level of self-control. As was said before, as long as provocation is viewed as a defence for "normal" people, the point of the objective test is that conduct that cannot be regarded as sufficiently provocative is not capable of supporting a claim of loss of control. What sort of

---

125 See S. Yeo, "Recent Pronouncements on the Ordinary Person Test in Provocation and Automatism", 33 *Criminal Law Quarterly* (1990-91) 280. Yeo argues that "It is difficult to appreciate why such a characteristic could not be relevant to the assessment of the gravity of the provocation if an ordinary person belonging to the same culture could have felt likewise" (at p. 290).

126 [1992] 4 All ER 889.

127 Ibid at 898.

128 [1995] 4 All ER 987.

129 [1995] 4 All ER 1008.

130 See, e.g., Nicolson and Sanghvi, "Battered Women and Provocation: The Implications of *R. v. Ahluwalia*" [1993] *Criminal Law Review* 728, pp. 732-3.

untoward behaviour should be seen as crossing the threshold of legal provocation is primarily a matter of moral judgment and as such it can only be determined by reference to the moral code that is current in society. The fact that the provocation is assessed in the light of certain personal attributes of the accused should not be seen as divesting the test in provocation of its objective character. In this respect, I do not see how mental conditions reducing a person's normal powers of self-control could fit into the provocation defence as "characteristics" that would modify but not preclude the objective test in provocation.

So, to conclude, the reasonable person provides a basis for answering the question of whether the provocation was capable of arousing anger to such a degree as to be likely to overcome, partly by reason of human frailty, the accused's capacity for self-control. Only provocations that are deemed serious enough to enrage an ordinary or reasonable person so that he may lose his self-control and kill could furnish a morally acceptable basis for a reduction of culpability. In this respect, the reasonable person is endowed with those individual characteristics of the accused that are deemed relevant to assessing the gravity of the provocation and hence to determining the degree of psychological pressure to which the accused was subjected. As to the forms of wrongdoing that may be regarded sufficiently provocative, the most straightforward cases would be those where the wrongdoing constitutes criminal behaviour of a serious nature. In addition to these, conduct that infringes commonly recognised standards of decent behaviour may satisfy the test of provocation, even though such conduct is not, strictly speaking, criminal. The reasonable person, as represented by the ordinary member of the jury, epitomises those commonly accepted standards of decent conduct the violation of which could support a claim of provocation and, at the same time, is seen as the vehicle of those common failings of human nature to which the provocation defence is said to be a concession.

## Proportionality and the Reasonable Person

At common law the judge could withdraw the defence of provocation from the jury, if he believed that there was no evidence suggesting that a reasonable person would have been provoked to lose his self-control and do as the accused did. In *Mancini*,[131] the accused, a manager of a club, stabbed the victim to death with a knife-like instrument during a fist fight. Charged with murder, the accused claimed that he was attacked by the victim, who had an open pocket-knife in his hand, and that he killed the victim while trying to defend himself. The accused's

---

131   *Mancini v DPP* [1942] AC 1, [1941] 3 All ER 272.

claim of self-defence was rejected by the jury, however, and he was convicted of murder. In his appeal the accused argued that, although he himself did not plead provocation, the judge should have directed the jury on the defence. The accused's appeal was dismissed by the House of Lords, however, on the grounds that the judge was under a duty to put the defence of provocation the jury only if he had a reason to believe that a reasonable or ordinary person, in the circumstances, would have lost his self-control and done as the accused did. The House adopted the view that an attack by fist "would not constitute provocation of a kind which could extenuate the sudden introduction and use of a lethal weapon like this dagger, and there was, therefore, ...no adequate material to raise the issue of provocation".[132] It was held, in other words, that the judge does not have to direct the jury on provocation unless the mode of the accused's retaliation bore a "reasonable relationship" to the provocation offered. In the words of Lord Simon

> The test to be applied is that of the effect of the provocation on a reasonable man...so that an unusually excitable or pugnacious individual is not entitled to rely on provocation which would not have led an ordinary person to act as he did. In applying the test, it is of particular importance...to take into account the instrument with which the homicide was effected, for to retort, in the heat of passion induced by provocation, by a simple blow, is a very different thing from making use of a deadly instrument like a concealed dagger. In short, the mode of resentment must bear a reasonable relationship to the provocation if the offence is to be reduced to manslaughter.[133]

The above passage expresses what has become known as the "reasonable relationship rule", a restatement of the early law's requirement of proportionality.[134] At common law it was recognised that where the accused's retaliation was greatly disproportionate to the provocation offered the killing should be attributed to the accused's malignity or self-indulgence rather than to human frailty.[135] The reasonable relationship rule required the judge to consider how a reasonable person would respond when confronted with different

---

[132] Ibid at 10 & 278.

[133] Ibid at 9 & 277.

[134] A similar approach has been adopted in a number of modern cases. See e.g. *McCarthy* [1954] 2 QB 105; *McPherson* (1957) 41 Cr App Rep 213; *Walker* [1969] 1 All ER 767; *Edwards v R* [1973] 1 All ER 152. The same position has been adopted in Scotland. See, e.g., *Thomson v H M Adv* (1986) SLT 281; *Fenning v HM Adv* (1985) SCCR 19.

[135] See East, 1 *Pleas of the Crown* 234; And see *Keite* (1697) 1 Ld Raym 139. But see *Ayes* (1810) R & R 166, cited by G. Williams in his article "Provocation and the Reasonable Man" [1954] *Criminal Law Review* 740.

forms of provocation. The provocation defence could not be relied upon unless, in the judge's opinion, the accused's reaction was proportionate, in terms of seriousness, to the gravity of the provocation. The rule suggests that some degree of self-control is still within the actor's power, notwithstanding his acting in the heat of passion. After the introduction of the Homicide Act 1957, however, if there is evidence that the accused was provoked to lose his self-control, the judge is under duty to put the defence of provocation to the jury, even though, in his view, the mode of the accused's reaction was disproportionate, or did nor bear a reasonable relationship, to the provocation. As Lord Diplock pointed out in *Camplin*,[136] considering the fact that, under s. 3, words alone are capable of amounting to provocation in law, the reasonable relationship rule, as expounded in *Mancini*, no longer applies.  Nevertheless, the judge is entitled to draw the jury's attention to those matters which, in his opinion, should be taken into consideration in determining whether the provocation was enough to make a reasonable person respond in the way the accused did (as s. 3 requires). In this respect, the relationship of the accused's response to the provocation received may still be considered.[137] What has changed is that, after 1957, it is for the jury, not for the judge, to determine whether the accused response to provocation was that expected from a reasonable person in the circumstances. In *Brown*, Talbot J. said

> [W]]hen considering whether the provocation was enough to make a reasonable man do as the accused did, it is relevant for the jury to compare the words or acts or both of these things which are put forward as provocation with the nature of the act committed by the accused. It may be, for instance, that a jury might find that the accused's act was so disproportionate to the provocation alleged that no reasonable man would have so acted. We think therefore that a jury should be instructed to consider the relationship of the accused's acts to the provocation when asking themselves the question: 'Was it enough to make a reasonable man do as he did?'.[138]

---

136  *Camplin* [1978] AC 705, [1978] 2 All ER 272.
137  In *Wardrope* [1960] Crim LR 770, *Church* [1965] 49 Cr App R 206, and the report in *Adams* [1961] CLY 1954, it was stated that the requirement of proportionality remains relevant after the 1957 legislation. In *Walker* [1969] 1 WLR 311, it was held that "one vital element for the jury's consideration in all these cases [of provocation] is the proportion between the provocation and the retaliation". Exceptionally, in *Southgate* [1963] Crim LR 570, it was held that the reasonable person cannot be relied upon to assess the way in which the accused responded to the provocation, that is, if it has been established that the accused was in fact deprived of his self-control at the time of the killing.
138  *Brown* [1972] 2 QB 229 at 234.

Talbot J. cited with approval Lord Devlin's statement in *Lee Chun-Chuen* that "Provocation in law consists mainly of three elements - the act of provocation, the loss of self-control, and retaliation proportionate to the provocation".[139]

Under s. 3 of the Homicide Act 1957 the jury, in applying the objective test, should consider whether the provocation offered was enough to make a reasonable person *do as he* [the accused] *did*. The phrase "do as he did" has been taken to suggest that the question for the jury is not whether a reasonable person might have lost his self-control if subjected to the provocation the accused was subjected to but, rather, whether a reasonable person would have responded to the provocation in the way the accused did.[140] As this suggests, even when acting in the heat of passion, the provoked actor must retain a degree of self-control, for only on such an assumption the requirement of proportionality in provocation would be meaningful. In *Phillips*, Lord Diplock, in rejecting the view that loss of self-control is an all or nothing concept, argued as follows

> Counsel contended, not as a matter of construction but as one of logic, that once a reasonable man has lost his self-control his actions ceased to be those of a reasonable man and that accordingly he was no longer fully responsible in law for them whatever he did. This argument was based on the premise that loss of self-control is not a matter of degree but is absolute; there is no intermediate stage between icy detachment and going berserk. This premise, unless the argument is purely semantic, must be based upon human experience and is, in their Lordships' view, false. The average man reacts to provocation according to its degree with angry words, with a blow of the hand, possibly if the provocation is gross and there is a dangerous weapon to hand, with that weapon.[141]

---

139 *Lee Chun-Chuen v R* [1963] AC 220 at 231.

140 As pointed out in *Phillips* [1969] 2 AC 130, 2 WLR 581, "section 3...in referring to the question to be left to be determined by the jury as being 'whether the provocation was enough to make a reasonable man do as he (the person charged) did' explicitly recognises that what the jury have to consider, once they have reached the conclusion that the person charged was in fact provoked to lose his self-control is not merely whether in their opinion the provocation would have made a reasonable man lose his self-control but also whether, having lost his self-control, he would have retaliated in the same way as the person charged in fact did". In the same case Lord Diplock remarked that the reasonable relationship rule, as expressed by Lord Simon in *Mancini*, is "an elliptic way of saying that the reaction of the defendant to the provocation must not exceed what would have been the reaction of a reasonable man" (at p. 137).

141 *Phillips v R* [1969] 2 AC 130 at 137.

The requirement of proportionality in provocation has been criticised on the grounds that it is contradictory to expect the provoked actor to respond as a reasonable person, that is in proportion to the provocation received and, at the same time, to hold him liable for manslaughter on the assumption that a reasonable person, when provoked, does not lose his self-control. The problem with the proportionality requirement is that it makes the provocation defence dependent upon an assessment of the accused's conduct after he lost his self-control rather than on his giving way to passion and losing control in the first place.[142] The requirement of proportionality, interpreted as relating to the accused's mode of retaliation, would appear to militate against the provocation defence where the provocation did not involve a threat to the accused's life. If the provocation did not involve such a threat, the defence should fail, unless it is accepted that the provoker's killing was not intended — a conclusion that would entail that the accused should be convicted of involuntary rather than voluntary manslaughter. It has been argued that, in so far as loss of self-control remains an important element of the provocation defence, the accused's mode of retaliation may be considered but only as relevant to answering the question of

---

This position regarding the issue of loss of control has been criticised by P. Brett, who has argued that it cannot be supported by the findings of modern psychological theory. According to Brett, "[T]he existence of what is called a 'fight-or-flight reaction' has been established beyond doubt, though the precise details of some aspects of the psychological functioning are still undergoing investigation and elucidation ... The all-or-nothing quality of the reaction makes it...pointless to draw distinctions of nicety between different types of provocative act. So, too, it demonstrates the folly of demanding a reasonable proportion between the provocative act and the reaction", "The Physiology of Provocation", *Criminal Law Review* [1970] 634, pp. 637-38. But, as Ashworth has remarked, Brett's argument is based on a theory (the Cannon-Bard theory) whose plausibility has been questioned. In Ashworth's words "There is nothing in psychological theory which compels the view that either the emotions or the normal controls must be completely dominant", "The Doctrine of Provocation", supra note 96, p. 306.

142 As G. Fletcher has remarked, "in the context of provocation, the reasonable person is hardly at home. First, as everyone is prepared to admit, the reasonable person does not kill at all, even under provocation. Therefore it is difficult to assess whether his or her killing should be classified as manslaughter rather than murder... The underlying question is whether the accused should be able to control the particular impulse or emotion that issues in the killing. Yet the intrusion of this mythical standard sometimes induces judges and legislative draftsmen to think that the issue is whether if the average person would have killed under the circumstances, the killing should be partially excused. The test cannot be whether the average person would have killed under the circumstances, for that test should more plausibly generate a total excuse", *Rethinking Criminal Law*, pp. 247-248.

whether the accused did in fact lose control. [143] The question, in other words, is not whether the accused, having lost his self-control, responded in proportion to the provocation, but whether the accused was provoked to lose his self-control to such a degree as to commit an intentional killing. Considering the accused's mode of retaliation in relation to the provocation offered is important in answering this latter question.[144]

The Criminal Law Revision Committee has proposed the reformulation of the test in provocation. The Committee has recommended that the jury should be invited to consider whether, as seen from the viewpoint of the accused, the provocation offered can reasonably be regarded as providing a sufficient ground for the loss of self-control leading the accused to react against the victim with intent to kill.[145] In answering this question the jury should take into account those characteristics of the accused, including any physical and mental disability from which he suffered, which, in their view, are relevant to determining the gravity of the provocation.[146] As Professor Williams has noted, "[this] rewording [of the test in provocation] would not solve the problem for the jury, but the committee thought it might express the question in slightly clearer words". He goes on to point out, nonetheless, that "[I]t is a logical improvement to make the word 'reasonably' refer to the jury's reasoning faculty instead of attaching to what the defendant did".[147] This approach consorts with the position that any reference to reasonableness or proportionality in the context of the provocation defence can only be relevant to answering the question of whether the provocation offered was such as to make the accused's giving way to anger and losing his self-control to such a degree as to lead him to commit an intentional killing appear a likely or not unexpected reaction.

---

[143] See Ashworth, "The Doctrine of Provocation", supra note 96, p. 305. See also S. M. H. Yeo, "Proportionality in Criminal Defences", 12 *Criminal Law Journal* (1988) 211.

[144] As was stated in the Australian case of *Johnson v The Queen* [1976] 136 CLR 619, "the proportion of the fatal act to the provocation is part of the material on which the jury should consider whether the provocation offered the accused was such as would have caused an ordinary man, placed in all the circumstances in which the accused stood, to have lost his self-control to the point of doing the act of the kind and degree of that by which the accused killed the deceased" (at 636 per Barwick CJ).

[145] CLRC/OAP/R, para. 81.

[146] Ibid, paras. 82, 83.

[147] G. Williams, *Textbook of Criminal Law* (1988), p. 342. See also Smith and Hogan, *Criminal Law* (8th ed. 1996), pp. 374-75.

An accused who argues that he lost his self-control and killed because he was provoked is providing a reason or explanation for his actions. But not all possible reasons are deemed sufficient to reduce culpability. The scope of the provocation defence is determined, to a great extent, by the need to limit the availability of the defence to those whose anger is morally warranted by the gravity of the provocation offered. Notwithstanding that the provoked killer is less to blame, the general assumption in the law is that, no matter how grave the provocation may have been, losing one's self-control and killing could have been avoided. We might well understand or sympathise with the accused who was subjected to grave provocation, but he has failed to live up to community standards which demand us to exercise self-restraint even when subjected to pressure. This explains why provocation is a partial defence rather than a complete defence. According to Ashworth:

> It is one of the fundamental postulates of English Criminal Law that individuals ought at all times to control their actions and to conduct themselves in accordance with rational judgment. Loss of self-control is therefore never capable of amounting to a [complete] defence to criminal liability.[148]

Killing as a response to provocation is always an overreaction, but how much an overreaction it is depends upon the gravity of the provocation the accused was subjected to. Where the overreaction is not great, in the light of the provocation offered, the accused's offence is mitigated. Admittedly, the more severe the provocation is the more the psychological effort the provoked actor needs to make in order to maintain control over his actions. Although every wrongful conduct that would pass the test of provocation in law may be capable of supporting the accused's plea for mitigation provided, of course, that his loss of self-control is not disproved as a matter of fact, the degree to which the accused is to blame should, in a sense, be proportionate to the degree of gravity of the provocation offered.[149] This is, surely, an important consideration which the sentencer cannot ignore in determining the appropriate degree of punishment for the lesser offence. Moreover, the gravity of the provocation is relevant to

---

[148]   A. Ashworth, "The Doctrine of Provocation", supra note 96, p. 317.

[149]   "Other things being equal, the greater the provocation, measured in that way [i.e. objectively], the more ground there is for attributing the intensity of the actor's passions and his lack of self-control on the homicidal occasion to the extraordinary character of the situation in which he was placed rather than to an extraordinary deficiency in his own character", Wechsler and Michael, "A Rationale of the Law of Homicide" 37 *Columbia Law Review* (1937) 701, p. 1251.

assessing the weight that certain circumstances surrounding the act of killing may have in establishing whether the accused did in fact lose his self-control as a result of provocation. Thus, matters such as the accused's mode of retaliation, or the time which may have elapsed between the provocation and the killing, are assessed as relevant to answering the question of loss of control by reference to the degree of wrongfulness of the provocation. For example, whereas in a case of a less serious provocation the lapse of some time should normally militate against the accused's claim of loss of self-control -. i.e. on the assumption that the time elapsed was sufficient for an average person to cool down - the opposite may obtain in a case where a more serious provocation was offered.

## A Comment on the Interrelationship between the Subjective and the Objective Questions in Provocation

As was said before, when the defence of provocation is raised, both the subjective or factual and the objective or evaluative questions are to be answered by the jury. In dealing with the question of whether the accused did in fact lose his self-control as a result of provocation the jurors will usually ask themselves whether they too may have lost control if faced with the alleged provocation. The more severe the provocation, assessed objectively, the more likely it is that the jury will believe that the accused actually lost his self-control as a result. Their decision as to whether the accused did in fact lose control may also be informed by considerations which are not directly related to the objective wrongfulness of the victim's conduct, such as the lapse of time between the provocation and the accused's response.

In the past much debate has revolved around the problem of distinguishing between the role of the reasonable person in dealing with questions of fact and its position as a legal standard of conduct. Some commentators have argued that the way the reasonable person has been treated in the doctrine of provocation provides an example of how a point of evidence has been allowed to slide into a point of law, and of the inevitable confusion which thereby results. According to Gordon

> Instead of being used as a way of testing the truth of the accused's statement that he lost self-control, the reasonable man has been turned into an objective standard of self-control. Even if the jury believe that the accused, in fact, lost control to an extreme degree, and that he killed because of this, they must convict him of murder unless they think that the reasonable man would have lost control to that degree, a result which, it is submitted, is clearly unjust, especially when what is in question is not the objective rightness of what was

done but the degree of punishment which should be inflicted on the particular accused. If the accused's alleged loss of self-control was something which the jury feel was quite unusual and unexpected in the circumstances this may properly lead them to refuse to believe that he did lose control, but if they do believe it, its unexpectedness seems unimportant - even the law must recognise that the unexpected can happen.[150]

Such criticism seems unfounded, however, especially in the light of the current approach to the provocation defence according to which all the questions, both factual and evaluative, pertaining to provocation are for the jury. As was explained before, the reasonable person is relied upon to answer the question of whether the accused lost his self-control and killed *as a result of provocation.* If the victim's wrongdoing is deemed serious enough to constitute provocation in law, and yet there is evidence suggesting that the accused did not in fact lose his self-control, the accused would not be able to rely on the defence. Moreover, even if there is evidence upon which it can be found that the accused did in fact lose control, the defence would fail unless the victim's conduct passed the test of provocation. Although evidence of any sort of wrongful conduct capable of amounting to provocation would suffice for the defence to be put to the jury, only those wrongdoings which are deemed grave enough, from the point of view of a reasonable person with the accused's characteristics, could be regarded as provocation sufficient to reduce the offence to manslaughter. In other words, neither provocation without loss of control, nor loss of control without sufficient provocation is enough for the defence to be accepted.

In provocation the reasonable person is relied upon in dealing with both the evaluative and factual aspects of the inquiry. Thus, in a case where the provocation was grave enough to lead a reasonable person to lose control and kill, the defence would be rejected if, for example, the time that elapsed between such provocation and the accused's response would be enough for a reasonable person to regain his self-control. On the assumption that the accused is a normal person, the latter consideration might lead the jury to believe that the accused, as a matter of fact, was not deprived of his self-control at the time of the killing. Here, the accused's plea may have passed the evaluative test — the victim's conduct did amount to provocation in law — but did not pass the factual test — the accused did not lose his self-control. In other words, considering how a reasonable person —

---

150  *Criminal Law* (1978), p. 783.
    See also *Kenny's Outlines of Criminal Law* (1966) p. 177; *Russell on Crime* (1964) pp. 534-5. A. Samuels, "Excusable Loss of Self-Control in Homicide", 34 *Modern Law Review* (1971) 163, p. 167.

with the accused's characteristics — would have interpreted, in terms of seriousness, the victim's conduct is crucial in answering the evaluative question: did the victim's conduct amount to provocation? At the same time, considering how a reasonable person might have reacted to the victim's provocation is important in answering the factual question: did the accused lose his self-control?[151]

## The Problem of Self-Induced Provocation

A question that has perplexed the courts for many years has been whether an accused could rely on the defence of provocation where it appears that the provocation has been induced by the accused's own offensive conduct towards the victim. At common law the judge could withdraw the defence of provocation from the jury if he believed that the provocation was self-induced. Under s. 3 the judge cannot withdraw the defence from the jury in such cases, although he may still draw the jury's attention to the fact that the provocation was self-induced as a factor militating against the accused's plea. It is for the jury to decide, however, whether the accused's claim that he was provoked should be accepted or not by taking into account everything both done and said according to the effect which, in their view, it would have on a reasonable person. However, in *Edwards*,[152] the Privy Council adopted the position that, in principle, an accused cannot rely on provocation when he himself had caused it. In that case the accused stabbed the victim to death during a struggle in the victim's hotel room. The accused had gone to the victim's room intending to blackmail the victim. He claimed that the victim became enraged when he heard the accused's demands and attacked him with a knife. The accused wrestled the knife from the victim and killed him in a fit of blind rage. At his trial for murder the accused raised self-defence and provocation. The accused's appeal against his conviction of murder was dismissed by the Full Court of Hong Kong. The accused then appealed to the Judicial Committee of the Privy Council. The accused's appeal focused on the trial judge's failure to direct the jury

---

151  As Hart has pointed out, "difficulties of proof may cause a legal system to limit its inquiry into the agent's 'subjective condition' by asking what a 'reasonable man' would in the circumstances have known or foreseen, or by asking whether a 'reasonable man' in the circumstances would have been deprived (say, by provocation) of self control; and the system may then impute to the agent such knowledge or foresight or control", "Legal Responsibility and Excuses", in *Punishment and Responsibility* (1968), p. 33.

152  [1973] AC 648, [1973] 1 All ER 152, PC.

on the issue of provocation. The Privy Council reduced the accused's offence to manslaughter stating

> On principle it seems reasonable to say that (1) a blackmailer cannot rely on the predictable results of his own blackmailing conduct as constituting provocation sufficient to reduce his killing from murder to manslaughter, and the predictable results may include a considerable degree of hostile reaction by the person sought to be blackmailed, for instance vituperative words and even some hostile action such as blows with fists; (2) but if the hostile reaction by the person sought to be blackmailed goes to extreme lengths it might constitute sufficient provocation even for the blackmailer; (3) there would in many cases be a question of degree to be decided by the jury.[153]

But as was said before, s. 3 requires that the jury, in deciding whether the accused was provoked to lose his self-control, are to take into account *everything* that, in their view, is capable of amounting to provocation, regardless of whether it was a predictable result of the accused's own conduct. If there is evidence that the accused was provoked the judge is required to put the issue to the jury, even if he has good reason to believe that the provocation was self-induced. The Privy Council's decision in *Edwards*, by adding the further condition that the provocation must not have been a predictable result of the accused's own actions, does not appear to accord with s. 3. Thus in *Johnson*[154] the accused was allowed to rely on the provocation defence, although the provocation was a predictable result of the accused's own offensive behaviour.[155] In that case the Court of Appeal expressed its disapproval of the position adopted in *Edwards* stating

> In view of the express wording of s. 3...we find it impossible to accept that the mere fact that a defendant caused a reaction in others, which in turn led him to lose his self-control, should result in the issue of provocation being kept outside a jury's consideration. Section 3 clearly provides that the question is whether things done or said or both provoked the defendant to lose his self-control. If there is any evidence that it may have done, the issue must be left to the jury.[156]

---

153  [1973] 1 All ER 152 at 158 (per Lord Pearson).

154  [1989] 1 WLR 740.

155  Ashworth has criticised this approach on the grounds that it leaves open the defence to an accused who deliberately induces provocation by another so that he may kill him and plead provocation as a defence. "Self-Induced Provocation and the Homicide Act",*Criminal Law Review* [1973] 483.

156  Ibid at 744. (per Watkins LJ)

The fact that the provocation was self-induced may nevertheless be taken into account by the jury in deciding whether the provocation was such as to make a reasonable person lose his self-control and act as the accused did. It may also be relevant in determining the appropriate amount of punishment, following the accused's conviction of manslaughter.

# 4 Provocation as a Partial Excuse

## Excuse, Justification and the Rationale of the Provocation Defence

Provocation has been described as a "failure-of-proof" defence, or as an "offence modification".[1] As a "failure-of-proof" defence, provocation is taken to negate the malice element of murder, without affecting the *mens rea* element of the lesser offence.[2] As we saw in chapter 3, in early law provocation was taken to negate the element of malice which an intentional killing implied, and as such, it operated as a "failure-of-proof" defence.[3] However, the interpretation of provocation as a "failure-of-proof" defence does not seem to accord with the current definition of malice aforethought as an intention to kill or to cause grievous bodily harm. Describing provocation as a "failure-of-proof" defence would presuppose a broader interpretation of the subjective element in murder — an interpretation that would encompass all morally relevant considerations bearing on culpability. From this point of view, an actual intention to kill or to cause grievous bodily harm, important though it may be, is not the only factor indicative of the degree of culpability required for murder. On the other hand, under the formulation "offence modification", provocation is portrayed as a defence capable of reducing culpability without affecting the *mens rea* and *actus reus* of murder.[4] This latter approach to provocation captures better the present understanding of the defence in English law. According to Wasik,

---

1    See P. Robinson, "Criminal Law Defenses: A Systematic Analysis", *Columbia Law Review* 82 (1982)199, pp. 232-3.
2    In Robinson's words, "[the failure of proof defense of provocation] is said to negate the required malice of murder, and thereby reduces the defendant's liability to manslaughter", ibid at pp. 205-6.
3    See Robinson, ibid at p. 233.
4    See T. Archibald, "The Interrelationship Between Provocation and Mens Rea: A Defence of Loss of Self-Control", *Criminal Law Quarterly* 28 (1985-86) 454, pp. 456-7.

The generally accepted view in English criminal law is that both provocation and diminished responsibility are seen as operating outside mens rea and actus reus. Thus it makes it easier to accept a reduction in offence category without questioning liability for that lesser offence, given that if the partial excuse negates mens rea for the most serious crime it would also affect the mens rea required for the lesser offence. [5]

This approach reflects what has been termed as the "cognitive" model of criminal responsibility, which focuses upon the issues of knowledge, intention and foresight of consequences as the main requirements of legal culpability.[6] Given that provocation does not negate any of these elements, the defence can only operate as an offence modification. On the other hand, the so-called "capacities" model of criminal responsibility centres on the actor's capacity to exercise control over his conduct and on whether the actor has the opportunity to exercise such control. From the point of view of the capacities theory, it is argued that the subjective element in crime should be viewed as broad enough to encompass requirements pertaining to both cognition and control. According to Fletcher,

> The spectrum of culpability teaches us that culpability is not only a matter of cognitive foresight, but also of self-control. The issue of self-control, we learn, requires subtle judgments of degree. In some cases of intentional homicide the actor exercises greater control, and in others, lesser. The grading of homicide disabuses us of the view that voluntariness and freedom of the will are black-and-white issues. Rather the shading develops by perceptible degrees from total dependence on circumstances to total independence of external influence.[7]

From the viewpoint of the capacities theory, provocation may be said to operate as a "failure-of-proof" defence by negating the degree of control over one's actions required for his or her conviction as a murderer. The notions of "failure-of-proof" defence and "offence modification" may be useful in describing the function of the provocation defence from different theoretical viewpoints. What remains to be considered further, however, is the moral basis upon which provocation reduces the gravity of an intentional homicide.

As was indicated earlier, the defence of provocation is understood to hinge upon two interrelated elements, namely, the wrongful act of provocation and impaired volition or loss of self-control. The first

---

5  "Partial Excuses in Criminal Law", 45 *Modern Law Review* (1982) 516, pp. 528-9.

6  See, e.g., G. Hughes, "Criminal Responsibility", *Stanford Law Review* 16 (1964) 470.

7  *Rethinking Criminal Law* (1978), p.353. And see C. Sistare, *Responsibility and Criminal Liability* (1989), pp. 18-19.

element is taken to be justificatory in character, for it focuses upon a condition that, on the face of it, is capable of affecting the wrongfulness of the actor's conduct quite independently of his or her state of mind. The second element, by placing the emphasis on the actor's state of mind and his inability to exercise control over his actions, is clearly excusative in nature. Because the provocation rests upon both excusative and justificatory considerations, the rationale of the legal defence has been difficult to locate.[8] As Alldridge has remarked

> The defence [of provocation] must be either a partial excuse (in which case the centre of the inquiry will be whether or not the defendant lost his/her self-control) or a partial justification (in which case the centre of the inquiry will be what was actually done by the deceased to the defendant — to what extent the deceased 'asked for it')...It is interesting to note that both these conditions obtained at common law. [9]

We saw in chapter 1 that justifications call in question the wrongfulness of an act; excuses deny the attribution of a wrongful act to the actor. But one might argue that provocation, as pertinent to determining the offence category in which an unlawful homicide is to be subsumed, is a matter neither of excuse nor of justification. Some commentators have argued that if a conviction of murder did not entail a fixed penalty, provocation would merely operate as a factor in the mitigation of sentence. If it were assumed that a defence could be treated as a justification or excuse only if it is aimed at complete exoneration from criminal liability, one may question the application of this sort of analysis to provocation. According to Hart

---

8    As J. L. Austin has noted, "It is arguable that we do not use the terms justification and excuse as we might; a miscellany of even less clear terms, such as 'extenuation', 'palliation', 'mitigation', hovers uneasily between partial justification and partial excuse; and when we plead, say, provocation, there is genuine uncertainty or ambiguity as to what we mean — is he partly responsible, because he roused a violent passion in me, so that it wasn't truly me acting 'of my own accord' (excuse)? Or is it rather that, he having done me such injury, I was entitled to retaliate (justification)? ", "A Plea for Excuses", in *The Philosophy of Action*, A. White (ed.), (1968) 19, p. 20.

9    "The Coherence of Defences", *Criminal Law Review* [1983] 665, p. 669. And according to Dressler, "careful analysis of the language and of the results of common law heat of passion cases demonstrates that there is an uncertainty whether the defence is a sub-species of justification or of excuse", "Rethinking Heat of Passion: A Defence in Search of a Rationale" , 73 *Journal of Criminal Law and Criminology* (1982) 421, p. 428. See also Dressler, "Provocation: Partial Justification or Partial Excuse?", *Modern Law Review* 51 (1988) 467.

> Provocation is not a matter of Justification or Excuse for it does not exclude conviction or punishment; but 'reduces' the charge from murder to manslaughter and the possible maximum penalty from death to life imprisonment.[10]

Nevertheless, given that a plea of provocation aims at reducing legal culpability, the theory of justification and excuse may still furnish the basis on which the rationale of the defence could be explained. Neither the formal limitations of legal doctrine, nor the genuine ambiguity surrounding legal decisions can detract from the valuable role of the theory of justification and excuse in elucidating the moral basis upon which criminal law defences operate. The fact that provocation operates as a "formal mitigation", to use Hart's terminology, does not preclude the defence from being considered in the light of the justification-excuse distinction, no matter how difficult the classification of the defence on this basis may be.

Provocation may be taken to operate as a partial excuse in so far as its mitigating function is set down to the assumption that the provoked actor is temporarily deprived of his or her self-control. Here, the lack of self-control, although it does not totally preclude moral blame, can still negative the degree of moral blame which a conviction for murder requires. Although provocation does not lead to complete acquittal, as other excuse-based legal defence do, its rationale may be explained in the light of excuse theory. As A. von Hirsch and N. Jareborg have noted

> Conduct is excused in certain situations where — although the outcome is not deemed desirable — the actor should be exempted from blame for acting as she or he did. Textbook examples are situations of duress and necessity, where the defendant injures an innocent victim, in order to avert a threat to his own life or safety from another source, human or natural. But the provoked actor faces no immediate threat from any such source if he refrains from retaliating. He is also claiming extenuation only, not complete exoneration. Theories of excuse in the substantive criminal law could thus be applicable only by analogy — to suggest why provocation constitutes a partial excuse, warranting reduction of punishment.[11]

Further, canvassing provocation as a partial justification should not mislead one to think that legal justification, in a strict sense, can be expressed in partial terms. Claims of legal justification dispute the unlawful character of an act in the circumstances and, in this respect,

---

10    "Prolegomenon to the Principles of Punishment", in *Punishment and Responsibility* (1968), p. 15.

11    A. von Hirsch & N. Jareborg, "Provocation and Culpability", in *Responsibility, Character, and the Emotions*, F. Schoeman (ed.), (1987), p. 242.

an act may be either legally justified or not justified at all. An analogy may be drawn, nonetheless, in so far as partial justification is understood to reduce the wrongfulness of the act by virtue of considerations independent of the actor's state of mind. From this point of view, the reason for reducing the level of criminal liability in provocation pertains not to the actor's loss of self-control as such but, rather, to the wrongfulness of the victim's provocative conduct that prompts the actor to retaliate in anger. Provocation operates as a partial justification on the assumption that the actor is to some degree morally justified to inflict punishment on the provoker. In Ashworth's words

> [T]he term [partial justification] does not necessarily imply a connection with the legal concept of justifiable force (i.e. in self-defence); its closest relationship is with the moral notion that the punishment of wrongdoers is justifiable. This is not to argue that it is ever morally right to kill a person who does wrong. Rather, the claim implicit in partial justification is that an individual is to some extent morally justified in making a punitive return against someone who intentionally causes him serious offence, and that this serves to differentiate someone who is provoked to lose his self-control and kill from the unprovoked killer.[12]

An accused who claims that he acted as he did because he was provoked is providing a reason for his actions. But not all possible reasons can be accepted as sufficient to reduce criminal liability. Provocation cannot be accepted as a defence unless the accused's anger at the victim is morally justified by the gravity of the provocation offered. As Horder points out, the defence of provocation "requires defendants to explain their conduct, in part, by reference to the 'moral warrant' that they believed the gravity of the provocation gave them for retaliating so violently in anger. The condition requires defendants to explain their conduct by reference to the *righteousness* of their angry retaliation in the circumstances".[13] In dealing with a claim of provocation, one needs to assess the moral judgments of the person who pleads a partial defence. Determining what amounts to grave provocation necessarily involves some sort of inquiry into community moral values and perceptions of wrongdoing. As was explained in the previous chapter, the reasonable person test in provocation is relied upon in answering this question.

---

12 "The Doctrine of Provocation", 35 *Criminal Law Journal* (1976) 292, p. 307.
13 J. Horder, *Provocation and Responsibility* (1992), p. 112.

## The Justificatory Element in Provocation: a Closer Look

The conception of provocation as a form of partial justification is said to have deep roots in the common law tradition.[14] Despite the important changes brought about in English law after the introduction of the Homicide Act 1957 and the increasing tendency to treat provocation as an excuse, the justificatory aspect of provocation cannot be ignored. Some commentators have argued that it is in the wrongful act of provocation, i.e. in the justificatory element, rather than in the actor's loss of control, that the true basis of the defence lies. The fact that the law has traditionally treated provocation as a legal defence in its own right, instead of subsuming provoked killings under a general "heat of passion" or "loss of self-control" excuse-based defence, is taken to lend support to this claim. According to McAuley

> while the defence of provocation may well be a concession to the natural human failings that are the lot of every defendant, it is submitted that its true basis is to be found in the contribution of the victim, in the fact that his wrongful conduct was the cause of the defendant's outburst. [15]

In this section it will be argued that, notwithstanding the indispensability of the justificatory element as a necessary conceptual element of provocation, the excuse theory provides a more satisfactory basis for justifying the role of the defence in law.

A provoked retaliation is, in essence, an act of revenge, although we not usually call it that, for the term "revenge" is most commonly used to denote retaliatory action that is premeditated or cold-blooded. Revenge is not just a blind expression of one's anger. It is based on reasons, and these have to do with the wrongfulness of a past action. A punitive action of this sort is always triggered by the wrongful conduct of some other person or persons. It is this necessary connection

---

14  It is pointed out that this is manifested by the fact that in early law special emphasis was placed on the need to establish provocation of a particularly grave nature before the defence could be accepted. See F. McAuley, "Anticipating the Past: The Defence of Provocation in Irish Law", *Modern Law Review* 50 (1987) 133, p. 150. See, e.g., *Keite* (1697) 1 Ld Raym 139; *Mawgridge* (1706) 17 St Tr 57; *Mason* (1756) Frost 132; *Bourne* (1831) 5 C & P 129; *Lynch* (1832) 5 C & P 324; *Kirkham* (1837) 8 C & P 115; *Selten* (1871) 11 Cox 674. As was stated in *Welsh* (1869) 11 Cox 336, "it is necessary that there should have been serious provocation in order to reduce the crime to manslaughter, as for instance, a blow, and a severe blow - something which naturally cause an ordinary man to lose his self-control and commit such an act" (at p. 336, per Keating J.).

15  "Anticipating the Past: The Defence of Provocation in Irish Law", supra note 14, p. 137.

between revenge and past wrongdoing that gives revenge a rational and moral status. Determining that certain conduct is provocative involves a judgement that such conduct constitutes a wrong or an injustice of some sort. Provocation, in other words, implies conduct objectively wrongful and as such capable of raising justified anger. Whether one's anger is justified depends upon the adequacy of the reasons for becoming angry — upon the accuracy of one's judgements as to what constitutes morally wrongful behaviour.

Of course, there is nothing wrong in becoming angry at wrongful conduct directed at us or others or in expressing our anger in some way. Indeed it is a sign of good moral character to become angry at the right things and at the right time.[16] According to Horder, feeling angry in accordance with reason "is a mean or proper display of the virtue of even-temperedness. The display of the virtue of even-temperedness involves the making of a correct judgment of wrongdoing, in the wake of which followed a commensurate desire for retaliation".[17] From this point of view, Horder points out, the validity of the reasons for a particular punitive response to wrongful conduct is judged "by the degree of conformity to, or departure from, the mean with regard to the virtues associated with anger, in the circumstances as angry people saw them...Where actions in anger are a mean or correct response, then the actions will be completely morally justified, being a display of good moral character. For defendants have made correct judgments of wrongdoing and/or appropriateness...in a particular set of circumstances, those judgments being correct concrete expressions of the good or acceptable moral reasons for action that are the mark of a good moral character".[18] Only where the provoked person's response is, in a sense, proportionate to the provocation received, his action can be said to be fully morally justified. If his response departs from the mean, then it may only be partially morally justified, and if the departure is great, it is not morally justified at all. Whether and to what degree a provoked person's response is partially justified thus depends upon the degree to which his action goes beyond the mean, in other words, beyond what a virtuous person would do when faced with similar provocation.

Killing as a response to provocation is always an over-reaction and, as such, it can never be fully morally justified, for a virtuous

---

16 In Aristotle's words, "Acts proceeding from anger are rightly judged not to be done out of malice; for it is not the man who acts in anger but he who enraged him that starts the mischief. Again, the matter in dispute is not whether the thing happened or not, but its injustice; for it is apparent injustice that occasions rage", *Nicomachean Ethics*, Bk. V, 8.

17 *Provocation and Responsibility*, pp. 128-9.

18 Ibid, at pp. 129-30.

person would not respond by killing, no matter how great the provoker's wrongdoing may have been. The reason why provocation is only a partial defence stems from this. The provoked killer remains blameworthy, although not blameworthy enough to justify his conviction as a murderer. The accuracy of the accused's judgment as to the wrongfulness of the provoker's conduct as well as the manner of his retaliation affect whether and to what degree the accused's response may be partially justified. This, in turn, will determine the amount of punishment imposed for the lesser offence. As Ashworth remarks

> An element of 'partial justification' thus enters into the moral evaluation of provoked crimes, and this inevitably brings the behaviour of the provoker under scrutiny; the more offensive, persistent and intentional the provocation given by the deceased, the greater the degree to which the offender was partially justified in retaliating.[19]

But it is only where the accused's over-reaction is not great, given the gravity of the provocation received, that a provoked killing may be mitigated. Where the accused's response in anger is grossly disproportionate to the provocation, "the action in anger will be almost completely without moral justification. It will be a glaring failure to reflect good or acceptable moral reasons for action in mean or correct concrete moral judgments of wrongdoing and/or appropriate response, and hence in action. Such a failure verges on a display of warped or bad moral character...and hence warrants conviction of murder".[20]

The interpretation of the provocation defence as a partial justification lays the emphasis on the assumption that it is the provoker who, by his wrongful conduct, triggers the accused's fatal response. Although such killings cannot be totally morally justified, the law cannot but take into account the role of the provoker in causing the accused to act as he did when determining the gravity of the offence committed. From this point of view, McAuley argues that

> the defence of provocation functions as a partial justification rather than a partial excuse. If it were merely a partial excuse, the defence would be limited to a denial that the defendant was entirely to blame for his actions, i.e. for wrongfully killing another intentionally, by reason of the impairment of his powers of self-control. As we have seen, however, the defence entails a denial that the defendant's actions were entirely wrongful in the first place, in the sense

---

19   "Sentencing in Provocation Cases", *Criminal Law Review* [1975] 553, p. 562.

20   Horder, *Provocation and Responsibility*, p. 131.

that it implies that the defendant was partially justified in reacting as he did because of the untoward conduct of the victim.[21]

McAuley's approach seems to consort with the idea that claims of justification focus, primarily, on the question of wrongfulness of an act, rather than on the blameworthiness of the actor. With regard to provocation, the justificatory factor is taken to reduce, not negate (as it is the case, e.g. with self-defence), the wrongfulness of the retaliation. Notwithstanding that the actor cannot here plead total justification, the wrongful character of the provocative conduct furnishes the main reason for reducing the killing from murder to manslaughter. However, from the point of view of the justification theory, it is not enough that the victim's conduct inflicts pain or harm. The accused's retaliation is a form of reaction that doubly involves intention: both the provoker and the provoked are viewed as acting intentionally. In other words, provocation as a partial justification presupposes that the provoker is in some way morally to blame for his conduct. The act of retaliation aims not only at paying back the harm by inflicting another harm, but also at conveying the feeling of reciprocal hate or malevolence. This explains why we do not avenge ourselves for action that is involuntary or unintentional, even when such action is substantially harmful. Under the justification theory, killing in self-defence cannot be morally justified unless the aggressor is morally responsible for his action. Similarly, in provocation the provoker's culpability is relevant to determining whether his killing in retaliation is partially morally justified. Thus, in a case where the author of the provocation is excusable, the provoked killer would not be able to rely on the defence if he is aware of the provoker's excuse. In such a case, no matter how wrongful the provocative conduct may seem, the accused's knowledge of the provoker's excuse would militate against the basic assumption of the partial justification theory, namely that the provoker, in the accused's eyes at least, deserves punishment. If, on the other hand, the accused is not aware of the provoker's excuse, the case should be treated as one of mistaken provocation.

According to the partial justification theory, in provocation the accused's claim for reducing the gravity of his offence turns on the assumption that the victim is, to some extent, morally responsible for his own death. From this point of view, it is argued that in those cases where the accused, acting in response to provocation, by mistake or accident killed an innocent party, the accused could still rely on the defence, provided that his intended victim was the author of the provocation. Further, the accused would be entitled to the defence if he

---

21    "Anticipating the Past: The Defence of Provocation in Irish Law", supra note 14, p. 139.

killed as a result of a mistaken belief as to the wrongful character of the victim's conduct. Under the justification theory, the issue of provocation in such cases of mistake should be assessed in the light of the circumstances as the accused believed them to be. Those cases of mistake in which no act of provocation in fact occurred may be referred to as cases of putative provocation. These should be distinguished from cases where an act of grave provocation did occur, but its author was someone else than the victim — i.e. cases of misdirected retaliation due to mistake or accident. In both kinds of cases the accused should be able to rely on the provocation defence. In McAuley's words

> the non-occurrence of the provocative event would seem, at least at first sight, to be fatal to the plea [of provocation], from the point of view of the theory of justification, as there would then be no prior wrong on which he could rely as a basis for his own retaliatory action. Yet this conclusion is counter-intuitive, as it removes the defence from a defendant who would have been entitled to it had the facts been as he reasonably supposed them to be...For while the paradigm case of a partial justification will, in the nature of things, rest on evidence of wrongful conduct on the part of the victim, it does not follow that retaliatory violence is always unjustified in the absence of such evidence. [22]

According to McAuley, under the justification theory, in cases of mistaken provocation the accused should still be able to rely on a partial justification defence, notwithstanding that the victim did nothing that could amount to provocation in law. A similar position is adopted in relation to cases of putative justification, e.g. putative self-defence, with the difference that in such cases the accused would be entitled to full acquittal. However, the overlap of the conditions of provocation and mistake of fact in such cases has led some commentators to speak of the accused's defence here as a variation of the excuse of mistake of fact. As Perkins has noted

> if the slayer is told of such great harm which he had not heard before, this may be sufficient for adequate provocation...even if the statement is untrue — provided it is made under circumstances calculated to cause it to be believed and it is actually believed by the slayer. This is merely a particular application of the reasonable mistake of fact doctrine.[23]

This view seems convincing but it does not represent the way putative self-defence (or putative justification) is treated in England and other

---

22   "Anticipating the Past: The Defence of Provocation in Irish Law", supra note 14, pp. 140-141.

23   *Criminal Law* (1957), pp. 50-51. And see P. Robinson, *Criminal Law Defenses* (1984), p. 8.

common law jurisdictions. At present the dominant position is that the right of self-defence arises where the actor *believes* that he or she is facing an unlawful attack, irrespective of whether such a belief is a mistaken one or not. In this respect, McAuley's reasoning on mistaken provocation, or mistaken partial justification, is compatible with current legal doctrine. Considering, however, that, from the point of view of the justification theory, the victim's culpability is crucial in turning the scales in favour of the defender, thus rendering his response justified, the current approach appears to confuse justification with excuse and therefore it misrepresents the theoretical basis of justification-based defences.

From the point of view of the partial justification theory, the provoked killer should be able to rely on the provocation defence only when the victim's transgression is sufficiently serious. It is argued that the law's insistence on the requirement of proportionality can best be explained in the light of the partial justification theory. The traditional position that words alone do not amount to provocation sufficient to reduce murder to manslaughter is taken as evidence that, at common law, the rationale of the provocation defence was to be found in the justification rather than the excuse theory. As we saw in the previous chapter, the requirement of proportionality indicates that, for a plea of provocation to be accepted, the act of retaliation must, in a sense, measure up to the gravity of the provocation offered. The more outrageous the provocation is the more justified the provoked person would be in retaliating violently. According to McAuley

> the principle of proportionality is generally invoked to deny the defence of provocation to a defendant who has fatally shot or stabbed an unarmed victim, or who has beaten his victim to death in an orgy of violence. But there is no reason in principle why it should not also be invoked to deny the defence to a defendant who kills his victim with a single blow of the fist if there is evidence that the latter's conduct did not warrant retaliatory violence of this order, in a word, in cases in which the victim's behaviour was insufficiently serious to justify a killing of any kind.[24]

According to the justification theory, killing as a response to provocation may be partially justified only in those cases where the victim's provocation is deemed serious enough to warrant a violent response. In this respect, the reasonable person test may be relied upon to answer the question of whether the victim's provocation was sufficiently grave to support a claim of partial justification: the killing of the provoker could be deemed partially justified only if a reasonable

---

[24]    "Anticipating the Past: The Defence of Provocation in Irish Law", supra note 14, pp. 154-5.

or ordinary person would regard the provocation offered as being very serious. Certain personal characteristics of the accused may be taken into account in determining the gravity of the provocative conduct. It is argued that, in so far as the emphasis is placed upon the justificatory element in provocation, the defence should succeed even if the accused was capable of exercising some degree of rational control over his actions when he killed the provoker. As McAuley puts it

> It makes perfect sense for the law to assume that an enraged defendant is capable of some measure of rational control. Perhaps for this reason it has traditionally been true that the critical question in a case of provocation is not whether the defendant has temporarily lost control in some absolute, irretrievable sense, but whether he was partially justified in killing his victim in the circumstances.[25]

But in so far as all that really matters is whether the provocation was serious enough to objectively reduce the wrongfulness of the provoker's killing, one may ask, what difference would it make whether or to what degree the provoked killer had lost his self-control? One cannot speak of the accused's reaction as being a provoked one unless the accused was deprived of his self-control to some degree but, from the viewpoint of the justification theory, this has little to do with the accused's plea for mitigation. As was noted before, moral judgments of justification are primarily concerned with the question of wrongfulness of conduct. If McAuley is correct, as long as the victim's provocation is serious enough, the accused should be entitled to a partial justification defence, whether or not he lost his self-control. Loss of self-control can only be relevant from the point of view of the excuse theory. Thus McAuley seems to contradict himself when he says that

> Undoubtedly, a defendant who kills after he has regained his composure, or when the effects of the provocation have more or less worn off, is not entitled to the defence, as he can hardly claim that it was the provocation which caused his violent outburst. A defendant who kills in these circumstances has plainly committed an act of revenge and consequently, is guilty of murder. But it is submitted that a defendant who can show that he killed in the face of substantial provocation should, *on this ground alone*, be entitled to the defence, provided that his conduct can be justified in the sense suggested above.[26]

What McAuley seems to be saying here is that one should distinguish between two types of provocation cases: a) cases in which the defence should fail unless the accused had, to some extent, lost his self-control — in such cases the wrongfulness of the victim's provocation alone

---

25   Ibid at p. 155.
26   Ibid at p. 156. (My italics)

would not be sufficient to partially justify a cold-blooded killing; and b) cases in which the victim's provocation is so grave as to reduce the wrongfulness of the accused's killing in retaliation, whether he lost his self-control or not. In the first case, however, one cannot speak of the accused's defence as a justification-based one, in the way McAuley suggests. In the second case it is questionable whether provocation could be the relevant defence for, as was said before, one cannot call a person's response as a provoked one unless he was deprived, to some extent, of his self-control. But if there may be cases where the victim's wrongdoing is so grave as to render the requirement of loss of self superfluous, I can see no reason why even those who kill out of sheer revenge should not be able to plead a partial justification defence if they could show that they were seriously wronged by the victim. Such a conclusion, it is submitted, would be morally and legally untenable. The desire to take revenge may be reinforced by the inability of the law to fully restore the previous situation, but revenge can never be part of the criminal justice system, nor can it be justified as "just". Further, as revenge is based on the subjective interpretation of the person wronged, rather than a publicly verifiable procedure of judgment, no rules can govern such practice and therefore no criteria of proportion can be formulated.

## Further Criticisms of the Partial Justification Theory

As was said in chapter 1, justification-based legal defences have been explained under different moral theories of justification. What needs to be considered further is whether the idea that provocation functions as a partial justification, rather than a partial excuse, can draw support from these theories. It has been said that under the *forfeiture* theory of justification, killing in self-defence is morally justified on the grounds that, by threatening another's life, the aggressor forfeits his own right to life.[27] Applied to provocation, the theory would suggest that the wrongful act of provocation weakens the provoker's right to life, although it does not completely negate it. Such an approach implies that any act of provocation would suffice to render the provoker's right to life less worthy of protection, provided that the provocation is deemed

---

27   For a discussion of the forfeiture theory of justification and its implications see Bedau, "The Right to Life", 52 *Monist* (1968) 550. See also G. Fletcher, "The Right to Life", *Georgia Law Review* 13 (1979); P. Montague, "Self-Defence and Choosing Between Lives", *Philosophical Studies* 40 (1981) 215; C.C. Ryan, "Self-Defence, Pacifism and the Possibility of Killing", *Ethics* 93 (April 1983) 508; Wasserman, "Justifying Self-Defence", *Philosophy and Public Affairs* (1985) 356.

grave enough and that the provoker can be held morally responsible for his actions. Moreover, if the provoker's right to life is weakened, not only the addressee of the provocation but anyone could take the provoker's life and plead partial justification.[28]

Strong objections can be raised against the forfeiture theory of justification as it applies to provocation. On the assumption that the provoker's right to life is weakened according to the gravity of his wrongdoing, any form of wrongdoing that passes the test of provocation in law could be said to weaken the provoker's right to life. Given the current definition of provocation, this would mean that even verbal provocations could have such an effect. Such a conclusion is morally untenable, however, for it contravenes commonly shared moral principles regarding the sanctity and inviolability of human life. As J. Dressler has remarked

> it might be claimed that a provoker who does not threaten the accused's life does not wholly forfeit his right to life but that, nonetheless, from society's perspective his life is entitled to less protection because of his wrongful behaviour. We value his life less than that of an innocent human being. Or, perhaps, we might say that our interest in protecting people from aggression is less intense when the defendant's own wrongful acts contributed to the attack. Such a claim has superficial appeal, but how strongly do we believe it? Do we really believe that a person's life should be less valued in the law because he slapped the face of the killer, uttered some opprobrium, blew smoke in his face, or committed a sexual impropriety with a member of the defendant's family? Is human life so easily alienated? It is one thing to proclaim that the provoker should be punished for his wrongdoing; it is another to suggest that his life can be taken with 'partial impunity'.[29]

On the other hand, if only very serious provocations were held to be capable of undermining the provoker's right to life, for example provocations involving physical violence or a real threat to life or limb, the scope of the provocation defence would get extremely narrow and, in most cases, provocation would appear to operate as a form of "imperfect" self-defence rather than as an independent defence in its own right.[30] Moreover, the application of the forfeiture theory to

---

28   This stems from the general assumption that claims of justification lend themselves to universalisation. See G. Fletcher, *Rethinking Criminal Law,* pp. 761-2.

29   "Provocation: Partial Justification or Partial Excuse?" 51 *Modern Law Review* (1988) 467, p. 478.

30   As we saw in the previous chapter, at common law only certain forms of wrongful conduct deemed extremely serious could amount to provocation in law. Although such an approach to the defence would be easier to explain in terms of the justification theory, most early commentators agreed that the

provocation leads to contradiction in so far as killing as a response to provocation constitutes a grave offence (manslaughter) and a wrongdoing far more serious than the victim's provocation. On the hypothesis that a culpable wrongdoing weakens the offender's right to life, the provoked person's right to life could also be said to be weakened as much as, or even more than, that of the provoker. Indeed, provoked aggression, especially when it involves a threat to life, can be resisted by force and the person who applies such force, whether the provoker or a third party, may be able to rely on self-defence or a similar justification-based defence. The defender's plea of justification in such cases is not necessarily weakened by the fact that he was defending against a provoked attack.[31]

Let us now consider whether the idea that the rationale of the provocation defence lies in the justification theory can draw some support from the other two moral theories of justification, namely the *lesser evil* theory and the theory based on the *enforcement of rights* principle (or the principle of the vindication of autonomy). As was said in chapter 1, the application of the lesser evil theory presupposes, firstly, a situation of conflict of values or interests wherein only one value or interest can possibly be preserved at the expense of the other; secondly, that the interests at stake can be evaluated and compared according to certain generally recognised criteria; and, thirdly, a rational agent who is called upon to make a reasonable choice as to which of the two values or interests should be preserved, that is, a choice in accordance with those objective criteria of evaluation. Notwithstanding its *prima facie* wrongful character, an act which preserves or promotes the superior interest is deemed morally and probably legally justified. As regards legal justification, in particular, it should be noted that the relevant judgment is not confined to the assessment of the competing interests at stake, but is informed also by considerations relating to the protection of the legal order as a whole. The conditions of provocation do not appear to meet the basic prerequisites of the lesser evil theory and the very idea of partial justification seems out of place here. Firstly, in provocation it cannot be said that the actor is confronted with an inescapable conflict of interests, as required for the application of the lesser evil theory. Depending upon the nature of the provocation offered, the provoked person may seek redress in an appropriate, i.e. fully justifiable,

---

defence constituted a concession to human frailty and, as such, its true basis was to be found in the excuse theory. See, e.g., East, 1 *PC* 238; Hawkins, I *PC* 97; Foster, *CC* 296.

31  Unless, of course, the provocation involved an actual threat to life.

manner.[32] And, secondly, if the killing of the provoker were regarded as less evil than putting up with the provocation, something which is hardly the case, the accused should be entitled to complete exoneration. As Dressler has remarked

> The lesser evil theory is also difficult to comprehend in partial terms. If the taking of a human life in response to nondeadly provocation is less evil or harmful than countenancing the provocation (an unlikely conclusion at that), the defendant should be acquitted of all homicide charges; if the defendant's actions are more evil, he should be punished fully for taking a human life.[33]

The third moral theory of justification rests upon the rights-enforcement principle, or the principle of vindication of autonomy. According to this theory, a person is entitled to defend his personal rights against attempted violations, even by inflicting harm on the transgressor. The idea that provocation operates as a partial justification cannot be supported by this theory either. The enforcement of moral or legal rights is not unconditional. On the contrary, such rights would remain in force only when pursued within certain limits. Unless a right is exercised in a way that is compatible with other people's rights, the right would fall in abeyance — what remains being a mere pretext of a right — and thus it could not warrant moral or legal justification. As Dressler puts it

> The right theory of justification is the least convincing basis in these circumstances [of provocation]. What right would we want to say the defendant is properly exercising when he kills the provoker? It cannot be the right to life, since the provoker does not jeopardise the defendant's (or anyone else's) right to life. If it is a dignitary right that the defendant seeks to exercise, it should certainly come as a surprise to us that such a right entitles the actor to take a human life in order to enforce it.[34]

As the above analysis suggests, none of the moral theories of justification is capable of providing enough support to the idea that the true basis of the provocation defence is to be found in the justification

---

32  As Robinson points out, "The triggering conditions of a justification defence do not in themselves give the actor the privilege to act without restriction. To be justified, the response conduct must satisfy two requirements: (1) it must be *necessary* to protect or further the interest at stake, and (2) it must cause only a harm that is proportional, or reasonable in retaliation to the harm threatened or the interest to be furthered", "Criminal Law Defences: A Systematic Analysis", supra note 1, p. 217.

33  "Provocation: Partial Justification or Partial Excuse?", supra note 29, p. 477.

34  Ibid, at p. 477.

theory. Although the justificatory element in provocation may in the past have played a part in the shaping of the legal doctrine of provocation, its role in modern law is greatly diminished. The current trend in the law towards placing more emphasis on the sanctity and inviolability of human life leaves very little room for any theory that views provocation as a partial justification. Moreover, the idea that an act of revenge may be partially justified conflicts with fundamental presuppositions of the criminal law system as a system whose very point is shifting the authority and moral basis of actions from the domain of subjective attitudes to general and impersonal norms of conduct.[35] Although for the defence of provocation to be accepted it must be established that the accused was somehow wronged by his victim, for only in such a case one could refer to the defence as "provocation", the rationale of the defence in law is more satisfactorily explained in terms of the excuse theory. The real basis of the provocation defence, traditionally regarded as a concession to human frailty, lies in the actor's loss of self-control in circumstances in which any ordinary person might also have lost control.[36] In this respect, the wrongful act of provocation is seen as providing a morally acceptable explanation for the accused's loss of self-control and killing rather than a reason for directly reducing the wrongfulness of his actions. It is to the analysis of the provocation defence in terms of the excuse theory that this discussion must now turn.

## The Excusative Element in Provocation

The traditional formulation of provocation as a concession to human frailty reflects the conception of the defence as an excuse.[37] This

---

35  As A.von Hirsch and N. Jareborg have pointed out, "Although the [provoker] might deserve punishment, the actor lacks authority to inflict it. Penalizing malefactors is not a legitimate role for an individual; it is a state function, to be undertaken with appropriate due process safeguards", "Provocation and Culpability", supra note 11, p.242.

36  As Devlin J. pointed out in *Duffy* [1949] 1 All ER 932, "circumstances which include a desire for revenge are inconsistent with provocation, since the conscious formulation of a desire for revenge means that a person has had time to think, to reflect, and that would negative a sudden and temporary loss of self-control, which is of the essence of provocation" (at 932).

37  See, e.g., *Holmes v DPP* [1946] AC 588: "the law has to reconcile respect for the sanctity of human life with recognition of the effect of provocation on human frailty" ( at 601 per Lord Simon ). According to O'Regan, "The doctrine of provocation is a concession to human frailty, a recognition that a lower standard of criminal responsibility should apply to one who kills when he is 'for the moment not master of his mind'", "Indirect Provocation and

approach to the provocation defence hinges on the notion of impaired volition or loss of self-control. Its governing assumption is that provocative conduct, when it is sufficiently serious, is capable of inflaming anger to such a degree as to be likely to lead the provoked person to lose his self-control and retaliate in violence. When the provoked person loses self-control he is unable to weigh up the consequences of his action according to reason. It is not that the provoked person lacks the *capacity* to reason. His judgment that there has been a wrongdoing is a reasoned judgement, but the reasoning then breaks down so that his actions that stem from that judgment are no longer the product of reason. As Horder puts it

> Action stemming from a loss of self-control...are the product of a judgment (of a certain degree of wrongdoing...) and a desire following in the wake of the judgment that controls the will without, for the moment, the restraining or guiding influence of reason.[38]

Although losing self-control and killing as a response to provocation is not totally excusable, the actor's degree of culpability falls short of that required to convict him of murder. From the point of view of the excuse theory, the gravity of the provocation is relevant to assessing the accused's claim that he was provoked to lose his self-control. There is no question here of whether the wrongful and culpable character of the provocative conduct should render the killing objectively less wrongful or partially justified. It is, rather, the accused's loss of self-control, *as a result of provocation*, that accounts for and justifies the reduction of culpability and, consequently, the reduction of the offence from murder to manslaughter. To gain some insight into the excusative element in provocation it is necessary to consider what human frailty means and how it relates to the loss of control requirement which, from the viewpoint of the excuse theory, constitutes the true basis of the provocation defence. I will begin by offering an account of the concept of loss of self-control as it figures in Aristotle's ethical theory.

## Aristotle on Akrasia, Loss of Self-Control and Responsibility

Aristotle distinguishes between what he calls as the "self-indulgent" man, that is the man whose choices and actions are guided by the wrong principle, and the akratic man. What Aristotle describes as

---

Misdirected Retaliation", *Criminal Law Review* [1968] 319, p. 320. And see R. Perkins, *Criminal Law* (1957), p. 42.
38   *Provocation and Responsibility*, p. 164.

*akrasia* refers to a state of character which tends to inhibit the agent from acting in a way that fully reflects the agent's moral beliefs.[39] The possibility of a discordance between external conduct and moral belief is manifested by the fact that the akratic man is more apt to repent of what he has done when carried away by passion; by contrast, the self-indulgent man generally persists in his choices.[40] Further, Aristotle draws a distinction between two kinds of akrasia, namely, impetuosity (*propeteia*), and weakness of will (*astheneia*).[41] Impetuosity pertains to those cases where the akratic agent, carried away by his passions, acts upon impulse and without deliberation. But not all actions that are performed upon impulse can be called impetuous, but only those that are contrary to choice.[42] Weakness of will, on the other hand, relates to those cases where the akratic agent, although he reaches the right choice[43] after deliberation, fails to act according to it.[44]

A further distinction Aristotle draws is that between the continent or self-restrained man — as contrasted with the akratic man — and the

---

39  In Aristotle's words: "[T]here is a sort of man who is carried away as a result of passion and contrary to the right rule — a man whom passion masters so that he does not act according to the right rule, but does not master to the extent of making him ready to believe that he ought to pursue such pleasures without reserve; this is the akratic man, who is better than the self-indulgent man, and not bad without qualification; for the best thing in him, the first principle is preserved. And contrary to him is another kind of man, he who abides by his convictions and is not carried away, at least as a result of passion. It is evident from these considerations that the latter is a good state and the former a bad one", *Nicomachean Ethics*, 1151a 20-25.

40  *Nicomachean Ethics*, 1146a 31-32.
    According to Alf Ross, "a person who has violated a system whose validity he himself recognises (i.e. experience as binding) in calm reflection, once the heat of the moment of action has subsided, must disapprove of his own conduct and become angry with himself. He must harbour with regard to himself the same feelings of anger, astonishment, sorrow or indignation that he would feel for another were he to have acted in the same way", *On Guilt, Responsibility and Punishment* (1975), p.7.

41  *Nicomachean Ethics*, 1150b 19.

42  Ibid at 1151, 5-7.

43  By right choice I am referring here to *orthe proeraisis* (1151a 34), or a choice in accordance with the *orthos logos* (1151a 21). According to Aristotle, right action is that "which is in accordance with right reason, and this is the mean between excess and defect relative to us", *Eudemian Ethics* 1222a 7.

44  As Aristotle puts it, "Of akrasia one kind is impetuosity, another weakness. For some men after deliberating fail, owing to their emotion, to stand by the conclusions of their deliberation, others because they have not deliberated are led by their emotion..." Ibid at 1150b, 20-25. And see D. Davidson, "How is Weakness of the Will Possible?", in *Essays on Actions and Events*, (Oxford 1980), p. 21.

temperate man. He explains that both the continent and the temperate man may comply with the same rule, or act according to the right principle; the temperate man, however, has no bad inclinations or urges to control, i.e. inclinations to act contrary to the rule, because, as Aristotle puts it, he does not feel any pleasure in doing so. The continent man, on the other hand, although he may be tempted or predisposed to act against the rule, does not allow himself to be carried away by his impulses. Patently, one may speak of the continent but not the temperate man as exercising self-control. Moreover, the akratic and the self-indulgent man resemble each other in that they both are inclined to act contrary to the rule; they differ, however, in that the self-indulgent man tends to act so primarily as a matter of choice, whereas for the akratic man this evinces weakness of will, i.e. a difficulty to bring one's actions into line with one's moral choices.[45] From this it becomes clear that it is the akratic man, not the self-indulgent one, who is capable of losing his self-control and acting contrary to the rule as a result.

Aristotle demonstrates, further, that people of a keen and excitable nature are in general more prone to the impetuous form of akrasia because, being easily overwhelmed by passion, they tend to act without taking time for deliberation and reflection. He calls our attention to the moral difference between the person who acts impetuously upon impulse and the one who has reached the right choice after deliberation but fails to regulate his conduct accordingly. In his words

> of the akratic men themselves, those who become temporarily beside themselves are better than those who have the rational principle but do not abode by it, since the latter are defeated by a weaker passion, and do not act without previous deliberation like the others...[46]

But not every action that is done upon impulse and without deliberation can be called impetuous, but only those that are contrary to choice.[47]

---

45   In Aristotle's words: "Since many names are applied analogically, it is by analogy that we have come to speak of the 'continence' of the temperate man; for both the continent and the temperate man are such as to do nothing contrary to the rule for the sake of bodily pleasures, but the former has and the latter has not bad appetites, and the latter is such as not to feel pleasure contrary to the rule, while the former is such as to feel pleasure but not to be led by it. And the akratic and the self-indulgent man are also like each other; they are different, but both pursue bodily pleasures — the latter, however, also thinking that he ought to do so, while the former does not think this", *Nicomachean Ethics*, 1151b 35, 1152a 5.

46   Ibid at 1150b 30-35, 1151a 5-10.

47   Ibid at 1151 5-7.

An action may be contrary to choice not only when it does not reflect the choice the actor has already made, but also when it goes against the choice the actor would have made, had he the time or opportunity to deliberate according to the principles which he would normally employ in making moral decisions. For example, a person who would normally not use violence against another, on a particular occasion does so carried away by anger. For such a person, resorting to violence is against his moral principles, and he would not have acted so by choice, had he kept his temper in check and taken the time to deliberate about it. In such a case the person is said to be acting upon impulse, or impetuously. In other words, acting impetuously is acting against choice (*para proairesin*) in the sense that the person acts, not contrary to a choice he actually made, but contrary to a choice he would have made, had he not acted impulsively.[48] From this point of view, a moral distinction is drawn between the person who, having been carried away by passion and lost his self-control, acts in a way that does not represent his all-things-considered choice, and the person whose action on the spur of the moment would be no different from that which he would have chosen under normal circumstances (i.e. the "self-indulgent" man).

Aristotle recognises that in both kinds of akrasia, i.e. impetuosity and weakness of will, the akratic agent acts both knowingly and intentionally, notwithstanding that his action does not accord with a fully-fledged moral choice. It is precisely the lack of correspondence between action and moral choice that accounts for the akratic agent's being morally less to blame than the one who chooses (or would have chosen, in normal circumstances) to act contrary to the rule. As Aristotle puts it

> [The akratic man] acts willingly (for he acts in a sense with knowledge both of what he does and of the end to which he does it), but is not wicked, since his purpose is good; so that he is half-wicked. And he is not a criminal; for he does not act of malice aforethought; of the two types of akratic man the one does not abide by the conclusions of his deliberation, while the excitable man does not deliberate at all.[49]

It is important to note that, according to Aristotle, the akratic agent acts voluntarily. For him, a person can be said to act voluntarily

---

48  Ibid at 1150b 25-28.

49  Ibid at 1152a 15-20. The moral difference between the akratic and the self-indulgent man is illustrated by Aristotle as follows: "the akratic man is like the state which passes all the right decrees and has good laws, but makes no use of them,...but the wicked man is like a state that uses its laws, but has wicked laws to use" (idem).

(*hekousios*) when (a) the moving principle is in the agent himself,[50] and (b) the agent is aware of the particular circumstances and probable consequences of his action.[51] It is clear that, when the akratic agent acts against his real decision, the moving principle, namely his desire for the act, is within him. Moreover the agent is aware of the circumstances of the act for it is his knowledge of these circumstances that gives rise to his desire or emotion and leads him to act against his decision.[52] It is the knowledge that he or someone else has been unjustly wronged that leads the akratic agent to retaliate in anger.

Aristotle remarks, further, that of the akratic men some act as they do in pursuit or defence of things often regarded as good and noble in themselves, i.e. worthy of being chosen as such, such as, for example, honour or duty. What these men are to be blamed for is not pursuing those things but, rather, doing so in the wrong way. Thus, we may speak of the akratic agent as, for example, "akratic in respect of honour", or "akratic in respect of duty", or "akratic in respect of gain", or "akratic in respect of anger". Of those akratic in respect of anger, Aristotle says that they are less to blame because their actions often stem from some sort of negative moral judgment of conduct that triggers off and, in a sense, justifies their anger. In Aristotle's words

> When [a man] acts with knowledge but not after deliberation, it is an act of injustice - e.g. the acts due to anger or to passions necessary or natural to man; for when men do such harmful and mistaken acts they act unjustly, but this does not imply that the doers are unjust or wicked; for the injury is not due to vice. But when a man acts from choice, he is an unjust and vicious man. Hence acts proceeding from anger are rightly judged not to be done of malice aforethought; for it is not the man who acts in anger but he who enraged him that starts the mischief. Again, the matter in dispute is not whether the thing happened or not, but its justice; for it is apparent injustice which occasions rage.[53]

Although his initial judgment of wrongdoing may have been a correct one, when the akratic agent gives way to anger and loses his self-control, his actions are no longer guided by reason. Nevertheless, because of the correctness of his initial judgment (whether that was based on the facts as they were or as he believed them to be makes no difference here), the akratic agent in respect of anger is less

---

50   Ibid at 1110a 15-17.
51   Ibid at 1110b 33-1a6.
52   Ibid at 1152a 15-16.
53   Ibid at 1135b 18.

blameworthy than the akratic agent who succumbs to a wanton impulse or appetite.[54]

According to Aristotle, both kinds of akrasia, i.e. impetuosity and weakness of will, manifest reprehensible character traits. But, one might argue, if the emotions or desires of the akratic person lead him to act in a way that does not represent his actual moral choices, these emotions or desires must be such that cannot be defeated. Indeed, one might seek to derive support for this argument from Aristotle's own explanation of the relationship between desire and reason — the rational element, as Aristotle calls it. According to him

[Both continent and akratic men] have a principle — a rational element in their souls — which we commend, because it urges them in the right direction and encourages them to take the best course of action; but there is also observable in them another element, by nature irrational, which struggles and strains against the rational. Just as in the case of the body paralysed limbs, when the person chooses to move them to the right, turn on the contrary to the left, so it is with the soul; the impulses (*hormai*) of the akratic person take them in the contrary direction. But while in the body we see that which moves astray, in the soul we do not.[55]

---

54  As Aristotle explains, "Anger seems to listen to argument to some extent, but to mishear it... so anger by reason of the warmth and hastiness of its nature, though it hears, does not hear an order, and springs to take revenge. For argument or imagination informs us that we have been insulted or slighted, and anger, reasoning as it were that anything like this must be fought against, boils up straightway; while appetite, if argument or perception merely says that an object is pleasant, springs to the enjoyment of it. Therefore anger obeys the argument in a sense, but appetite does not. It is therefore more disgraceful; for the man who is akratic in respect of anger is in a sense conquered by argument, while the other is conquered by appetite and not by argument", Ibid, 1149a 25-35. Aristotle adds that "no one commits wanton outrage with a feeling of pain, but every one who acts in anger acts with pain, while the man who commits outrage acts with pleasure. If, then, those acts at which it is most just to be angry are more criminal than others, the akrasia which is due to appetite is more criminal; for there is no wanton outrage involved in anger", idem, at 1149b 20-25.

55  Ibid at 1102b6 28.
    And according to T. Aquinas, "He that has knowledge of the universal is hindered, because of passion, from reasoning in the light of that universal, so as to draw the conclusion; but he reasons in the light of another universal proposition, suggested by the inclination of the passion, and draws his conclusion accordingly...Hence passion fetters the reason, and hinders it from thinking and concluding under the first proposition; so that while passion lasts, the reason argues and concludes under the second", *Summa Theologica*, Part II, Q. 77.

What this seems to suggest is that just as the paraplegic person makes a real choice but his movement is contrary to it, so the akratic person makes a real choice to act in a certain way but his impulses lead him to act against it. This might be taken to imply that the akratic person, just like the paraplegic, psychologically cannot help acting the way he does and hence he is not responsible for his action. But this is not what Aristotle really says, since for him the akratic person acts akratically, i.e. against his moral choices, only occasionally or exceptionally, not all the time.[56] If a person follows his desires all the time he is not akratic but bad.[57] Moreover, even if it were true that in some cases the akratic agent may find himself overwhelmed by his desires or emotions in the way that the paraplegic is overcome by his illness, the akratic agent may still be held morally responsible for allowing himself to get into a situation where he loses control of his actions. The akratic agent, in other words, is to blame for allowing his passion to become so strong as to overcome his own moral choices.[58] Unlike the condition of the paraplegic, what causes the akratic agent to act against his best judgement is not regarded as an irresistible or permanent pathological condition. This may be true with regard to the impetuous agent, who acts upon impulse without taking time for deliberation. In such a case, as noted before, the agent acts against a choice which he would have made had he not acted upon impulse. But what of the akratic agent who acts against his own best judgment, after going through deliberation and choice?[59] How is it possible that a person who has reached a correct decision, taking into account his desires and feelings, and has decided to act on it, then loses control of his actions and acts contrary to his decision? Aristotle's answer to this question is that "desire leads towards [the object] for it {the desire] can move each of our bodily parts".[60] So, for Aristotle, desire has the power to move the parts of the body, as it has direct access to these parts. In the case of the akratic agent a desire, if it is sufficiently strong, can find its way to the bodily parts and result into action, circumventing the agent's prior decision or choice to act otherwise.[61]

Aristotle's analysis of the phenomenon of akrasia and of the way in which it affects the attribution of responsibility provides a basis for

---

[56]   *Nicomachean Ethics*, at 1152a 26-27.

[57]   Ibid at 1151a 20-24.

[58]   Ibid at 1113b 30-33.

[59]   I.e. the one who exhibits weakness of will (astheneia), as acting contrary to his own best judgment. Ibid at 1148a 6-10, 1151a 29-35.

[60]   Ibid at 1147a 34-35.

[61]   See on this D. Wiggins "Weakness of Will, Commensurability, and the Objects of Deliberation and Desire", in A. D. Rorty (ed.), *Essays on Aristotle's Ethics* (1980), 246.

understanding the character of the excusative element in provocation.[62] In particular, his account of the relationship between justified anger — as a result of a moral judgment of conduct — and loss of self-control is illuminating, for it explains why a provoked person is less to blame for the wrongful action that results from his loss of self-control. It is the moral justification of the provoked person's anger that furnishes a good reason for recognising loss of self-control as an excuse. This is what distinguishes the person who loses his self-control as a result of provocation from the one who tends to lose control all the time — the so called "bad tempered" or, to use Aristotle's terminology, the "self-indulgent" man.[63] Excusing those who succumb to anger in the face of grave provocation and lose control of their actions constitutes a concession to the failings of human nature, and it becomes possible precisely because these failings are common to all men.[64] At the same time, Aristotle's theory explains why provocation cannot provide a complete excuse: it is because the provoked actor is still to blame for allowing himself to be carried away by his passion. While the provoked agent might not be able or not want to suppress his anger, he is taken to be capable of stifling the behaviour stemming from it. In the absence of mental impairment, the provoked agent is deemed capable of exercising self-control, i.e. for recognising that there are overriding reasons for not acting on the desire to retaliate which arises in his emotional state.

According to Aristotle, of the two kinds of akratic men, those who act upon impulse and without deliberation are in general less to blame than those who give way to a desire after going through

---

62  For a more detailed account of this aspect of Aristotle's ethical theory see L.A. Kosman, "Being Properly Affected: Virtues and Feelings in Aristotle's Ethics", in *Essays on Aristotle's Ethics*, Amelie Oksenberg Rorty (ed.), (1980); A.O. Rorty, "Plato and Aristotle on Belief, Habit, and Akrasia", *American Philosophical Quarterly* 7 (1970) 50; G. Mattheus, "Weakness of Will", *Mind* 75 (1966) 405; O.G. Ritchie, "Aristotle's Explanation of AKRASIA", 6 *Mind* (1897) 536; R. Robinson, "Aristotle on Acrasia" in his *Essays in Greek Philosophy* (Oxford 1969); W.W. Fortenbauch, "Aristotle: Emotion and Moral Virtue", *Arethusa* (1969). And see J.L. Ackrill (ed), *Aristotle's Ethics* (1973).

63  As A. von Hirsch and N. Jareborg have remarked, the provoked agent is less to blame because he "was moved to transgress in part because of, rather than despite, his sense of right and wrong", "Provocation and Culpability", supra note 11, p. 251.

64  As J. Feinberg has noted, "Provocations are essentially causal mechanisms They exploit the known tendency of a certain class of words [or actions] to evoke emotional responses, and the presumed tendency of certain classes of persons (nearly all persons in some circumstances or other) to respond passionately to them", *The Moral Limits of the Criminal Law*, (Oxford 1985), p. 226.

deliberation, because their action precedes the formation of a fully informed decision. Anger experienced as loss of self-control tends to involve an immediate or spontaneous response — i.e. a response not preceded by deliberation and choice. The underlying assumption here is that the impulsive agent, blameworthy though he may be, acts against his all-things-considered judgment — a judgement which he would have reached had he given himself time to deliberate. In the light of this assumption, law's insistence on the requirement of loss of self-control (of acting "in the heat of passion", or "on the spur of the moment") can be understood. But could the second type of akrasia, the one which Aristotle calls weakness of will (*astheneia*), provide a basis for partially excusing a provoked killing, given that, in such a case, the agent acts after going through the process of deliberation? Here the actor knows what would be an appropriate level of punitive response, but give in to the desire to inflict more punishment. While this weakness might seem not different from that involved in one's giving way to lust or greed, it is not, because of the nature of anger as stemming from a morally warranted judgment of conduct. Extreme anger may feel like a great pain, and the retaliatory actions are done to relieve this, not to satisfy more "base" emotions (such as greed or lust). In this respect, one might assert that such actions are understandable and deserve some forgiveness. This way of looking at the issue leaves room for some deliberation prior to the provoked actor's response and might be relevant when dealing with cases involving persons who have killed after they have been subjected to a long term of abuse in the victim's hands. However, such an approach is difficult to accept as a valid one for the purposes of the provocation defence for, as long as the actor is regarded as a normal person, it would open the way for bringing within the scope of the defence cold-blooded or revenge killings normally thought inconsistent with the loss of control element in provocation. In general the criminal law does not leave room for excusing violations committed as a result of the agent's giving way to temptation. Thus a thief cannot claim on the grounds that, although he knew that what he was doing was wrong, he succumbed to the temptation to steal (no matter what his real motive for doing so may have been). Similarly, it will not be a defence for an accused to claim that, because he had been attacked by the victim, he gave in to the temptation to inflict harm greater than was needed to defend himself, or to retaliate after the attack was over.[65] However, as is explained in chapter 5, if the distress the agent is experiencing as a result of some grave wrong he suffered at the victim's hands is so acute as to seriously impair his normal capacity for self-control, then he may be able to rely on diminished responsibility or a similar

---

[65]   See, e.g., *Palmer v R* [1971] 1 All ER 1077, 1088.

defence. Moreover, the fact that the provoked agent has had time to deliberate on what the appropriate response to the victim's provocation should be, would not necessarily preclude the provocation defence if, on a subsequent occasion, the agent loses his self-control and kills as a response to fresh provocation offered by the victim.

## Loss of Self-Control as a Basis for Excusing

In provocation it is not required that the actor loses his self-control to the extent that he does not know what he is doing, or what his action is aimed at; but self-control must be lost to such an extent that for the moment his action is being guided by passion rather than by reason. Indeed, it is an important prerequisite for pleading provocation as a partial defence to murder that the accused have acted with the requisite *mens rea* for murder, i.e. an intention to kill or to cause grievous bodily harm. If the provoked agent loses his self-control to such an extent as to be unaware of the nature or quality of his act, or unable to exercise control over his bodily movements, then he or she may be entitled to full acquittal on the basis of a lack of *actus reus* or *mens rea* defence. Other things being equal, if the provoked agent suffers a total loss of self-control, automatism may provide the appropriate basis for a complete defence to the charge of murder.[66] As Archibald explains

> for automatism to be applicable, there must be a complete loss of self-control and a concomitant involuntary and unconscious state on the part of the accused. In provocation, a loss of partial control is presupposed but only to the extent that the accused gives way to his inflamed passions. His cognitive processes are not impaired nor is his physical ability to control his conduct.[67]

---

66   As T. Archibald has remarked, "it may be possible to argue in extremely exceptional cases where there is some evidence pointing towards the inference that the accused suffered a total loss of control, that his conduct was involuntary and unconscious; therefore, the actus reus of the crime might be negatived and the accused could be acquitted on the basis that the automatic conduct gives rise to the defence of automatism", "The Interrelationship Between Provocation and Mens Rea: A Defence of Loss of Self-Control", *Criminal Law Quarterly* 28 (1985-86) 454, pp. 454-455. And see A. Ashworth, "Reason, Logic and Criminal Liability", *Law Quarterly Review* 91 (1975) 102, pp. 128-9.

67   "The Interrelationship Between Provocation and Mens Rea: A Defence of Loss of Self-Control", supra note 66, p. 470. And see C. T. Sistare, *Responsibility and Criminal Liability*, (1989), p. 78; R. Berger, "Provocation and the Involuntary Act", *McGill Law Journal* 12 (1967), 202.

Nevertheless, in those cases of provocation where the actor is totally deprived of his ability to control his conduct, the victim's provocation might perhaps be regarded as a triggering factor of the excusing condition — i.e. automatism — providing the basis of his defence to murder. Thus, although another excuse takes the priority over provocation here, the latter might be granted a role peripheral to or supportive of the defence relied upon.[68]

The role of loss of control in the theory of excuses is understood in the light of the important distinction between involuntariness and moral or normative involuntariness. The term involuntariness is used to denote one's total inability to direct one's conduct or to exercise control over one's bodily movements. One might say that, in such cases, the agent acts only in appearance because the conduct is no longer subject to conscious determination by the agent.[69] Normative or moral involuntariness, on the other hand, pertains to those cases where the agent, although he is able to direct his external conduct (to "act", in a strict sense), is unable to act as he chooses — or would have chosen — due to external or internal constraints on his freedom to choose (cases of "overpowered will"). According to Fletcher

> Excuses arise in cases in which the actor's freedom of choice is constricted. His conduct is not strictly involuntary as if he suffered a seizure or if someone pushed his knife-holding hand down on the victim's throat. In these cases there is no act at all, no wrongdoing and therefore no need for an excuse. The notion of involuntariness at play is what we should call moral or normative involuntariness. Were it not for the external pressure, the actor would not have performed the deed. In Aristotle's words, he 'would not choose any such act in itself'.[70]

The distinction between involuntariness and moral or normative involuntariness is allied to that between compulsion and coercion. The person acting under compulsion is unable to exercise physical control

---

68    As Colvin puts it, "extreme rage may produce a state of dissociation under which conduct is no longer being directed by a reasoning mind and there is therefore no voluntary actus reus. Similarly, provocation may induce a state of impaired cognition which negatives mens rea", *Principles of Criminal Law* (1991), p. 253.

69    As Jerome Hall has noted, with regard to conduct whose cause is "entirely outside the person, where his 'self' does not participate in the slightest degree, the legal rules represent the traditional judgement that the defendant has not acted at all, i.e. 'act' implies volition", *General Principles of Criminal Law*, 2nd ed. (1960), p. 422. See also, S.C. Coval & J.S. Smith, *Law and its Presuppositions: Actions, Agents and Rules*, (1986), esp. chapters 1 and 2.

70    *Rethinking Criminal Law* (1978), p. 803. And see Holland, *Jurisprudence* 13th ed. (Oxford 1924), p. 103. See also C.T. Sistare, supra note 67, p. 77.

over his bodily movements, in other words, is not free to act. The coerced person, by contrast, although he is free to act in a strict sense, is not free to choose the direction of his action.[71] Compulsion provides the basis for claims of exculpation contesting authorship-responsibility and hence, indirectly, moral responsibility. Claims of exculpation (or mitigation) stemming from coercion challenge directly the actor's being morally responsible for a wrongful act. From the point of view of the excuse theory, the classification of the various exculpatory claims in law turns on the source and nature of the relevant external or internal impediments precluding the agent's acting in compliance with the law. H. Gross explains the distinction between different excusing conditions, according to the source, as follows

> Instead of denying a *prima facie* imputation of conduct to some occurrence, we admit that the occurrence is an act — that is, an occurrence for which someone might be held responsible. But because the actor could choose only with inordinate difficulty to do otherwise — or could not choose to do otherwise at all — we deny that he is in fact fully responsible, or responsible at all. In this sense the following are not (or are not fully) voluntary acts: (1) acts done only because coerced by others; (2) acts done only because of one's own uncontrollable urges; (3) acts done only because circumstances left no choice; (4) acts done when one is in an abnormal mental state that leaves one unable to appreciate what he is doing. [72]

The excusative element in the provocation defence pertains to the idea of moral or normative involuntariness. Although the provoked agent acts, in a strict sense, voluntarily, i.e. both knowingly and intentionally, he is less to blame because, being overcome by passion, his freedom to choose is constricted. Freedom of choice in action, as a requirement of moral and legal responsibility, presupposes, among

---

71    As D. Hoekema remarks, "What the victim of coercion is able to do despite the threat is to control his actions in the usual way. His control over the movements of his own body has not been taken from him, as it is in cases of compulsion. He is *free to act*. What has been taken from the victim of coercion is the ability to determine his future condition by his actions, to bring about future conditions which he desires by his present acts. Of course, his acts still determine in part what his future condition will be; but the normal control that we have and expect over what happens to us as a result of our actions has been disrupted by the threat. The victim of coercion, then, is subjected to extraordinary constraints on his choice; in short, he is not free to choose", *Rights and Wrongs*, (1986), p. 75. For an analysis of the distinction between compulsion and coercion see J. Edwards, "Compulsion, Coercion, and Criminal Responsibility", *Modern Law Review* 14 (1951) 297; H. G. Frankfurt, "Coercion and Moral Responsibility", in *Essays on Freedom of Action*, T. Honderich (ed.), (1973) 63.

72    *A Theory of Criminal Justice* (1979), p. 69.

other things, that the actor is "master of his mind", or that he is acting in a "normal" frame of mind. Heat of passion and loss of self-control imply that the contribution of reason in the psychological process towards the formation of the will is precluded or substantially diminished.[73] There are two ways in which passion may affect a person's ability to choose freely. In some impetuous acts the urge does not circumvent the conscious self but, in a sense, passes through it. Because of its intensity, however, the urge overrides the actor's ability to exercise rational judgment, or defeats his moral resistance.[74] One might also consider as relevant here the so called *short-circuited reactions*. These pertain to cases where an intense psychological urge is activated so abruptly that, in a way, circumvents the conscious self and affects directly the agent's motivational system. In such cases the agent's moral inhibitions are bypassed rather than overcome. Depending upon the degree to which self-control is lost, the provoked agent's response may be described as an impetuous act of the first type or as a "short-circuited reaction". In the latter case loss of self-control tends to involve a spontaneous, immediate reaction to the provocation received. The desire to inflict punishment on the provoker which is triggered by the judgment of wrongdoing is translated into action immediately, i.e. without going through any process of deliberation. In this case the agent reacts almost without thinking, like the person who, when another raises his hand to hit him, instinctively ducks his head or raises his hands to protect himself. In the former case, by contrast, the provoked agent appears to be making a choice in anger to inflict a certain kind of punishment on the provoker. The exercise of choice here, however, does not necessarily require us to draw the inference that the provoked agent is in control of his actions, for the choice he makes, distorted by emotion, involves a misjudgment as to what form and degree of retaliation is appropriate. Depending upon the perceived gravity of the provocation, this misjudgment is to some extent excusable because people are fallible and often leap before they look,

---

73    According to Kant, in those cases where reason succumbs to passion, the will is determined by something external to it — a relation which Kant terms the *'heteronomy of the will'*. In such cases the person's reasons for acting in a certain way pertain only to what he or she desires, independently of his moral beliefs. On the other hand, when the person's will is determined by reason, the will is said to be 'self-ruled', for reason is viewed as something 'internal' to the will. A will which is determined by reason is at one with itself. According to Kant, such a will can override passion and desire.

74    See N. R. F. Maier, "Frustration Theory: Restatement and Extension", *Psychological Review* 63 (1956) 370, p. 382. The author suggests that there are intermediate states between being totally emotional and totally rational, wherein emotion and reason may conflict with each other.

especially when they are conquered by passion. Both impetuous acts involving deliberation and short-circuited reactions should be distinguished from what is referred to as "reflex actions". The latter lack a concrete psychological basis and therefore relate to the conditions of involuntariness rather that to those of moral or normative involuntariness. The "impetuous acts" and, arguably, the "short-circuited reactions" are not irrelevant to the attribution of moral and, possibly, legal responsibility for both may be taken to manifest undesirable character traits or dispositions.

What do we mean, then, when we say that the provoked agent who acts "in the heat of the moment" is not entirely free to choose? To answer this question one would need to look more closely at the interrelation between free agency and self-control. It has been asserted that freedom of choice presupposes that what motivates the agent to act in a certain way accords with his or her all-things-considered evaluations. G. Watson draws a distinction between the agent's "valuational" and "motivational" systems. He defines an agent's valuational system as

> that set of considerations which, when combined with his factual beliefs, yields judgements of the form: the thing for me to do in these circumstances, all things considered, is a. To ascribe free agency to a being presupposes it to be a being that makes judgements of this sort. To be this sort of being, one must assign values to alternative states of affairs, that is, rank them in terms of worth.[75]

Moreover, Watson defines the motivational system of an agent as that set of considerations which moves the agent to action. From this point of view, an action is held not to be free if the agent's motivational system is not aligned with, or correspond to, his evaluational system. In Watson's words

> The possibility of unfree action consists in the fact that the agent's valuational and motivational system may not completely coincide. Those systems harmonize to the extent that what determines the agent's all-things-considered judgements also determines his actions...The free agent has the capacity to translate his values into action; his actions flow from his evaluational system.[76]

As has been pointed out earlier, provocation may provide the grounds for a partial excuse only if the victim's conduct is considered to be sufficiently wrongful, i.e., capable of raising legitimate anger or

---

[75] "Free Agency", in *Free Will* (1982), p. 105.
[76] Ibid at p. 106.

indignation.[77] It is precisely his disapproval of the victim's conduct that motivates the agent to respond. In provocation the actor often appears to be making a choice to retaliate — a choice preceded and precipitated by a negative moral judgment of the victim's conduct. In other words, the provoked agent does not merely judge that there has been a wrongdoing, but also, to some extent, deliberates on what retaliatory action is required. But, where there is an overreaction, the agent judges that more retaliation is appropriate than it is in fact justified by the seriousness of the provocation. Thus, although acute anger or indignation does not always preclude the agent's making a choice (in a strict sense), it may greatly undermine his capacity to weigh up or to properly evaluate the moral significance of his choice of action in the light of its (intended) consequences. Debilitating anger may sometimes preclude choosing altogether, but more often the person acting in the heat of passion claims to have been unable to choose differently than to have been unable to choose at all. The provoked agent acting under an irresistible urge makes choices but cannot control the choosing process or resist the choices he makes. In short, the provoked agent makes a choice, yet the conduct chosen is not morally voluntary.

Freedom of action as a requirement of responsibility presupposes not only that what motivates a person to act concurs with his or her evaluations; it presupposes, in addition, that the person's evaluations that move him to action take place in a "normal" frame of mind. As A. Mele has noted

> A self-controlled person is disposed to bring his motivations into line with his evaluations and to maintain that alignment. But there is more to being self-controlled than this, for one's evaluations themselves can be warped in various ways by one's wants and motivations. Hence, a self-controlled person must also be disposed to promote and maintain a structure of evaluations or values which is not unduly influenced by his motivations.[78]

---

77   In provocation the assumption that only justified anger may render the provoked agent partially excusable on the basis of his loss of self-control implies that not only the provoked agent's response to the provocation but also his assessment of the victim's conduct is subject to judgment. As C. Taylor has remarked, "Naturally we think of the agent as responsible, in part, for what he does; and since he is an evaluator, we think of him as responsible in part for the degree to which he acts in line with his evaluations. But we are also inclined to think of him as responsible in some sense for these evaluations themselves", "Responsibility for Self", in *Free Will* (1982), p. 118.

78   "Self-control, Action, and Belief", *American Philosophical Quarterly* 22, 2, (April 1985) 171.

In provocation, although the agent's judgment of wrongdoing motivates his choice to take punitive action, the ensuing urge to retaliate in a sense overrides the agent's own evaluational system, or his ability to assess correctly both the provoker's misdeed as well as his own response to the provocation. Thus, we might say that the provoked agent is not fully free to choose because his capacity for rational evaluation is undermined by the overwhelming emotional pressure which he is experiencing.[79] In this respect, the provoked agent who overreacts in an outbreak of anger is similar to the victim of coercion who acts morally involuntarily.

As was indicated above, the excusative element in provocation rests on the assumption that provocative conduct may give rise to such an emotional state wherein the agent's freedom to choose is temporarily suspended. Provocation is understood as a condition likely to occasion a form of internal coercion that precludes the agent from acting morally voluntarily. Nevertheless, unlike other defences based upon the idea of moral or normative involuntariness, loss of self-control as a result of provocation falls short of totally excluding moral and legal culpability. Giving way to anger — justified though such anger may be — or allowing one's reasoning ability (and hence his freedom to choose) to be overcome by passion furnishes sufficient grounds for holding the provoked agent partially responsible for his wrongdoing. The provoked agent who kills is still to blame for violating the general norm requiring that people should always hold their anger in check, even when faced with the most severe provocation. The agent remains morally and legally responsible for the lesser crime of manslaughter because, as a "normal" person, he is assumed capable of resisting his impulse to kill the provoker. The provoked agent's inability to defeat his urge to kill shows that he lacks the power of reason to view his response to provocation in the context of a system of values and an assessed set of circumstances. Because that power of reason is lacking the provoked agent finds it impossible to control his impulse, since the stifling of the impulse cannot be made the objective of a voluntary choice. As long as the provoked person is regarded as a "normal" person, giving way to anger can only be due to a defect of character, manifested by his inability to view the impulsive action in the light of a given system of norms that proscribes the taking of human life. This is

---

[79] As R. Brandt has remarked, "Strong emotional disturbance is known to primitivize thinking (much as does alcohol). A state of anger notoriously enhances one's aggressive tendencies, and reduces one's empathetic or sympathetic concern about injuring its target", "A Motivational Theory of Excuses in the Criminal Law", *Criminal Justice Nomos* XXVII (1985) 165 at pp. 183-184; reprinted in *Justification and Excuse in the Criminal Law*, M.L. Corrado (ed.), (1994) 95, p. 114.

precisely what justifies the provoked killer's being held, to some extent, morally and legally responsible for his actions.

In provocation the attribution of responsibility for the lesser offence can be explained on the basis of the theory of responsibility which focuses on the relationship between external conduct and human character. As we saw in chapter 2, this theory postulates that moral praise or blame pertains not directly to acts but, rather to the character traits. By character trait is understood any socially desirable or undesirable disposition or attitude that an act may be taken to reflect.[80] Although not all acts manifest character traits in a way that is morally or legally relevant, an actor cannot be held blameworthy or legally culpable unless his harmful conduct reflects a socially undesirable attitude. If it does, the degree of blame and punishment which the actor deserves is to be determined by reference to the extent to which his or her attitude is deemed undesirable; if it does not, blame and punishment would be inappropriate, although certain non-punitive measures preventive of similar conduct in the future might be taken. Notwithstanding that attitudes may be volatile or unstable, the general assumption of this theory is that, other things being equal, a wrongful and unlawful act does manifest an undesirable character trait or attitude. From the point of view of the character theory of responsibility, the role of excuses is to block the normal inference from a wrongful act to an undesirable trait of character. Determining whether a wrongful act reflects a defect in the actor's character requires consideration of the actor's state of mind at the time of his act and of his ability to exercise control over his conduct. In this respect, the admission of loss of self-control in provocation is taken to block the normal inference from the act of killing to the character fault associated with the crime of murder. Nevertheless, the excusing condition here cannot preclude the actor's conviction for the lesser crime of manslaughter, for losing control and killing is still taken to reflect a defect in the actor's character.

Under the character theory of responsibility one could also explain why losing control and killing in the face of a trivial provocation, or when no provocation has been offered, should not entitle the actor to a partial excuse. One might say that, if the provocation is not regarded as serious enough to raise justified anger to such a degree as to cause an ordinary person to lose his self-control and kill, the actor's response, on the spur of the moment though it may have been, manifests the same degree of character fault as that normally ascribed to a premeditated killing. The same may be said about those

---

80   As W. Lyons has remarked, "we are blamed for character traits and their expression only in so far as it is considered that a character trait has given rise to actions which have had an undesirable upshot. If character traits did not ever do anything, they could never do harm", *Emotion* (1980), p. 194.

cases in which the actor is deemed responsible for creating a situation wherein a provocative event is highly likely to occur.[81] As Dressler has pointed out

> under excuse theory, we do not (fully) blame a person who (partially) loses self-control if, *but only if,* he is not to blame for his anger and for his homicidal actions which result from it...A person who becomes sufficiently enraged to kill because the decedent acted in a nonwrongful manner arguably does not deserve to be excused. At the least the nonwrongfulness of the decedent's actions is highly pertinent in determining whether the actor's loss of self-control was excusable. Thus the individual who becomes angry and responds violently when another *justifiably* strikes him in self-defence and the person who unjustifiably creates the situation in which the provocation gives birth are blameworthy and should not be excused.[82]

If sufficient provocation cannot be shown or where the actor is deemed responsible for creating the conditions of provocation, the fact that the actor killed after he lost his self-control cannot on its own entitle him to an excuse on the grounds of the provocation defence. One might argue, however, that if a general loss of control defence was recognised, establishing provocation would not be necessary in order to reduce the actor's culpability for homicide. Nevertheless, where the actor's loss of self-control cannot be attributed to provocation, such a general loss of control defence may hold good only in so far as another acceptable reason for losing control can be brought forward. Let us examine this issue further.

## Provocation and Loss of Self-Control: a Double Test in Law?

In an essay entitled "Provocation and Culpability",[83] Andrew von Hirsch and Nils Jareborg have proposed the replacement of the traditional objective test in provocation with two separate tests which, in their view, will allow us to deal better with the two different aspects of the provocation defence — the excusative and the justificatory

---

81   As was indicated in Chapter 3, however, this does not represent the current position in English law. Provocation may be accepted as a defence even though it was self-induced, provided that the objective and subjective requirements of the defence are met. That the provocation was self-induced, however, may be relevant as an aggravating factor in determining the appropriate sentence imposed for the lesser offence.

82   "Provocation: Partial Justification or Partial Excuse?", supra note 29, p.475.

83   In *Responsibility, Character, and the Emotions,* F. Schoeman (ed.), (1987), 241.

aspect. They have argued that the reasonable person test is inadequate, for what is at issue when a plea of provocation is at stake is not the reasonableness of the accused's choices but, rather, "the choices not being fully the person's own".[84] The first of the proposed tests hinges on the requirement of impaired volition or loss of self-control; the second rests on what the authors refer to as the *principle of resentment*. An accused's plea of extenuation would satisfy the first test whenever a strong case of impaired volition or loss of control can be made. It is submitted, nonetheless, that the scope of this test should remain narrow so as to cover only those cases wherein the actor is totally deprived of his capacity to exercise self-control. The second test, which is the true one of provocation as ordinarily understood, may come into play if the first test fails. A claim of extenuation will be warranted under the resentment principle if the accused can put forward a good reason for feeling angry at the victim. And this would presuppose the accused's being able to show that he or she suffered a serious wrong at the victim's hands. If such a twofold test were introduced, it is argued, one would need not to speculate about how a reasonable person would have reacted to the provocation received.[85] The authors point out that speaking of the provoked person's anger as being warranted or justified according to the resentment principle does not imply the justification of the ensuing act of retaliation. In their own words

> What is crucial to [the actor's] claim of extenuation is his having a *good reason* for his anger, stemming from some misdeed committed by the victim against him or someone close to him. Let us emphasize, however: It is only [the actor's] anger that is warranted, not the deed that results from it. The criminal act, we should recall, is not justified, but only, perhaps, less culpable because of the nature of the sentiment involved. [86]

In order to determine whether a claim of extenuation on grounds of provocation is warranted under the resentment principle one would have to consider the nature and degree of the victim's wrongdoing. The authors suggest that "[t]he most straightforward cases are those where the victim's acts constituted criminal behaviour of a significant nature...The next cases comprise those where the victim behaved toward the actor in a manner that is not criminal, but nevertheless infringes commonly recognised standards of decent behaviour".[87]

---

84    Ibid at p. 252.
85    Ibid at pp. 253-4.
86    Ibid at pp. 248-9.
87    Ibid at p. 254.

The authors argue that the resentment principle need not be invoked in those cases where the actor was deprived of his self-control in a sudden outburst of rage. In such cases, it is pointed out, the actor's plea of extenuation may be dealt with under a general impaired volition or loss of control defence. Nevertheless, for such a defence to succeed, the actor would have to put forward a good reason for losing his self-control, i.e. a reason that would make it morally possible to allow an excuse on this basis. It is suggested, therefore, that one need not have recourse to the resentment principle — as the basis of the test of provocation — unless it is established that the accused's reaction was preceded by some form of forethought and deliberation on what retaliatory action is required. According to the authors, in these cases

> the 'hot anger' requirement of common law ceases to make sense. Since the claim no longer is that the person had his capacity for choice impaired, the momentary shock of the event is immaterial. What now matters is [the actor's] being angry for good reasons — and the sense of grievance may grow. The anger is not just a momentary emotional turbulence, and involves as much cognition as feeling; it may last, reinforced by the sense of having been aggrieved.[88]

Although it is true that provocation cannot furnish a basis for excusing unless the accused was seriously wronged by his victim, it seems questionable whether granting an excuse can be justified on the grounds of the resentment principle alone. If the test of provocation were taken to rest on this principle only, it would be difficult to distinguish between a voluntary act of revenge carried out in anger and a partially excusable act of retaliation, given that in both cases the actor's anger at the victim may be morally justified on account of the latter's wrongdoing. In so far as it is accepted that the wrongfulness of the provocation does not allow us to speak of the actor's homicidal response as partially justified, demonstrating that the actor's anger at the victim was morally warranted is a necessary but not a sufficient condition of excusing. Under the excuse theory the central question is not merely whether the actor was morally justified to feel angry or resentful; it is, rather, whether those feelings significantly impaired the actor's capacity to exercise control over his actions.[89] The actor's sense of justified anger provides the required link between provocation and impaired volition but it cannot furnish any grounds for excusing

---

[88]  Ibid at p. 252.

[89]  As Ashworth has remarked, "It is the elements of suddenness and impulsivity which serve to distinguish provocation as a mitigating factor from revenge, which may be treated as an aggravating factor because it is usually accompanied by planning and deliberation", *Sentencing and Penal Policy* (1983), p.169.

unless the actor did in some way lose his self-control. This is not to say that the actor must have lost his self-control in an absolute sense for, as was indicated earlier, loss of control is a matter of degree. Thus the fact that the enraged actor may appear, in some cases, to be making a choice to kill his provoker, or to be deliberating on what punitive response is required, does not necessary imply that he is in control of himself for his choices are guided by passion rather than by reason. In other words, in such cases the actor can still be said to be acting morally involuntarily.[90]

Although the authors are correct in placing emphasis on the resentment principle as a condition for excusing, they fail to explain adequately how this principle relates to the excusative element in provocation for, surely, speaking of the actor's having a good reason for feeling angry does not necessarily entail lack of self-control.[91] One cannot conclude from the fact that the agent's choice of action was made in anger that the agent was carried away by anger so that he was no longer master of his mind. Nevertheless, it is only in the latter case that the provoked agent should be able to rely on a partial excuse. Separating the test of provocation from the test of impaired volition would misrepresent the true basis of the excusative claim in provocation.[92] Provocation cannot be regarded as an excuse-based defence without reference to the element of impaired volition and this applies also to those cases which do not appear to satisfy the requirement of acting "on the spur of the moment". However, in some cases where the "heat of passion" requirement is not met, the grounds for excusing might shift from provocation to diminished responsibility if the agent's impaired capacity for self-control is attributed to an abnormality of mind — an abnormality possibly triggered off by the victim's wrongdoing — rather than to provocation as such.

The authors have argued, moreover, that an accused could not rely on the resentment principle unless the wrongful act of provocation was directed at him or someone close to him. It is submitted that if the act

---

90   See the discussion of the distinction between two different types of impetuous acts in the previous section.

91   "It may happen that a man is abnormally cool under gross provocation but none the less extremely resentful of any kind of personal affront; if he were to kill at once, but in cold blood, he cannot be excused by the fact that the acts of provocation would have been expected to cause an ordinary man to lose his self-control", *Kenny's Outlines of Criminal Law*, 19th ed. J.W.C. Turner (ed.), (1966), p. 179.

92   As Ashworth points out, "Surely it is the combination of the elements of partial excuse and partial justification which raises sufficient exculpation to warrant a reduction to manslaughter", *Principles of Criminal Law* (1991), p. 246.

of provocation was aimed at a third party not related to the accused, the latter should not be able to shelter under the provocation defence. In their words

> Where the wronged individual is someone having no particular connection to the actor, however, the principle [of resentment] would not apply. The actor might still be indignant — but the notion of justified personal resentment no longer holds. Having in no fashion been wronged by the victim, the actor has no good reason for responding with such anger that the normal moral restraints are understandably compromised. The actor cannot claim the principle of resentment when he 'punishes' someone for wrongdoing directed at third persons.[93]

The position a plea for extenuation could not be warranted under the resentment principle when the victim's wrongdoing is directed at a third party unduly restricts the scope of the excuse in provocation. Depending on the gravity of the victim's offence, the actor may be fully entitled to an excuse on the grounds of provocation, even though no particular relationship obtains between him and the target of the provocation. It seems correct to say, nonetheless, that in such cases the gravity of the provocation offered should be expected to be significantly greater than in those cases where the provocation is directed at the actor or a close friend or relative of his. Consider, for example, a case where the actor sees another indecently assaulting a child. Although the wrongful act is not directed at the actor, nor is he somehow related to the victim, one could see no reason why he should not be able to rely on provocation if he loses his self-control in the face of such an outrage and kills the assailant in a fit of anger. The actor's claim for extenuation would be even stronger if he could offer an additional, personal reason for getting enraged — for example, if he himself had been similarly assaulted when he was a child. It seems clear, therefore, that the resentment principle, as providing the basis of the test of provocation, is applicable to cases both of direct and of indirect provocation, irrespective of whether there is a special connection between the actor and the victim of the provoker's wrongdoing.[94] As O'Regan has pointed out

---

93   "Provocation and Culpability", supra note 83, p. 254.

94   As Pape J. stated in *Terry* [1964] VR 248, "[indirect provocation] did not prevent the operation of the principle that provocation will reduce murder to manslaughter provided that the provocation was offered in the presence of the accused and provided that all the other elements of provocation are present. ...I do not see any reason why the doctrine should be confined to relatives, for the relationship between the person attacked and the accused must be a relevant factor when the question whether an ordinary man would be likely to lose his self-control is being considered by the jury (at pp. 250-1). See also *Mouers*

An ordinary man who witnesses a brutal attack on a small child, an elderly woman or a dear friend may well lose his self-control whether the person attacked be a relative or not. Once this is conceded the limitation of provocation to acts done to a relative seems arbitrary and inconsistent with fundamental doctrine. It is submitted that in all cases of indirect provocation the correct approach is to ask not whether the person attacked is a relative of the accused but whether an ordinary man, seeing what the accused saw, would have been provoked in the same manner. [95]

As the above discussion suggests, von Hirsch's and Jareborg's claim that the objective test in provocation should be abolished lacks sufficient grounds of support. As the authors themselves have noted, in provocation, the reasonable person provides a basis for assessing the accused's judgment of wrongdoing that led him to lose his self-control and kill.[96] Only provocations that are deemed grave enough to enrage an ordinary or reasonable person so that he may lose his self-control and kill could furnish a morally acceptable basis for a partial excuse. As was pointed out in chapter 3, the reasonable person epitomises those commonly accepted standards of decent behaviour whose violation could support a claim of provocation and, at the same time, is seen as the vehicle of those common failings of human nature to which the provocation defence is said to be a concession.

Let us now consider a little further the idea that an accused might perhaps be able to rely on a general loss of control defence in some cases where the test of provocation cannot be met. As was pointed out earlier, in such cases the accused's plea for extenuation should not be accepted unless the accused offers a good reason for his losing his self-control in the circumstances. We might say that for an excuse to be allowed the accused's claim of impaired volition must be supported by evidence of a particular condition which is put forward as its triggering factor or "cause". Although a number of such conditions have been singled out as providing the grounds for formulating general defence categories, a claim of impaired volition might perhaps be brought forward which may be difficult to subsume or treat under one of the existing categories. In this respect, a general loss of control or impaired volition defence would serve to accommodate claims of

---

(1921) 57 D. L. R. 569. And see our reference to indirect provocation in Chapter 3, p. 76, above.

95  R. S. O'Regan, "Indirect Provocation and Misdirected Retaliation", *Criminal Law Review* [1968] 319, p. 321.

96  In the authors' words, in provocation "[the reasonable person] serves as a proxy — although a clumsy and imprecise one — for something that is essential to the resentment principle: namely, that the actor should have a good reason for his anger", "Provocation and Culpability", supra note 83, p. 252.

excuse based on conditions lying outside the scope of the existing excuse-based legal defences. An excuse-based defence of this kind would be open-ended, in the sense that, although it would rest upon the requirement of impaired volition, no specific condition or triggering factor would be laid down as the cause of the actor's impairment. It would rest upon the accused to bring forward evidence of an acceptable condition, or set of conditions, accounting for his (partial or total) lack of control over his conduct. Such a general impaired volition defence may be introduced either to complement or even to replace (i.e. as encompassing) an existing defence category. For example, the American Model Penal Code provides the reduction of homicide from murder to manslaughter in those cases where the accused acted "under the influence of extreme mental or emotional disturbance for which there is reasonable explanation or excuse". It is added that "The reasonableness of such explanation or excuse shall be determined from the viewpoint of a person in the actor's situation under the circumstances as he believes them to be".[97] Many American jurisdictions have adopted the MPC's approach, replacing the common law defence of provocation with the broader defence of "extreme emotional disturbance".[98] Under this provision there are no special limitations as to what sort of circumstances that may give rise to such an excuse-based defence. It is upon the jury to decide whether the accused in fact acted under the influence of extreme mental or emotional disturbance, and it is upon them to determine whether the disturbance was one "for which there is reasonable explanation or excuse".[99] An excuse-based defence similar to the MPC's 'extreme emotional disturbance' defence may be relied upon to deal, for

---

[97] Model Penal Code, para 210.3(1)(b) (1980).

[98] See, e.g., Ark Stat Ann para 41-150 (1) (a) (1977); Conn Gen Stat Ann paras 53a-54a, 53a-55 (West Cum Supp 1983-84); Del Code Ann tit 11, paras 632 (3), 641 (1979); Mont Code Ann para 45-5-103(1) (1981); N Y Penal Law, paras 125.20(2), 125. 25(1)(a), 125.27(2)(a); Utah Code Ann, para 76-5-205(1)(b) (1978).

[99] Supra note 91. And see MPC para 210.3 (1)(b), Comment 62 (1980): "[I]t is clear that personal handicaps and some external circumstances must be taken into account. Thus, blindness, shock from traumatic injury, and extreme grief are all easily read into the term 'situation'. This result is sound, for it would be morally obtuse to appraise a crime for mitigation of punishment without reference to these factors. On the other hand, it is equally plain that idiosyncratic moral values are not part of the actor's situation. An assassin who kills a political leader because he believes it is right to do so cannot ask that he be judged by the standard of a reasonable extremist. Any other result would undermine the normative message of the criminal law". And see P. Robinson's analysis of the defence of extreme emotional disturbance in his *Criminal Law Defenses* (1984), Vol. 1, pp. 481 ff.

example, with some cases of cumulative provocation lying on the borderline between provocation and diminished responsibility where neither provocation nor diminished responsibility seem capable of providing the basis of the accused's plea for a partial excuse. In these cases, the lapse of time between the last provocative incident and the accused's response, or the admission of forethought and deliberation, would appear to militate against the "hot anger" requirement of provocation. On the other hand, the assumption that the accused is a "normal" person, or the relatively uncertain or temporary nature of his psychological impediment, may render the defence of diminished responsibility difficult to accept. Here, the accuse might nevertheless be able to rely on a defence of impaired volition, on the grounds of extreme mental or emotional disturbance, by drawing attention to the psychological effect that continued abuse or violence has had on him or her and the ensuing difficulties in checking, through rational judgment, the disruptive force of the ensuing emotions.

## Concluding Note

The excusative element in the provocation defence pertains to the assumption that the provoked agent who loses his self-control acts morally or normatively involuntarily. In so far as the actor's anger at the author of the provocation is morally justified, an intentional killing committed in the "heat of passion" does not reflect the moral disposition or trait of character which is normally associated with murder. Although the so called "resentment principle", as part of the objective test in provocation, may be relevant to establishing a good reason for the accused's feeling angry at his victim, this principle alone cannot entitle the accused to an excuse, at least from the viewpoint of excuse theory, unless the requirement of impaired volition or loss of self-control is also met. Impaired volition does not mean that the provoked agent must have lost his self-control in an absolute sense, for loss of self-control is a matter of degree and, as such, it does not always preclude deliberation or choice. What must be precluded or, at any rate, seriously affected, however, if provocation is to provide a partial excuse, is the actor's capacity of assessing the moral significance of his actions or of bringing his actions into line with his all-things-considered moral choices. In this respect it seems correct to say that for the accused's plea of extenuation to be accepted, the tests of provocation and impaired volition should both be satisfied. If a case does not meet the "hot anger" requirement of provocation, considering the wrong which the accused may have suffered at his victim's hands and the effect this may have had on the actor's state of mind may be relevant to establishing another excusing condition, such as diminished responsibility, as the true basis of the actor's defence to a murder charge.

# 5 Cumulative Provocation and Diminished Responsibility

## The Problem of Cumulative Provocation

The term cumulative provocation is used to describe cases involving a prolonged period of maltreatment of a person at the hands of another which culminates in the abuser's killing by his or her victim. In such cases the gravity of each provocative incident is increased by what has taken place before. A long course of domestic violence which ends up in the killing of one spouse by the other provides the typical example here.[1] When a person charged with murder pleads an excuse on grounds of provocation, his argument may be that the provocation he was subjected to was the abuse he suffered at the victim's hands. He might claim that the abusive behaviour would have had the same effect on just anyone, or he might argue that, as a result of his previous experiences of maltreatment, he was provoked to lose his self-control and kill by something which would not have provoked a reasonable or ordinary person. He might also claim, either alternatively or instead of this, that the abuse he suffered at the victim's hands had such an effect on him as to make him different from other people in some important respects, and that this should be taken into consideration when his plea is assessed. With regard to cumulative provocation, a distinction should be drawn between cases in which the accused's retaliation was immediately preceded and precipitated by some sort of provocative conduct, and cases in which no such final provocation did in fact occur. The accused's plea for a partial excuse in both types of cases turns upon the whole of the victim's abusive behaviour towards the accused; it does not hinge upon a single act of provocation deemed sufficient by itself to trigger off a punitive reaction likely to involve an intent to kill.

A number of theoretical issues arise in relation to claims of extenuation stemming from the circumstances of cumulative

---

1    The issue of cumulative provocation may also arise in cases where the accused was subjected to a long course of abuse by a third party. See, e.g., *Davies* [1975] QB 691, [1975] All ER 890.

provocation. Some of these issues pertain to the incident or conduct relied upon as constituting provocation. The incident may be of a type that is not normally recognised as provocation, or it may not be a serious enough example of a recognised type. What is the basis of any decision that a certain form of behaviour can or cannot amount to provocation in law? In relation to cumulative provocation one may argue that provocation can consist of a course of conduct over time, rather than a single, isolated incident. Further, even where a single incident of provocation can be identified, a history of abuse might be relevant to assessing the gravity of the provocation offered by putting it into context. Are these approaches to defining provocation compatible with the current understanding of the defence in law?

Another set of questions arise in relation to the way in which an accused has retaliated, even where a provocative event can be demonstrated. Indeed, of the cases of cumulative provocation the most problematic are those in which the hot anger requirement of provocation is not met. The accused may have responded calmly and after deliberating on what retaliatory action is required. Often the lapse of time between the last provocative incident and the accused's retaliation would appear to suggest that he or she acted with forethought and deliberation. Could the accused rely on the defence even if his response did not follow immediately upon the provocation, or if the accused did not lose his self-control, in the sense of ceasing to act calmly and rationally? There have been cases where the accused's plea of provocation was accepted, despite the absence of a final act of provocation or the admission of some degree a planning and deliberation prior to the killing. One might perhaps say that such cases would best be explained if provocation was taken to operate as a partial justification rather than a partial excuse. As was indicated in chapter 4, if this approach to the defence were adopted, at least in some cases, the fact that the accused did not lose control would not necessarily preclude the defence if the victim's wrongdoing — as reflected either in a particular act or in a series of acts — is deemed sufficiently grave to warrant the partial justification of the wrongdoer's killing. From the point of view of the excuse theory, on the other hand, one might say that such cases require a broader interpretation of the element of impaired volition in provocation — an interpretation capable of encompassing different types of response. A better approach might perhaps be to treat the circumstances of cumulative provocation as likely to bring about the conditions of different legal excuses. In this respect, identifying the relevant legal defence would require one to consider the nature of the excusing condition stemming from the circumstances of the particular case.

## In Search of the Rationale of Excusing in Cumulative Provocation Cases

From the point of view of the excuse theory it may often seem problematical whether the circumstances of cumulative provocation furnish sufficient grounds for relying on provocation as a partial defence to murder, particularly where the accused's retaliation cannot be connected with a final provocative incident. In a number of provocation cases involving a history of abuse the jury was directed to take into account the previous maltreatment of the accused by his or her victim as relevant to assessing the gravity of the provocation offered. Thus an act which, on its own, may not be sufficient to amount to provocation, when considered in the light of previous provocative acts or words may be regarded as serious enough to cause the accused to lose his self-control.[2] Although considering the previous mistreatment of the accused by the victim may be considered relevant to assessing the seriousness of the provocation offered, such a consideration would be very difficult on its own to support a partial excuse on the basis of provocation. If a final wrongdoing triggering off the accused's reaction cannot be identified, the accused's claim that he or she was provoked would be difficult to accept. Even in some cases where a final act of provocation can be identified, it may seem questionable whether the accused's plea of provocation should succeed.[3] The assumption that the act of provocation was, in the circumstances, foreseeable, or that the accused was in a sense used to the victim's untoward behaviour, may seem to militate against the loss

---

2   As Widgery CJ stated in *Davies* [1975] QB 691, the "background is material to the provocation as the setting in which the state of mind of the defendant must be judged" (at p. 702). And see *Simpson* [1957] Crim LR 815; *Fantle* [1959] Crim LR 584; *McCarthy* [1954] 2 QB 105; *Bullard* [1957] AC 635. In Canada the general principle under which cases of cumulative provocation are treated was explained in *Conway* (1985) 17 CCC (3rd) 481 as follows: "[P]resent acts or insults, in themselves insufficient to cause an ordinary person to lose self-control, may indeed cause such loss of self-control when they are connected with past events and external pressures of insult by acts or words and accordingly in considering whether an ordinary man would have lost self-control [the jury] must consider an ordinary man who had experienced the same series of acts or insults as experienced by the appellant" (at p. 487, per Howland CJO).

3   As Ashworth points out in relation to sentencing "the circumstances of cumulative provocation may be considered as either a mitigating or an aggravating factor, although the former seems more likely". "Sentencing in Provocation Cases", *Criminal Law Review* [1975] 553, pp. 556-7.

of self-control requirement of provocation.[4] In general, evidence of planning and deliberation would be fatal to the accused's plea, as it would tend to negative the element of loss of control or impaired volition as required by the current definition of the defence. As Devlin J. pointed out in his direction to the jury in *Duffy*

> Severe nervous exasperation or a long course of conduct causing suffering and anxiety are not by themselves sufficient to constitute provocation in law. Indeed the further removed an incident is from the crime the less it counts. A long course of cruel conduct may be more blameworthy than a sudden act provoking retaliation, but you are not concerned with blame here — the blame attaching to the dead man. You are not standing in judgment on him. Circumstances which induce a desire for revenge, or a sudden passion of anger, are not enough. Indeed, circumstances which induce a desire for revenge are inconsistent with provocation since the conscious formulation of a desire for revenge means that the person has had time to think, to reflect, and that would negative a sudden, temporary loss of self-control which is the essence of provocation.[5]

An accused cannot rely on provocation, as the defence is usually formulated, if his killing of the victim was planned or controlled. Provoked killings are expected to be impulsive, because loss of self-control is inconsistent with planning or premeditation. They are also expected to happen quickly, following immediately upon the act of provocation. Where there was premeditation, the intention to kill must have been formed prior to the killing itself and this is strictly inconsistent with the loss of self-control requirement. It is assumed that, where there was a provocative incident, a delay amounts to time in which the accused should have cooled down and regained his composure. The position expressed by Devlin J. in *Duffy* has been

---

4    According to Gordon, "It is doubtful whether a long course of provocative conduct can found a successful plea of provocation, unless there is also some final act of provocation which, albeit because it follows on the earlier provocation and is the last straw, actually provokes a loss pf control — it is not sufficient that it should merely provide an occasion for [the accused] to exact revenge for the deceased's prior provocation. The fact that the deceased had indulged in a course of provocative conduct may indeed in some circumstances militate against the plea of provocation, as showing that [the accused] had become so used to this type of behaviour that it no longer affected his self-control", *Criminal Law*, 2nd ed. (1978), p. 766.

5    *Duffy* [1949] 1 All ER 932 at p. 933.

adopted in a number of subsequent cases.[6] In *Ibrams*,[7] the defendants, who had been terrorised by the victim over a period of time, formed a plan and killed the victim. There was no evidence suggesting that, immediately prior to the killing, the victim had done anything to provoke them. The Court of Appeal adopted the position that the time that had elapsed after the final provocative incident as well as the formulation of a plan negated any claim by the accused that they lost their self-control. As we saw in chapter 3, in *Thornton* [8] the Court of Appeal took the view that loss of self-control remained an essential element of the provocation defence. The same position was adopted in *Ahluwalia*,[9] where the loss of self-control requirement was described as an "essential ingredient" of the provocation defence, serving "to underline that the defence is concerned with the actions of an individual who is not, at the moment when he or she acts, violently, master of his or her own mind". [10] As was indicated in the latter case, delayed action is not inconsistent with provocation, but a sudden and temporary loss of self-control at the time of the killing is vital to the defence. In general, s. 3 of the Homicide Act 1957 is understood not to have altered the traditional position that provocation requires a sudden a temporary loss of self-control. This means that in a case where there is no evidence suggesting that the accused was provoked to lose his self-control the judge is still entitled to withdraw the defence from the jury.[11] The Criminal Law Revision Committee has recommended

> no change in the present rule, whereby the defence [of provocation] applies only
> where the defendant's act is caused by the provocation and is committed suddenly
> upon the provoking event, not to cases where the defendant's reaction has been

---

6    See, e.g., *Brown* [1972] 2 All ER 1328; *Davies* [1975] 1 All ER 890.
     See also *Ibrams* (1981) 74 Cr App Rep 154; *Turner* [1975] QB 834, [1975]
     All ER 70; *Burke* [1987] Crim LR 336; *Newell* [1980] 71 Cr App Rep 331;
     . *Raven* [1982] Crim LR 51; *Cocker* [1989] Crim LR 740.
7    *Ibrams* (1981) 74 Cr App R 154.
8    *Thornton* [1992] 1 All ER 306.
9    *Ahluwalia* [1992] 4 All ER 889.
10   Ibid at p. 895.
11   In Samuel's words, "The trial judge can still withdraw the issue of provocation
     from the jury if he is satisfied that as a matter of law there is no evidence of
     loss of self-control by the accused sufficient to lay the foundation of such a
     defence so as to require the prosecution to dispose of it, but he cannot
     withdraw the issue from the jury on the ground that there is evidence of loss of
     self-control but not such as would affect a reasonable man", "Excusable Loss
     of Self-Control in Homicide", 34 *Modern Law Review* (1971) 163, p. 165.

delayed, but the jury should continue to take into consideration previous provocations before the one which produced the fatal reaction.[12]

The CLRC's recommendation is consistent with the traditional position, as expressed in *Duffy*, that loss of self-control is an essential element of the provocation defence. Moreover, it is recognised that in so far as there is evidence that the accused was provoked to lose his self-control, evidence of cumulative provocation should be taken into consideration in determining whether the accused was sufficiently provoked.

The position expressed by the CLRC has been criticised on the grounds that it is based on a very narrow definition of the provocation defence.[13] The CLRC's approach, it is argued, overlooks the important requirement that a conviction of murder should be avoided unless the accused fully deserves to be stigmatised as a murderer. In some cases of cumulative provocation, evidence of forethought and deliberation is not sufficient to warrant, morally, the accused's conviction of murder.[14] It is pointed out that the position — also adopted by the CLRC — that the scope of the crime of murder should be narrowed down to include only those killings which deserve to be stigmatised as murders militates against the outright rejection of the provocation defence where the hot anger requirement is not met. Strict adherence to this requirement may lead, in some cases of cumulative provocation, to convictions of murder that are deemed morally unfounded. As Wasik puts it

> cases of cumulative provocation should fall outside the scope of 'new murder'. The law should recognise that there are degrees of culpability even in deliberate killings. Whilst evidence of forethought and premeditation must always tell against the defendant on sentence, the more lenient approach evident in some sentencing cases, which regards cumulative provocation as mitigating the offence rather than making it more serious, is recommended. The traditional view of provocation as a 'concession to human frailty' is clearly important both on liability and on sentence, but in cases [of cumulative provocation] there must be proper weight given to the justificatory as well as the excusative element.[15]

---

12    CLRC, 14th Rep (1980), para 84.
13    See M. Wasik, "Cumulative Provocation and Domestic Killing", *Criminal Law Review* [1982] 29, pp. 34-5.
14    According to Wasik, "in defining the ambit of the defence [of provocation] a balance has to be struck between the reflection of contemporary attitudes of sympathy towards the defendants in such cases [of cumulative provocation] and the duty of self-control upon every citizen by the law", ibid at p. 35.
15    Ibid at p. 37. And see CLRC, 14th Rep (1980), paras 15,19,84.

Admittedly, the tendency in English law is towards treating the accused in cases involving cumulative provocation with leniency. Often the judge is prepared to accept the accused's plea of not guilty to murder but guilty to manslaughter directly. There have been cases in which the accused was found guilty of manslaughter only, in spite of evidence suggesting that he did not kill his victim "on the spur of the moment". For example, in *Maw and Maw*,[16] the accused, two sisters, killed their violent and drunken father by stabbing him with a kitchen knife. On the night of the killing, the father assaulted and abused the accused and their mother. In the fight that followed he was struck on the head by a heavy mirror and was knocked unconscious. While he was unconscious the accused agreed that, if he used violence on them or their mother again, they would kill him. When the victim regained consciousness and began using violence, he was stabbed to death by one of the sisters with a knife. The jury found the two accused guilty of manslaughter and not murder on the grounds that they have acted under provocation.[17] Feelings of sympathy towards an accused who has been subjected to a long period of abuse by his victim might lead the jury to acquit the accused altogether or to convict him of manslaughter directly instead of convicting him of murder.[18] In many cases involving cumulative provocation what seems to justify a reduction of culpability is the extreme distress or depression which the accused was experiencing as a result of his or her long ill-treatment at the victim's hands.

But what is the precise nature of the legal defence or defences that may stem from the circumstances of cumulative provocation? Wasik puts forward three possible ways in which this question may be answered. First, cases of cumulative provocation may be dealt with under the existing defence of provocation. This, he argues, would presuppose an interpretation of the provocation defence broader than the one currently adopted — an interpretation that would place sufficient emphasis on the justificatory as well as on the excusative element in provocation. Under this broader interpretation, provocation would not always depend upon a sudden and temporary loss of self-control. Despite evidence of forethought and deliberation, the defence could succeed if the accused's resentment against the victim is justified in the light of the abuse he or she suffered at the latter's hands.

---

16   *The Times*, August 20, November 18, 19, 20, 21, 22, Dec. 4, 15, 16 (1980)

17   See also *Wright, The Times*, October 14, (1975); *Ratcliffe, The Times*, May 13, (1980); *Bangert, The Times*, April 28, (1977). Quoted by Wasik, supra note 13.

18   See, e.g., *Pulling, The Times*, April 27, (1977); *Fuller, The Times*, November 19, (1980). Quoted by Wasik, supra note 13.

Secondly, cases involving cumulative provocation may be treated under the defence of diminished responsibility or, perhaps, under a combined defence of provocation and diminished responsibility. However, according to Wasik, such an approach to the matter might result in a misunderstanding as regards the rationale and purpose of the diminished responsibility defence. Thirdly, such cases might be dealt with under a separate defence to murder. The ambit of such a defence should be drawn wide enough to encompass a variety of extenuating circumstances that may justify the reduction of culpability for homicide.[19] Wasik regards the first of these three possible approaches to the problem of cumulative provocation as comparatively the least troublesome.[20]

It seems difficult, however, to view all cases of cumulative provocation as capable of being treated under a single legal defence. Rather, cumulative provocation should be regarded as a situation likely to give rise to the conditions of different legal defences. Instead of widening the scope of the existing defence categories in order to accommodate all cumulative provocation cases, it would perhaps be better if we distinguished between different possible pleas that may arise in such cases. Those pleas might be either for extenuation or, possibly in some cases, exoneration, depending upon the nature of the particular defence raised.[21] It may be true that the majority of the claims stemming from the circumstances of cumulative provocation would meet the conditions of provocation and diminished responsibility or, probably, of an intermediate defence sharing characteristics of both (such as a general defence of extreme emotional disturbance). Nevertheless, neither provocation nor diminished responsibility on its own appears capable of providing a single basis for dealing with all cases of cumulative provocation in law. One would have too high a price to pay, in terms of loss of coherence and consistency, if the scope of either defence were stretched beyond a certain point to cover the variety of claims likely to arise from the circumstances of cumulative provocation.

In a case involving cumulative provocation, a plea for mitigation on grounds of provocation should not be accepted unless all the conditions of the defence, as this is currently defined, are satisfied. As was indicated before, from the point of view of the excuse theory, this would presuppose that the accused has retaliated in the heat of passion and that his reaction was triggered off by a provocative incident of

---

19   See, e.g., MPC's defence of 'extreme emotional disturbance' discussed in chapter 4 above.

20   "Cumulative Provocation and Domestic Killing", supra note 13, pp. 35-6.

21   In some cases of cumulative provocation the accused may be able to plead, e.g., self-defence, or insanity.

some sort. However, the gravity of that final provocative incident or, to put it otherwise, the accused's judgment of certain conduct or words as gravely provocative, should be assessed in the light of previous provocation from the same source. According to Ashworth

> the significance of the deceased's final act should be considered by reference to the previous relations between the parties, taking into account any previous incidents which add colour to the final act. This is not to argue that the basic distinction between sudden provoked killings and revenge killings should be blurred, for the lapse of time between the deceased's final act and the accused's retaliation should continue to tell against him. The point is that the significance of the deceased's final act and its effect upon the accused — and indeed the relation of the retaliation to that act — can be neither understood nor evaluated without reference to previous dealings between the parties. [22]

In a case of cumulative provocation, the final act of provocation, however trivial it might appear to have been, should be regarded as in a sense epitomising or reflecting in the accused's eyes all the previous abuse he or she suffered at the victim's hands. In this respect, such a provocation may be seen as being serious enough to support a partial excuse on the grounds of impaired volition or loss of self-control. From this point of view it seems correct to say that the circumstances of cumulative provocation should be taken into account as relevant to establishing the required connection between the final provocative incident and the accused's loss of self-control. It seems clear that, in so far as the accused's plea in such cases pertains to his or her loss of control, the wrongfulness of the victim's conduct can only be taken to provide a good reason or explanation for the accused's giving way to passion.

## Diminished Responsibility

It was indicated earlier that provocation is traditionally described as a defence for "normal" people.[23] On the assumption that the accused is a normal person, evidence of planning and deliberation prior to the killing should normally militate against his claim of loss of self-control. Although some degree of forethought and deliberation is not necessarily incompatible with the loss of self-control element, in so far

---

22    "Sentencing in Provocation Cases", supra note 3, pp. 558-9.
23    In Ashworth's words, "The defence of provocation is for those who are in a broad sense mentally normal. Those suffering from some form of mental abnormality should be brought within the defence of diminished responsibility", "The Doctrine of Provocation", 35 *Criminal Law Journal* (1976) 292, p. 312. And see *Ward* [1956] 1 QB 351.

as the latter element is viewed as a matter of degree, if the accused appears to have regained his composure at the time of the killing his plea of provocation should normally fail. In such a case the accused may be able to rely on a different kind of legal excuse, namely diminished responsibility, but surely not on one that rests on the assumption that he or she is a 'normal' or 'reasonable' person. As G. Williams has remarked

> Provocation is traditionally a defence for 'normal' people. Abnormal people can shelter under it, but only on the same conditions as apply to normal ones. If they want their abnormality to be taken into account they must raise a defence appropriate to them — insanity or diminished responsibility.[24]

There may be cases involving cumulative provocation in which the accused may be able to plead diminished responsibility or, arguably, a combined defence of provocation and diminished responsibility. Like provocation, diminished responsibility operates as a partial defence to murder reducing murder to voluntary manslaughter.[25] The defence, which was introduced in response to the recommendation of the Royal Commission on Capital Punishment for a broader insanity defence,[26] is provided for by s. 2 of the Homicide Act 1957.[27] According to s. 2

---

24   *Textbook of Criminal Law*, 2nd ed. (1983), p. 544.
25   The defence of diminished responsibility appeared first in the law of Scotland. See *HM Adv v Dingwall* (1867) 5 Irv, 466.
26   Cmnd 88932, 1949-1953. The proposed broadening of the defence of insanity was rejected, however, on the grounds that it would greatly complicate the application of the insanity defence.
27   Similar defences are found in the codes of many jurisdictions. For example, Para 22 of the German Penal Code provides: "If, at the time of the commission of a crime, the capacity of the perpetrator to understand the wrongfulness of his conduct or to act in accordance with this understanding is substantially diminished due to the existence of grounds set forth in Paragraph 21 [a psychotic or similar serious mental disorder, a profound interruption of consciousness, feeblemindedness], his punishment shall be mitigated according to Paragraph 61 (1) of this Code". Under this provision, diminished responsibility operates as a mitigating factor with regard to all criminal offences but, instead of reducing the offence category, it is taken into account as a factor in the mitigation of sentence. The American Model Penal Code distinguishes the defence of diminished capacity, as described in para 101(c), from that of extreme emotional disturbance (para. 210.3 (1)(b)). Although both defences serve to reduce murder to manslaughter, the defence of extreme emotional disturbance applies to mentally healthy, normal, people who kill as a result of an extreme emotional disturbance caused by certain circumstances; the defence of diminished capacity, by contrast, applies to persons who suffer from an abnormality of mind but who are not sufficiently insane to be totally

(1) Where a person kills or is a party to the killing of another, he shall not be convicted of murder if he was suffering from such abnormality of mind (whether arising from a condition of arrested or retarded development of mind or any inherent causes or induced by disease or injury) as substantially impaired his mental responsibility for his acts and omissions in doing or being party to the killing.

(2) On a charge of murder, it shall be for the defence to prove that the person charged is by virtue of this section not liable to be convicted of murder.

(3) A person who but for this section would be liable, whether as principal or as accessory, to be convicted of murder, shall be liable instead to be convicted of manslaughter.

(4) The fact that one party to a killing is by virtue of this section not liable to be convicted of murder shall not affect the question whether the killing amounted to murder in the case of any other party to it.[28]

As with provocation, it must first be established that the accused has had the *mens rea* for murder before the defence of diminished responsibility is put to the jury. However, the trial judge cannot raise the defence if the accused does not wish to do so. If evidence of diminished responsibility comes to light during the trial the judge should draw the attention of the defence counsel to that evidence and

---

excusable on the grounds of the insanity defence.In Australia, the criminal law of South Australia and Victoria does not recognise a diminished responsibility defence. In New South Wales, Queensland and the Australian Capital Territory diminished responsibility is defined by statute: s. 23A Crimes Act 1900 (NSW), s. 304A Queensland Criminal Code, s. 14 Crimes Act 1900 (ACT). The statutory definitions adopted are based largely on s. 2 of the English Homicide Act 1957. For example, s. 304(1) of the Queensland Criminal Code provides: "When a person who unlawfully kills another under circumstances which, but for the provisions of this section, would constitute murder, is at the time of doing the act or making the omission which causes death in such a state of abnormality of mind (whether arising from a condition of arrested or retarded development of mind or inherent causes or induced by disease or injury) as substantially to impair the person's capacity to understand what the person is doing, or the person's capacity to control the person's actions, or the person's capacity to know that the person ought not to do the act or make the omission, the person is guilty of manslaughter only". See, e.g., *Rolph* [1962] Qd R 262; *Miers* [1985] 2 Qd R 138.

28  Consideration should also be given to the Law Commission's Draft Criminal Code. Clause 56 of the Code provides: (1) A person who, but for this section, would be guilty of murder is not guilty of murder if, at the time of his act, he is suffering from such a mental abnormality as is a substantial enough reason to reduce his offence to manslaughter.(2) Mental abnormality means mental illness, arrested or incomplete development of mind, psychopathic disorder, or any disorder or disability of mind, except intoxication. (3) Where a person suffering from mental abnormality is also intoxicated, this section applies only where it would apply if he were not intoxicated.

leave it to the defence to decide whether the issue should be put to the jury.[29] As with the defence of insanity, it rests upon the accused to prove the defence on a balance of probabilities.[30] For the defence to succeed it is important that medical evidence is brought forward to support the claim that the accused was suffering from an abnormality of mind arising from one of the causes specified in s. 2(1).[31] If the medical evidence supports a finding of diminished responsibility, the jury must find the accused guilty of manslaughter only. The question of whether the accused was suffering from an abnormality of mind is ultimately one for the jury, not the medical expert, to decide.

Under s.2, it must be proved, first, that the accused, at the time of the killing, was suffering from an abnormality of mind. As was indicated above, this is a question for the jury to decide on the basis of the medical evidence brought forward and all the other relevant evidence. In *Byrne* [32] the term "abnormality of mind" was defined by Lord Parker CJ as follows

> 'Abnormality of mind', which has to be contrasted with the time-honoured expression in the M'Naghten Rules, 'defect of reason', means a state of mind so different from that of ordinary human beings that the reasonable man would term it abnormal. It appears to us to be wide enough to cover the mind's activities in all its aspects, not only the perception of physical acts and matters, and the ability to form a rational judgment whether an act is right or wrong, but also the ability to exercise will-power to control physical acts in accordance with that rational judgment.[33]

As this statement makes clear, an irresistible urge, or an inability or extraordinary difficulty to hold one's impulses in check, could be treated under the diminished responsibility defence. In *Byrne* the accused killed a young woman and then mutilated her body. Medical evidence suggested that he was subject to perverted sexual urges which he found impossible or extremely difficult to resist, and that he had committed the killing while under the influence of such urges. In the light of the existing evidence, it was clear that, at the time of the

---

29   Where the accused raises the defence of insanity it is possible for the prosecution to raise the issue of diminished responsibility. And, conversely, where the accused pleads diminished responsibility the prosecution may, on the basis of the available evidence, raise the issue of insanity. See s.6 of the Criminal Procedure (Insanity) Act 1964.

30   See *Dunbar* [1958] 1 QB 1. See also *Ahmed Din* (1962) 46 Cr App Rep 269; *Bathurst* [1968] 2 QB 99; *Vinagre* (1979) 69 Cr App Rep 104; *Bradshaw* (1985) 82 Cr App Rep 79, [1985] Crim LR 733;

31   See *Dix* (1981) 74 Cr App R 306.

32   [1960] 2 QB 396.

33   Ibid at p. 403.

killing, not only did the accused know what he was doing, but that he was also fully aware of the wrongful character of his actions. Nevertheless, the Court of Criminal Appeal quashed his conviction for murder and found him guilty of manslaughter only, on the grounds that, due to his condition, it was extremely difficult for him to control his impulses. It was pointed out that "the step between 'he did not resist his impulse' and 'he could not resist his impulse' is...one which is incapable of scientific proof. A fortiori there is no scientific measurement of the degree of difficulty which an abnormal person finds in controlling his impulses". The jury should seek to resolve this problem by approaching it "in a broad common-sense way".[34] In this case the Court of Appeal recognised that mental responsibility for the accused's acts requires consideration by the jury "of the extent to which the accused's mind is answerable for his physical acts which include a consideration of the extent of his ability to exercise will-power to control his physical acts". This question, as being one of degree, can only be decided by the jury. In Lord Parker's words

> Medical evidence is, of course, relevant, but the question involves a decision not merely as to whether there was some impairment of the mental responsibility of the accused but whether such impairment can properly be called 'substantial', a matter upon which juries may quite legitimately differ from doctors.[35]

In *Byrne* the Court accepted that the accused's condition was correctly described as "partial insanity" or as a condition "bordering on insanity". Judges used similar expressions in their directions to juries in subsequent cases, but such expressions may lead to confusion as they appear to connect diminished responsibility with insanity. Thus, in *Seers*,[36] the Court of Appeal adopted the position that judges should avoid comparing diminished responsibility to insanity for there may be cases in which the abnormality of mind upon which the accused's defence is based has nothing to do with any of the conditions relating to the insanity defence.[37] For example, a depressive condition may provide a sufficient basis for the defence of diminished responsibility, although the sufferer could not be described as insane or partially insane.[38]

---

34    Ibid at p. 406. And see *Walton v R* [1978] AC 788, [1978] 1 All ER 542.
35    Supra note 29, at p. 403.
36    (1984) 79 Cr App Rep 261.
37    Consider also *Rose v R* [1961] AC 496; [1961] 1 All ER 859. In this case it was held that if the word insanity is used in relation to diminished responsibility it must be used in "its broad popular sense".
38    But there is still much confusion surrounding the definition of mental abnormality in the context of the diminished responsibility defence. This

It is required, further, that the abnormality of mind from which the accused claim to suffer arises from one of the causes laid down by s. 2(1).[39] Although no clear description is given of the causes referred to in s. 2, it appear that "disease or injury" most likely pertains to physical injury or illness and that "inherent cause" includes functional mental disorder.[40] Examples of abnormalities of mind that were sufficient for the defence of diminished responsibility to be put to the jury range from arrested intellectual development combined with psychopathic tendencies,[41] a disorder of personality induced by psychological injury,[42] reactive depression caused by marital difficulties,[43] chronic alcoholism,[44] and "Otello syndrome", described as morbid jealousy for which there was no cause.[45] Intoxication by drugs or alcohol is generally excluded as a basis of the diminished responsibility defence.[46] In such cases the jury are required to ignore the fact that the accused was intoxicated. As was pointed out in *Atkinson* ,[47] the jury must be asked the following question: "Has [the accused] satisfied you on the balance of probabilities that, if he had not taken drink, (i) he would have killed as he in fact did? and (ii) he would have been under diminished responsibility when he did so?". Alcoholism or the use of drugs may however be relevant if there is evidence suggesting that they have caused damage to the accused's brain amounting to "disease or injury".[48] Although emotions such as

---

confusion stems, in part, from the difficulties in drawing clear distinctions between different mental and psychological states and assessing them in terms of moral responsibility. See e.g. S.L. Morse, "Undiminished Confusion in Diminished Capacity", *Journal of Criminal Law and Criminology* 75 (1984) 1; and see J. Dressler's reply in "Reaffirming the Moral Legitimacy of the Doctrine of Diminished Capacity: A Brief Reply to Professor Morse", *Journal of Criminal Law and Criminology* 75 (1984).

39　See, e.g., *King* [1965] 1 QB 443 at 450.

40　See *Sanderson* (1993) 98 Cr App Rep 325; *Fenton* (1975) 61 Cr App Rep 261; *Gittens* [1984] QB 698. See also *Tandy* (1987) 87 Cr App Rep 45; *Inseal* [1992] Crim LR 35; *Egan* [1993] Crim LR 131.

41　*Egan* [1992] 4 All ER 470.

42　*Gittens* [1984] QB 698.

43　*Sanders* (1991) 93 Cr App Rep 245.

44　*Tandy* [1989] 1 WLR 350.

45　*Vinagre* (1979) 69 Cr App Rep 104.

46　*Tandy*, supra note 44. See also *Egan*, supra note 41.

47　[1985] Crim LR 314.

48　As was stated in *Tandy*, alcoholism will only assist the accused if it "had reached the level at which her brain had been injured by the repeated insult from intoxicants so that there was gross impairment of her judgment and emotional responses", supra note 44, at 356. See also *Inseal* [1992] Crim LR 35.

envy, anger or resentment are not supposed to come under s. 2, there have been cases in which such emotions were deemed sufficient to support a diminished responsibility defence.[49]

The defence of diminished responsibility operates as a partial excuse on the assumption that the accused's impaired capacity reduces his moral responsibility for his actions. But this does not mean that a third, intermediate level, between full responsibility and complete lack of responsibility should be recognised. Speaking of a substantial impairment of the capacity for rational judgment and self-control does not imply that the actor could only "partially" perceive the wrongful character of his act, or that he could only "partially" control his actions. Diminished responsibility refers, rather, to a special type of being responsible, one that presupposes a capacity for both perception and control. Due to the actor's mental condition, however, perceiving the character of his actions correctly, or exercising self-control, is regarded as being extraordinarily difficult, that is "as compared to normal people normally placed".[50] This is precisely what justifies the reduction of culpability and, consequently, legal liability in such cases. According to E. Griew, for the defence of diminished responsibility to be accepted, it must be demonstrated that

the defendant had an abnormality of mind (of appropriate origin). This had a substantial effect upon one or more relevant functions or capacities (of perception, understanding, judgment, feeling, control). In the context of the case this justifies the view that his culpability is substantially reduced. His liability is on that account to be diminished. More shortly: his abnormality of mind is of such consequence in the context of this offence that his legal liability for it ought to be reduced.[51]

For the defence to succeed, it is required that the accused's difficulty in exercising control over his conduct was substantially greater than that of a reasonable or normal person. In determining whether the accused's responsibility for the killing was "substantially impaired" the jury are expected to adopt a broad, commonsense approach. In

---

49    See e.g. *Miller, The Times*, May 16, 1972; *Asher, The Times*, June 9, 1981; *Coles* (1980) 144 JPN. 528.
50    HLA Hart, "Prolegomenon to the Principles of Punishment" in *Punishment and Responsibility* (1968), p. 15.
51    "The Future of Diminished Responsibility" [1988]*Criminal Law Review* 75, p. 82. See also G.E. Dix, "Psychological Abnormality as a Factor in Grading Criminal Liability: Diminished Capacity, Diminished Responsibility and the Like", *Journal of Criminal Law, Criminology and Police Science*, (1971) 313; R.F. Sparks, "Diminished Responsibility in Theory and Practice", 27 *Modern Law Review* (1964) 9.

general, "substantial impairment" means an impairment that is more than minimal but less than total impairment.[52]

When the defence of diminished responsibility is raised, its success or failure depends, largely, on whether the jury believes that the accused deserves to be convicted as a murderer. This, in turn, depends upon the extent of their sympathy for the accused and the circumstances and gravity of the killing. As Glanville Williams has remarked, "the defence...is interpreted in accordance with the morality of the case rather than  as an application of psychiatric concepts. Where sympathy is evoked...it seems to be dissolving into what is virtually the equivalent of a mitigating circumstance".[53]  This explains why the defence has been accepted, despite the absence of clear evidence of abnormality of mind, in some cases involving mercy-killings, or killings committed in conditions of reactive depression or association, where the accused has killed in response to extreme grief, stress or anxiety.

Diminished responsibility may provide the legal basis for dealing with cases of cumulative provocation that cannot be treated under the provocation defence. Having been subjected to a long course of cruel and violent behaviour, the accused may claim that he or she is experiencing such grave distress or depression as to substantially diminish his capacity for self-control and, hence, his moral responsibility for his actions.[54] Pleading diminished responsibility, instead of provocation, in a case involving a long history of abuse would seem more appropriate where no final provocative incident, occurring immediately prior to the killing, can be demonstrated, or where the accused's retaliation was preceded by planning and deliberation.[55] The same approach might be adopted in a case where the conduct that triggered off the accused's fatal response is not regarded as being capable of amounting to provocation (i.e. on the basis of the objective test as it applies in the circumstances of cumulative provocation). Here the circumstances of cumulative provocation may provide a sufficient basis for supporting the

---

52   See *Simcox* [1964] Crim LR  402; *Lloyd* [1967] 1 QB 575; *Gittens* [1984] QB  698; *Campbell*  (1987) 84 Cr App Rep  255; *Egan* [1992] 4 All ER 470.

53   *Textbook of Criminal Law*,  2nd ed. (1983), p. 693.

54   Crimes  of passion are often the result of intense anxiety or depression leading into a psychotic state of morbid resentment or jealousy.

55   Thus in *Ahluwalia* [1992] 4 All ER 889, although the defence of provocation was rejected, the accused's appeal was allowed and a retrial ordered on the grounds that diminished responsibility had not been raised at her trial despite medical evidence suggesting that she was suffering from an abnormality of mind (endogenous depression) when the offence was committed.

accused's plea of diminished responsibility, even in those cases where no clear evidence of an abnormality of mind (in a strict medical sense) can be brought forward.

## Pleading Provocation and Diminished Responsibility Together

In some cases, especially those involving cumulative provocation, the accused may be able to plead a combined defence of provocation and diminished responsibility. The practical effect of raising such a combined defence would be the reduction of the offence from murder to manslaughter if it is found that the accused was suffering from an abnormality of mind and was provoked to lose his self-control. The possibility of setting up a combined defence of this kind has been recognised by the Criminal Law Revision Committee. According to them

It is now possible for a defendant to set up a combined defence of provocation and diminished responsibility, the practical effect being that the jury may return a verdict of manslaughter if they take the view that the defendant suffered from an abnormality of mind and was provoked. In practice this may mean that a conviction of murder will be ruled out although the provocation was not such as would have moved a person of normal mentality to kill.[56]

The problem with reducing the accused's legal liability on the grounds of both provocation and diminished responsibility is that the basic assumptions upon which these defences are based appear to be incompatible: provocation presupposes a reasonable or normal person driven to the act of killing by angry passion; diminished responsibility presupposes a person suffering from an abnormality of mind and who, for that reason, cannot be called "normal" or "reasonable".[57] Nevertheless, a number of cases may be cited in which this problem has not prevented the courts from accepting such a combined defence.[58] In *Matheson*[59] the Court of Criminal Appeal adopted the position that when a combined defence is raised the jury, in returning a

---

56 CLRC, Working Paper on Offences Against the Person, August 1976, para. 53.
57 This does not mean, however, that the defences are necessarily mutually exclusive. See N. Morris and L. Blom-Cooper, *A Calendar of Murder* (1964), p. 298, n.4.
58 See, e.g., *McPherson,The Times*, June 18, 1963; *Holford, The Times*, March 29, 30, 1963;*Whyburd* (1979) 143 JPN 492.
59 *Matheson* [1958] 2 All ER 87.

verdict of manslaughter, should state the ground upon which their decision is based. According to Lord Goddard CJ

> It may happen that on an indictment for murder the defence may ask for a verdict of manslaughter on the ground of diminished responsibility and also on some other ground such as provocation. If the jury returns a verdict of manslaughter, the judge may and generally should ask them whether their verdict is based on diminished responsibility or on the other ground or on both. [60]

As a defence strategy, pleading provocation and diminished responsibility together is considered to be to the accused's advantage. As was indicated above, the reduction of murder to manslaughter in such cases rests on the assumption that the accused suffered from an abnormality of mind and was provoked. This would render admissible medical or psychiatric testimony which the jury would not be allowed to consider if the accused had chosen to rely on provocation alone.[61] A combined plea of provocation and diminished responsibility entails a further advantage for the accused as regards the sentence imposed for the lesser offence of manslaughter. According to Professor Williams

> Success in the combined defence of provocation and diminished responsibility has an advantage for the defendant in respect of sentence: it may result in a more lenient outcome than a defence of provocation alone; and it is virtually free from the risk of life sentence that attends a defence of diminished responsibility by itself.[62]

As we saw in chapter 3, when the defence of provocation is raised the jury has to assess the accused's plea by deliberating upon how a reasonable or normal person may have reacted to the provocation offered, relying on their collective common sense and everyday experience.[63] As Lord Simon explained in *Camplin*

---

[60]  Ibid at p. 90. And see *Solomon and Triumph* (1984) 6 Cr App Rep (S) 120.

[61]  As R. D. MacKay has remarked, "where there is some psychiatric evidence which supports the contention that at the time of the killing the accused may have been suffering from an abnormality of mind, then if this evidence also mentions provocation or some similar term, it will be advantageous for the accused to plead both defences. The pleading of provocation alone will almost certainly mean that the psychiatric evidence will be inadmissible, at least in so far as the 'ordinary man' criterion is concerned", "Pleading Provocation and Diminished Responsibility Together", *Criminal Law Review* [1988] 411 at p. 422. And see *Campbell* (1986) 84 Cr. App. Rep. 255; [1987] Crim.L.R. 257.

[62]  *Textbook of Criminal Law*, 2nd. ed (1983), pp. 544-5.

[63]  See, e.g., *Smith (Stanley)* [1979] 3 All ER 605 at 611.

whether the defendant exercised reasonable self-control in the totality of the circumstances ...would be entirely a matter for consideration by the jury without further evidence. The jury would, as ever, use their collective common sense to determine whether the provocation was sufficient to make a person of reasonable self-control in the totality of the circumstances (including personal characteristics) act as the defendant did.[64]

In *Turner*, Lawton L.J. pointed out that "Jurors do not need psychiatrists to tell them how ordinary folk who are not suffering from any mental illness are likely to react to the stresses and strains of life".[65] In *Campbell* [66] the defence was allowed to introduce psychiatric testimony regarding the accused's state of mind in order to assist the jury in answering the question of provocation. It was argued that, in this case, the issue was restricted to whether the particular accused — not a reasonable person — may have lost his self-control as a result of the provocation offered. The defence of provocation was rejected, however, and the accused was convicted of murder. In his appeal the accused claimed that, given the medical evidence, the trial judge should have directed the jury as to the issue of diminished responsibility. The appeal was dismissed, however, on the grounds that diminished responsibility can only be raised by the defence, who also bears the burden of proving it before the jury. The Court of Appeal held, further, that there was no *prima facie* evidence of diminished responsibility in this case because the medical witness "never even addressed himself in his evidence to the final matter which would have to be proved by the defence in order to establish diminished responsibility, namely that the abnormality was such as substantially to impair the mental responsibility of the appellant for his acts...".[67] In a case where the accused chooses to plead a combined defence of provocation and diminished responsibility, it is recognised that he should bear the burden of proof only as to the latter defence. It should be noted, however, that in most cases where provocation and diminished responsibility are raised together the jury may find it difficult to keep the two issues separate. This seems true, particularly with regard to some cases of cumulative provocation in which the elements of provocation, abnormality of mind and loss of self-control appear to be interrelated or interdependent.

One reason for pleading provocation and diminished responsibility together has to do with the uncertainty that surrounds the application of the objective test in provocation. This uncertainty is

---

64    *Camplin* [1978] 2 All ER 168, at pp. 182-3.
65    *Turner* [1975] 1 QB 834, at pp. 841-2.
66    (1987) 84 Cr App Rep 255.
67    Ibid at 259.

often the result of the difficulty in differentiating between individual characteristics or peculiarities of the accused that may be taken into account as modifying the reasonable person test and those peculiarities that lie outside the scope of the test. Thus, pleading a combined defence of provocation and diminished responsibility would be a better defence strategy in a case where it is unclear whether the reasonable person may be endowed with a particular mental characteristic of the accused or not.[68] There may be cases in which the accused's plea of provocation may be accepted independently of the fact that he or she was suffering from an abnormality of mind — i.e. where the provocation is deemed serious enough to provoke an ordinary person to lose his self-control and kill. However, in those cases where the provocation was not serious enough to provoke an ordinary person, the acceptance of the accused's claim that he was provoked to lose control may be seen as in a sense conditional upon establishing diminished responsibility. In such cases the accused may be able to rely on a partial excuse if it is accepted that he or she was provoked to lose his self-control precisely because he suffered from an abnormality of mind that substantially impaired his ability to control his behaviour. Here, however, the legal excuse turns primarily on the conditions of diminished responsibility rather than on those of provocation. Provocation may be regarded as a factor triggering off the accused's reaction, but not as the true basis for the reduction of culpability for homicide. A verdict accepting the accused's plea for extenuation on the grounds of both provocation and diminished responsibility might be more appropriate where the conditions of both defences are satisfied. One might envisage a case in which evidence suggests that the accused was suffering from an abnormality of mind  and was sufficiently provoked — i.e. according to the objective test, as it applies to normal people. In such a case it is  clear that if the accused had chosen to rely only on provocation his plea would have been successful on this

---

68  In *Taaka* [1982] NZLR 198, the New Zealand Court of Appeal adopted the view that the obsessively compulsive personality of the accused should be regarded as a characteristic relevant to the issue of provocation and, as such, it should be taken into account by the jury in applying the objective test. In some cases it has been suggested, moreover, that a post-traumatic stress disorder or battered woman syndrome may be regarded as a 'characteristic' for the purposes of the provocation defence. See, e.g., the New Zealand case of *Gordon* (1993) 10 CRNZ 430. Some commentators have concluded that these cases suggest a departure from the traditional jurisprudence of provocation, as the position adopted indicates that mental peculiarities may be viewed as a discrete exculpatory factor in defining provocation in law. One should note, however, that New Zealand law does not provide for a separate defence of diminished responsibility and this might explain the more liberal approach to the application of the objective test adopted in these cases.

ground alone. The same would be the case if the accused had raised diminished responsibility only. Unless the accused's loss of control is somehow attributed the conditions of one of these defences exclusively, a verdict reducing murder to manslaughter on both grounds would be the best way of dealing with the accused's plea here.

## Concluding Note

So, to summarise, if there is evidence suggesting that, at the time of the killing, the accused suffered from an abnormality of mind and was provoked — as it is often the case in cases involving cumulative provocation — the accused may be able to raise a combined defence of provocation and diminished responsibility. Such a combined defence would make it possible for the jury to consider medical or psychiatric evidence that would be inadmissible if provocation alone was raised. It is recognised that where the accused pleads provocation and diminished responsibility together his culpability for homicide may be reduced on either basis or on both. It has been noted that one must distinguish between cases in which accepting the accused's claim that he was provoked to lose his self-control in a sense presupposes establishing diminished responsibility and cases in which it is unclear which the exact basis of the partial excuse should be — i.e. those cases in which the conditions of both provocation and diminished responsibility obtain. A verdict of manslaughter on both grounds would be most appropriate with regard to these latter cases.

# 6 Self-Defence, Provocation and Mistake of Fact

## Introduction

Provocation operates as a partial excuse on the assumption that the accused's loss of self-control (and hence his or her inability to act morally voluntarily) was caused, in part, by the victim's wrongdoing. Determining the threshold of legal provocation presupposes a moral judgement about what sort of offensive conduct is capable of arousing in a person such a degree of justified anger or indignation that might defeat his or her capacity for self-control.[1] As was indicated earlier, the moral and legal assessment of an alleged provocation is based on a test that combines both "objective" and "subjective" criteria. Although legal wrongdoings of a significant nature should for the most part provide a sufficient basis for the defence, non-legal, moral wrongdoings may also be considered serious enough to pass the threshold of provocation in law.[2] Over this threshold, provocations may vary from the less serious ones (e.g. verbal provocations) to those involving very serious wrongdoings (e.g. provocations involving physical violence). Provocations involving different forms and degrees of wrongdoing may equally support a partial defence to murder, provided that the requirement of loss of self-control is also satisfied.[3] There may be

---

[1] According to Fletcher, "Determining this threshold is patently a matter of moral judgment about what we expect people to be able to resist in trying situations. A valuable aid in making that judgment is comparing the competing interests at stake and assessing the degree to which the actor inflicts harm beyond the benefit that accrues from his action. It is important to remember, however, that the balancing of interests is but a vehicle for making judgment about the culpability of the actor's surrendering to external pressure", *Rethinking Criminal Law* (1978), p.804.

[2] See A. von Hirsch and Nils Jareborg, "Provocation and Culpability", in *Responsibility, Character and the Emotions* (1987) 241, at pp. 253-4.

[3] The gravity of the provocation offered is taken into account at the sentencing stage in determining the appropriate degree of punishment for the lesser

cases where, depending upon the nature and gravity of the victim's wrongdoing, the accused's response to provocation may appear to verge on action taken in self-defence. This chapter draws together and examines questions that arise in some cases lying on the borderline between provocation and self-defence. The discussion focuses, for the most part, on the question of culpability for homicide in imperfect or excessive self-defence cases, and on how such cases are dealt with under current legal doctrine. Although a detailed analysis of self-defence and related defences is beyond the compass of the present work, attention is drawn to doctrinal issues that emerge from a comparative examination of self-defence and provocation in the light of the theory of justification and excuse.

## Self-Defence and Criminal Liability

We saw in chapter 1 that when an accused raises  self-defence, or another justification-based defence, his claim is that his harm-causing conduct was, in the circumstances, lawful or permissible. A distinction has been proposed between what is referred to as the "implicit elements" approach and the "licence" approach to legal justification.[4] According to the implicit elements approach, when an accused acts under a valid justification, e.g. self-defence, he or she cannot commit the offence charged. His conduct may have satisfied all the explicit elements of the offence, as provided for by the offence definition, but it has not satisfied the implicit elements of the offence. Thus, for an accused to be convicted e.g. of murder it is required that he caused the death of another with an intention to kill or to cause grievous bodily harm (the explicit elements); it is required, moreover, that he did so in the absence of certain justificatory circumstances, e.g. self-defence (the implicit elements).[5] An offence cannot be committed unless all the explicit and implicit conditions are met. The licence approach, on the other hand, treats a justification such as self-defence as providing a licence or liberty to commit a criminal offence. From this point of view, the person who kills another in self-defence commits an offence, but the commission of that offence is considered, in the circumstances, permissible.

A justification-based defence may arise where the accused have acted in order to prevent the commission of an offence, to ward off an unlawful attack against himself or another, to effect a lawful arrest or to

offence. See A. Ashworth, "Sentencing in Provocation Cases", *Criminal Law Review* (1975) 555.

4   See D.H. Husak, *Philosophy of Criminal Law* (1987).
5   Ibid at p. 190.

protect his or another's property. In English law, the Criminal Law Act 1967 regulates these defences, previously governed by common law rules.[6] Section 3 of the Act provides

(1) A person may use such force as is reasonable in the circumstances in the prevention of crime, or in effecting or assisting in the lawful arrest of offenders or suspected offenders or of persons unlawfully at large.

(2) Subsection (1) above shall replace the rules of common law on the question when force used for a purpose mentioned in the subsection is justified by that purpose.

It is recognised that, as regards self-defence, defence of others and defence of property, the common law defence survives but only to the extent that it is not incompatible with the statutory defence.[7] Under both the common law and s. 3, for such a defence to succeed it is required that the force used was reasonable in the circumstances as they existed or as the accused believed them to be. It is accepted that a person will be entitled to the defence where he honestly believed that he was under attack, irrespective of whether such a belief was reasonable or not.[8] If the accused honestly believed that he was being attacked, or about to be attacked, even though that was not in fact the case, the jury will be invited to consider whether his use of force was proportionate to the threat which the accused believed to be created by the attack under which he believed himself to be.[9] If, taking into account all the circumstances of the case, the jury concludes that the accused used too

---

6    As was said in chapter 1, under common law self-defence has traditionally been treated as a justification, covering not only defence of oneself but also defence of others. See e.g. *Rose* (1884) 15 Cox CC 540; *Duffy* [1967] 1 QB 63.

7    See *Cousins* [1982] QB 526, [1982] 2 All ER 115; *Devlin v Armstrong* [1971] NI 13. However, it has been argued that, in cases involving putative or mistaken self-defence, or where the aggressor is excusable, only the common law defence will apply, as in these cases the actor cannot be said to be acting in the prevention of crime. See A. W. Mewett, "Murder and Intent: Self-Defence and Provocation", *Criminal Law Quarterly* 27 (1984-85) 433.

8    See also Clause 44 of the Law Commission's Draft Criminal Code.

9    See *Williams* (Gladstone ) (1984) 78 Cr App Rep 276. In this case it was held that "If the jury came to the conclusion that the defendant believed, or may have believed, that he was being attacked or that a crime was being committed, and that force was necessary to protect himself or to prevent crime, then the prosecution have not proven their case" (at p. 281). See also *Jackson* [1985] RTR 257; *Asbury* [1986] Crim LR 258; *Fisher* [1987] Crim LR 334; *Beckford v R* [1988] AC 130, [1987] 3 All ER 425. Where however the accused's mistake as to the need to use force in defence, or as to the degree of force needed, was caused by his voluntary intoxication, his defence will fail. See, e.g., *O'Grady* [1987] 3 WLR 321; *O'Connor* [1991] Crim LR 135.

much force, his plea of self-defence will fail. The same will be the case if the accused did not know or believe that circumstances existed which would justify his use of force, irrespective of whether those circumstances actually existed or not.[10] When a justification-based defence is raised the burden is on the prosecution to disprove that defence beyond reasonable doubt.[11]

The use of force is not reasonable if it is not necessary. For the use of force to be necessary it is required that the danger or threat which the accused apprehends must be sufficiently specific and imminent,[12] and must be such that it could not be reasonably met without resorting to force.[13] This, however, does not mean that a person cannot use force before an attack actually takes place. As Lord Griffiths remarked in *Beckford*, "a man about to be attacked does not have to wait for his assailant to strike the first blow or fire the first shot; circumstances may justify a pre-emptive strike".[14] If the jury think that the use of force was necessary then they will proceed to compare the harm caused by the accused with the harm prevented by his or her action. If the harm caused was grossly disproportionate to the harm prevented, the accused's defence should fail. As was stated by Lord Diplock in *Attorney-General for Northern Ireland's Reference (No 1 of 1975)*,[15] in considering whether the use of force was reasonable the jury should ask themselves the following question

Are we satisfied that no reasonable man (a) with knowledge of such facts as were known to the accused or...believed by him to exist (b) in the circumstances and time available to him for reflection (c) could be of the opinion that the prevention of the risk of harm to which others might be exposed if the suspect were allowed to escape [or the defence of himself or another, or the prevention of crime or the defence of property] justified exposing [the accused's victim] to the

---

10     See *Dadson* (1850) 4 Cox CC 358;*Chapman* (1988) 89 Cr App Rep 190. See also J. C. Smith, *Justification and Excuse in the Criminal Law* (1989), pp. 38-41; B. Hogan, "The Dadson Principle", *Criminal Law Review* [1989] 679.

11     As Lord Griffiths stated in *Beckford. v. R.* [1988] A.C. 130, "It is because it is an essential element of all crimes of violence that the violence or the threat of violence should be unlawful that self-defence, if raised as an issue in a criminal trial, must be disproved by the prosecution. If the prosecution fail to do so the accused is entitled to be acquitted because the prosecution will have failed to prove an essential element of the crime namely that the violence used by the accused was unlawful" (at p. 144).

12     See, e.g., *Devlin v. Armstrong* , supra note 7.

13     See, e.g., *Fegan* [1972] NI 80.

14     *Beckford v R*, supra note 9, at p. 144.

15     [1977] AC 105.

risk of harm to him that might result from the kind of force that the accused contemplated using?[16]

As the above statement suggests, the use of force in self-defence must satisfy the test of reasonableness or proportionality. In dealing with this question the jury are expected to imagine themselves acting under the circumstances in which the accused had to act, i.e. under all the stresses to which the accused was exposed and with the time which the accused had available to him in which to decide whether to use force and how much force to use. In other words, the question of whether the force used was reasonable or not must be answered by the jury in the light of the circumstances in which the accused decided to use force.[17] If, after considering all the relevant evidence, the jury conclude that, although some force may have been necessary to repel an attack, the accused used too much force, his plea of self-defence will fail.

Killing in self-defence or defence of another may be justified only if the accused believed that the attack posed an immediate threat on his or another person's life. Under common law it was recognised that a person could not rely on self-defence unless he had retreated as far as possible before using force. According to the current approach to the defence, however, the duty to retreat is not a condition laid down by law, but only a factor to be considered by the jury in deciding whether it was necessary for the accused to use force, and whether the force used was reasonable.[18] However, an accused would not be able to rely on self-defence if he deliberately provokes an attack on himself or another so that he may be able to justify his use of force on the grounds of self-defence.[19]

---

[16]  Ibid at 137.

[17]  *Palmer v R* [1971] AC 814, at p. 832. See also *Shannon* [1980] 71 Cr App Rep 192, [1980] Crim LR 410;*Whyte* [1987] 3 All ER 416.

[18]  As Lord Lane pointed out in *Bird* [1985] 1 WLR 816, "If the defendant is proved to have been attacking or retaliating or revenging himself, then he was not truly acting in self-defence. Evidence that the defendant tried to retreat or tried to call off the fight may be a cast-iron method of casting doubt on the suggestion that he was the attacker or the retaliator or the person trying to revenge himself. But it is not by any means the only method of doing that" (at p. 820). And see *McInnes* [1971] 3 All ER 295. It is recognised, moreover, that a person is under no duty to refrain from going where he may rightfully go because he is knows that there is a risk that he might be attacked. See *Field* [1972] Crim LR 435.

[19]  As was stated in *Browne* [1973] NI 96, "The need to act must not have been created by conduct of the accused in the immediate context of the incident which was likely or intended to give rise to that need" (at p. 107, per Lowry LCJ). However, where the accused's conduct was only likely to provoke an

So, to summarise, the test that applies when self-defence or a related defence is being considered has a subjective and an objective aspect. The subjective aspect pertains to the assumption that question of whether the use of force was necessary should be answered in the light of the facts as the accused believed them to be. If the accused acted under an honest although mistaken belief that the use of force was necessary for his or another person's protection, he is no more criminally responsible than if that force was in fact necessary for defence. The objective aspect pertains to the requirement that the degree of force used must be necessary and reasonable in view of the circumstances as the accused (mistakenly or not) believed them to be. If the harm caused by the accused was grossly disproportionate to the harm prevented the defence would fail.

In both self-defence and provocation the situation giving rise to the conditions of the legal defence is brought about — most often culpably — by the victim. According to Wasserman, when self-defence is pleaded as a defence to a murder charge, the accused's claim of justification has to do with the fact that he was forced by the victim to choose between lives.[20] Modern commentators agree that the aggressor's culpability in endangering the accused's or another person's life renders the use of lethal force in self-defence legally justified. In Fletcher's words

> Necessary defence is founded on the principle that it is right and proper to use force, even deadly force, in certain circumstances. The source of the right is a comparison of the competing interests of the aggressor and the defender, as modified by the important fact that the aggressor is the only party responsible for the fight.[21]

As was indicated earlier, as a justification, self-defence is concerned primarily with the societal approval, or permissiveness, of the harm-causing conduct rather than with the blameworthiness of the actor as such. With regard to provocation, although the trend in modern law is towards treating the defence as a partial excuse, there is still some backing for the idea that provocation operates as a partial

---

attack, it is doubtful whether the defence should be denied to him. See Smith and Hogan, *Criminal Law*, 8th ed. (1996), p. 264.

20 "Justifying Self-Defence", *Philosophy and Public Affairs* (1985) 378.

21 *Rethinking Criminal Law*, (1978), pp. 857-8. And according to G. Williams, "Self-defence is classified as a justification on the basis that the interests of the person attacked are greater than those of the attacker. The aggressor's culpability in starting the fight tips the scales in favour of the defendant", "The Theory of Excuses", *Criminal Law Review* [1982] 739. See also P. Robinson, "Criminal Law Defences: A Systematic Analysis", 82 *Columbia Law Review* (1982) 199.

justification.[22] We saw in chapter 4 that, according to some commentators, the provoker's culpability may also be said to render his killing in retaliation partially justified.[23] Such an approach to provocation implies that a provoked killing attaches less blame to the actor than an unprovoked one, irrespective of the actor's frame of mind — as relating to his capacity to exercise self-control — at the time of his retaliation. The argument that provocation operates as a partial justification would appear to gain some support in those cases in which the wrongful act of provocation involves a serious threat of physical violence, in other words, in those cases where provocation borders on self-defence. It has been pointed out that

> When provocation takes the form of physical assault of such nature as would be expected to arouse overwhelming passion in the person attacked, it will not always be easy to distinguish the victim's immediate retaliation from a resistance by way of self-defence. It is therefore not surprising that the early authorities did not always keep homicide under provocation separate from homicide in self-defence.[24]

However, any attempt to elicit support for the idea that provocation operates as a partial justification by drawing an analogy between provocation and self-defence runs up against serious difficulties. Although the conditions of self-defence and provocation may, in some cases, appear to overlap to a considerable extent, it is important to recognise that the theoretical bases of the two defences are very different. Provocation is based on the assumption that the victim's conduct deprived the accused of his power of self-control. The victim's conduct is relevant to deciding whether the accused has provoked to lose his self-control, and whether a reasonable person in the position of the accused may have been similarly provoked. Loss of control presupposes anger. Self-defence, by contrast, focuses not on anger or loss of self-control, but on a morally worthy motive, i.e. self-preservation. Further, using force in self-defence is justified not merely as an act aimed at the protection of the defender's interests, but also as an act which vindicates the legal order in general. The superior interest which is protected by the act of defence pertains not only to the

---

22  As G. Gordon has remarked, "The tendency of the modern law is in theory to allow the plea of provocation only where the accused has lost control, but the idea that provocation is a form of unjustifiable self-defence is not altogether dead", *Criminal Law*, 2nd ed. (1978), p. 769.

23  See F. McAuley, "Anticipating the Past: The Defence of Provocation in Irish Law", *Modern Law Review* 50 (1987) 137.

24  *Kenny's Outlines of Criminal Law* (1966), p.172. And see *Letenock* (1917) 12 Cr App Rep 221; *Cobbett* (1940) 28 Cr App Rep II.

immediately defended personal interest, which may be superior but also inferior to the interest of the attacker, but also to the prevention of crime. The vindication of the legal order pervades the rationale of self-defence and other justification-based defences but this, surely, is not the case as regards provocation. With respect to the latter defence, establishing a serious wrongdoing on the victim's part is not by itself sufficient to support the reduction of culpability. What is required is that the provocation has deprived the accused of his capacity to exercise control over his conduct.

Besides the traditional understanding of self-defence as a justification, the same defence may also be interpreted as a form of excusing necessity. As we saw in chapter 1, early law recognised this version of the defence under the principle of *se defendendo*.[25] This approach to the defence draws support from the common sense view that the person whose life is threatened has no choice but to kill his attacker.[26] Like in all cases in which the actor's will is overpowered by external factors, the person defending himself can be said to act morally involuntarily. Considering that, from the point of view of justification theory, the aggressor's culpability plays a crucial role in turning the scales in favour of the defender, treating self-defence as an excuse may gain acceptance in some cases involving non-culpable aggression. In such cases the use of force in self-defence, especially deadly force, can be said to be excused, rather than justified, just as in cases of excusing necessity. From the point of view of the excuse theory, self-defence and provocation may be said to share a common basis: both defences could be seen as operating on the assumption that the actor lacks the freedom to choose — he acts morally involuntarily. What distinguishes self-defence as a complete excuse from provocation as a partial excuse is that in provocation the actor succumbs to a form of coercion — the emotional pressure caused by anger — that is not regarded as being irresistible.

## Self-Defence and Excusing Conditions

As was noted before, an accused's plea of self-defence will be judged in the light of the facts that existed or that the accused believed to exist, whether they actually existed or not. English law recognises that the accused's belief need not be reasonable, just honest. Thus, if the

---

25   See Coke 55; Hale 479-87; Foster 275; 1 Hawkins 113; 4 Blackstone 184.
26   See G. Fletcher, *Rethinking Criminal Law* (1978), pp. 856 ff.; "Proportionality and the Psychotic Aggressor: A Vignette in Comparative Criminal Theory", *Israel Law Review* 8 (1973) 367; P. Robinson,"Criminal Law Defences: A Systematic Analysis", supra note 21, p. 240.

accused was totally mistaken in thinking that he was about to be attacked he will be judged on the basis of that mistaken belief.[27] In Australian and North American jurisdictions a different test has been adopted, one that requires the accused's belief to be founded on reasonable grounds.[28] The same approach was adopted in English law prior to the decisions of the English Court of Appeal in *Williams* [29] and the Privy Council in *Beckford*.[30] [31] The difference between the two approaches may not be as significant at it may appear, however, for, as stated in *Williams*, "The reasonableness or unreasonableness of the defendant's belief is material to the question of whether the belief was held by the defendant at all".[32] As was said in the previous section, if the prosecution can prove that the accused employed more force than was reasonably necessary in order to ward off an attack, the defence of self-defence will normally fail. Exceeding the limits of necessary force in self-defence or defence of another is fatal to the accused's claim of justification. The right to use force in defence is restricted by the proportionality principle. This principle requires that the degree of force used in defence must be reasonable or proportionate to the threat posed by the attack. Thus, although lethal force may be necessary to ward off a minor assault, such force is clearly grossly disproportionate to the threat and, for that reason, unjustifiable.[33]

In English law, the reasonableness of the force used in defence is a question of fact to be determined by the jury. It is upon them to decide whether the prosecution has proved, beyond reasonable doubt, that the accused exceeded the degree of force needed to avert the attack. If the prosecution is successful in establishing that the accused

---

27    New Zealand law adopts a similar approach. See s. 48 of the NZ Crimes Act 1961.

28    See, e.g., ss 271 and 272 of the Queensland Criminal Code, ss 248 and 249 of the Criminal Code of Western Australia. And see *Zecevic* (1987) 61 ALJR 375, 162 CLR 645; *Dziduch* (1990) 47 A Crim R 378. And see D. O'Connor and P. A. Fairall, *Criminal Defences* (1996) 191. Consider also the American Model Penal Code, paras 3.04, 3.09 (2); Canadian Criminal Code ss 27, 34, 35, 37. And see S.M H. Yeo, *Compulsion in the Criminal Law* (1990), ch. 6.

29    [1987] 3 All ER 411, 78 Cr App Rep 276.

30    [1988] AC 130, [1987] 3 All ER 425, [1987] 3 WLR 611, 85 Cr App Rep 378.

31    See, e.g., *Rose* (1884) 15 Cox CC 540; *Chisam* (1963) 47 Cr App Rep 130; *Fennell* [1971] 1 QB 428.

32    *Williams* [1987] 3 All ER 411, at p.415.

33    See G. Fletcher, *Rethinking Criminal Law* (1978), pp. 859-60; P. Robinson, "Criminal Law Defences: A Systematic Analysis", supra note 21, p. 219.

exceeded the limits of necessary force, the defence will fail, even if it is accepted that the accused was actually acting in response to an unjustified attack.[34] With respect to criminal offences other than murder, if the plea of self-defence fails on the grounds that the force used by the accused was unreasonable or disproportionate to the threat, the fact that the accused was defending himself against an unjustified attack may be taken into account as a factor in the mitigation of sentence. However, where the accused is charged with murder, the rejection of his defence on such a basis would necessarily entail a sentence of life imprisonment.

It is recognised, further, that the question of whether the degree of force used in defence was reasonable or not should be answered in the light of the circumstances in which the accused decided to use force. The jury should be directed to take into account that, under the stress of the situation, the accused might not have been able to make out the exact degree of force needed to ward off the attack. As was stated by Lord Morris in *Palmer*

> If there has been an attack so that defence is reasonably necessary it will be recognized that a person defending himself cannot weigh to a nicety the exact measure of his necessary defensive action. If a jury thought that in a moment of unexpected anguish a person attacked had only done what he honestly and instinctively thought was necessary that would be most potent evidence that only reasonable defensive action had been taken.[35]

As the above statement suggests, a plea of self-defence may be accepted even if the accused used more force than was in fact necessary if the jury recognises that, in the circumstances, the accused was unable to calculate correctly the amount of force actually needed.

---

34   According to Professor Smith, "Where [the accused], being under no mistake of fact, uses force in public or private defence, he either has a complete defence or if he uses excessive force, no defence. If the charge is murder, he is guilty of murder or not guilty of anything...He may have believed the force was reasonable but if, even by the relaxed standard applied in this context, it was not, he was making a mistake of law, which is not a defence, and he is guilty of murder", *Criminal Law*, 8th ed. (1996), p. 268. And see *Clegg* [1995] 1 All ER 334; *Palmer v R* [1971] AC 814, [1971] 1 All ER 1077; *McInnes* [1971] 3 All ER 295, [1971] 1 WLR 1600.

35   *Palmer v R*, supra note, at p. 832. And see *Shannon* [1980] 71 Cr App Rep 192. In that case it was stated that "if the jury concluded that the stabbing was the act of a desperate man in extreme difficulties, with his assailant dragging him down by the hair, they should consider very carefully before concluding that stabbing was an offensive and not a defensive act, albeit it went beyond what an onlooker would regard as reasonably necessary." (at p. 196).

In so far as the reasonableness of the accused's response to an attack is assessed by reference to his state of mind in the circumstances, the justification of self-defence would appear to hinge on considerations that are clearly excusative in nature. If the accused had been acting in a state of fear, panic or extreme anger, no blame is attributed to him for exceeding the limits of necessary force in self-defence. This is what the phrase "reasonable defensive action" in Lord Morris's statement seems to imply. One might envisage an analogy between cases of excessive self-defence where the defence is accepted on the ground that the accused, given his state of mind in the circumstances, could not make out the exact degree of force actually needed to repel the attack and those cases of putative or mistaken self-defence. In the latter cases the accused believes, mistakenly, that he is being attacked and uses force (sometimes deadly force) in self-defence. It has been argued that, contrary to the current approach in Anglo-American law, in such cases the accused's defence should be regarded as excuse- rather than as justification-based. The accused's action remains wrongful, as there is no real attack justifying the use of force in defence, but the accused may be excused on the grounds of his mistaken belief. According to Fletcher,

> Mistakes as to justificatory elements, however, do not affect either the violation of the norm or the wrongful nature of acting in ignorance. If an actor believes that he is being attacked and responds with force, his injuring the putative aggressor is a wrongful but excused battery.[36]

Treating the use of force in defence as justified where the accused mistakenly believes that he is being attacked, or where he exceeds, due to stress or fear, the limits of necessary force, is incompatible with the basic assumption that justification negates, from an objective point of view, the wrongfulness of the act.[37]

---

[36]  *Rethinking Criminal Law* (1978), p. 696.

[37]  The traditional common law position that putative self-defence operates as a justification has been adopted by the drafters of the American Penal Code. Para 3.04 provides that the right of self-defence arises when "the actor believes that such force is immediately necessary for the purpose of protecting himself against the use of unlawful force". Para 3.09 (2) provides, further, that, in cases of putative self-defence, for the plea of self-defence to be accepted the accused's mistake must be reasonable. Fletcher remarks that "The Common law and now the Model Penal Code and its progeny interweave criteria of justification and excuse in cases in which the defending actor, reasonably, but mistakenly believes that he is being attacked. Those situations, which we shall call putative self-defence, are regularly called cases of justification. Assimilating a putative justification to an actual justification undermines the matrix of legal relationships affected by a claim of justification", *Rethinking*

In self-defence, the psychological pressure that the defender experiences when his life or limb is under immediate threat should be taken into account in considering whether he should be excused for exceeding the limits of necessary force. Stress, fear, mistake, or a combination of these factors, may provide a good reason for excusing the actor for employing more force than is actually necessary to repel an unlawful attack. As was noted before, however, English law adopts a different, subjectivist, approach to the question of justification — an approach that places the emphasis on whether the accused himself, mistakenly or not, believed that his action was justified. With respect to putative self-defence this implies that accepting the accused's claim of justification in a way presupposes that the jury must be satisfied that the accused was acting under a mistake of fact. A more coherent approach to the matter, it is submitted, would be to treat as justified only those cases of self-defence where the degree of defensive force employed was actually necessary and proportionate to the threat posed by the attack. Cases of putative self-defence, as well as those in which the accused due to stress or fear uses more force than is actually necessary should be dealt with under the excuse theory.

## Excusing the Use of Excessive Force in Self-Defence

It was said before that, in English law, the use of unreasonable or excessive force in self-defence will normally defeat the accused's claim of justification.[38] This all-or-nothing character of the defence of self-defence has been criticised as likely to result in morally controversial convictions, especially where the accused is charged with murder — an offence that entails a fixed penalty of life imprisonment. Some common law jurisdictions introduced a qualified defence to murder resulting in a conviction of manslaughter where an accused was justified to use some force in self-defence but he used more force than was reasonably necessary in the circumstances. Such a partial defence

---

*Criminal Law* (1978), pp. 762-3. Similarly P. Robinson argues that "Under such provisions, the actor who mistakenly believes that his conduct meets the requirements of a justification defence will be justified, when it seems clear that such an actor is properly only excused. His conduct has not, in fact, avoided a greater harm or furthered a greater good; it has not caused a net benefit, but rather a net harm. On the other hand, he may well be blameless, especially if his mistake is reasonable", "Criminal Law Defenses: A Systematic Analysis", supra note 21, p. 239.

38    *Palmer v R* [1971] AC 814; *McInnes* [1971] 1 WLR 1600; *Clegg* [1995] 1 All ER 334, [1995] Crim LR 418.

was recognised by the Supreme Court of Victoria in *McKay*,[39] and was confirmed by the High Court of Australia in *Howe*.[40] As Lowe J stated in *McKay*, "...if the occasion warrants action in self-defence or for the prevention of felony or the apprehension of the felon but the person taking action acts beyond the necessity of the occasion and kills the offender the crime is manslaughter — not murder".[41] In *Howe*, Menzies J expressed this position as follows

> The law is that it is manslaughter and not murder if the accused would have been entitled to acquittal on the ground of self-defence except for the fact that in honestly defending himself he used greater force than was reasonably necessary for his self-protection and in doing so killed his assailant.[42]

For such a partial defence to apply the following conditions had to be met: (a) the accused must have honestly and reasonably believed that he was being attacked; (b) the accused must have honestly believed that the degree of force used was necessary in the circumstances to protect himself; (c) the accused's action would have been fully justified if excessive force had not been used. The defence of excessive self-defence could be relied upon, in other words, where the accused's plea of self-defence failed to satisfy the objective test. The doctrine of excessive defence, as was formulated in *Howe*, applied mainly to cases of self-defence. It has been asserted, however, that the doctrine should logically apply to any case where the accused was legally entitled to use force.[43] Although there have been cases in early English law in which a similar approach was adopted,[44] the partial defence of

---

39  [1957] ALR 648.

40  (1958) 100 CLR 448. See also *Bufalo* [1958] VR 363; *Haley* (1959) 76 WNNSW 550; *Enright* [1961] VR 663; *Turner* [1962] VR 30; *McNamara* [1963] VR 32; *Tikos* (No. 1) [1963] VR 285; *Tikos* (No. 2) [1963] VR 306. The same doctrine has been adopted in Irish law. See e.g. *People (A-G) v Dwyer* [1972] IR 416. The doctrine was also followed in some Canadian cases (see, e.g., *Brisson* (1983) 139 DLR 685) but was finally rejected by the Supreme Court of Canada. See *Gee* (1982) 2 SCR 286, 29 CR (3d) 347; *Faid* [1983] 1 SCR 265, 33 CR (3d) 1. In the latter cases the proposed defence was referred to as a "partial justification".

41  Supra note 39, at p. 649.

42  Supra note 40.

43  Indeed *McKay*, the case in which the doctrine was for the first time introduced, was concerned with the use of excessive force in the arrest of a felon and the defence of property. See Smith and Hogan, *Criminal Law*, 8th ed. (1996) p. 269.

44  See, e.g., *Cook* (1639) Cro Car 537; *Whalley* (1835) 7 C & P 245; *Patience* (1837) 7 C & P 775; *Weston* (1879) 14 Cox CC 346; *Biggin* [1918-19] All ER 501. In the cases of *Whalley* and *Patience* , for

excessive self-defence was clearly rejected by the Privy Council in *Palmer*.[45] In *Viro*,[46] the High Court of Australia once more confirmed the doctrine of excessive defence, refusing to follow the decision of the Privy Council in *Palmer*.[47]

---

example, the accused used deadly force to resist an unlawful arrest; in both cases the accused were found guilty of manslaughter.

45   [1971] 1 All ER 1077. In that case it was held that "If in any of the above cases there is a suggestion that a measure of dispensation or tolerance, where a death is intentionally and unnecessarily caused, is to be found in the circumstances that someone is acting on an illegal warrant or is executing process unlawfully (Cook) it is not one that commended itself to their Lordships" (at 1083D). And see *Cascoe* [1970] 2 All ER 833; *Emelogue*, May 2, 1971, No. 7044/69 (unreported); *McInnes* [1971] 3 All ER 295, [1971] 1 WLR 1600; *Edwards* [1973] 1 All ER 152; *A-G for Northern Ireland's Reference* (No. 1 of 1975) [1977] AC 105 at 148; *Clegg* [1995] 1 All ER 334, [1995] Crim LR 418.

46   (1978) 141 CLR 88. In this case Mason J. explained the operation of the defence of excessive defence in the context of murder as follows: "(1) It is for the jury first to consider whether when the accused killed the deceased the accused reasonably believed that an unlawful attack which threatened him with death or serious bodily harm was being or was about to be made upon him. By the expression 'reasonably believed' is meant, not what a reasonable man would have believed, but what the accused himself might reasonably believe in all the circumstances in which he found himself. (2) If the jury is satisfied beyond reasonable doubt that there was no reasonable belief by the accused of such an attack no question of self-defence arises. (3) If the jury is not satisfied beyond reasonable doubt that there was no such reasonable belief by the accused, it must then consider whether the force in fact used by the accused was reasonably proportionate to the danger which he believed he faced. (4) If the jury is not satisfied beyond reasonable doubt that more force was used than was reasonably proportionate it should acquit. (5) If the jury is satisfied beyond reasonable doubt that more force was used, then its verdict should be either manslaughter or murder, that depending upon the answer to the final question for the jury — did the accused believe that the force which he used was reasonably proportionate to the danger which he faced? (6) If the jury is satisfied beyond reasonable doubt that the accused did not have such a belief the verdict will be murder. If it is not satisfied beyond reasonable doubt that the accused did not have that belief the verdict will be manslaughter", (at pp. 146-7). See also *Lawson and Forsythe* (1985) 18 A Crim R 360.

47   For a fuller account of the defence of excessive force see *Howard's Criminal Law*, 5th ed, (1990) pp. 99 ff; N. Morris and C. Howard, *Studies in Criminal Law* (1964), ch. IV; C. Howard, *Australian Criminal Law* (1965), pp. 80-83; "An Australian Letter: Excessive Defence", *Criminal Law Review* [1964], 448; "Two Problems of Excessive Defence", 84 *Law Quarterly Review* (1968) 343; N. Morris, "A New Qualified Defence to Murder", 1 *Adelaide Law Review* 23 (1960); I. Elliot, "Excessive Self-Defence in Commonwealth Law: A Comment", 22 *International and Comparative Law Quarterly* (1973) 727.

However, in *Zecevic*,[48] the High Court of Australia reversed its own earlier decisions, bringing Australian law into line with the law of England as expressed in *Palmer*. It was held that this change was necessary in order to facilitate the jury's task in applying the law and not because the previous approach was in principle wrong.[49] As was indicated before, the defence of excessive force was open only to the accused who acted under an honest mistake as to the degree of force needed to repel the attack. On the other hand, such a partial defence was not recognised in cases of putative self-defence where the accused honestly but unreasonably believed that he was being attacked. Under Australian law, in the latter cases the accused may be entitled to a complete defence only if his or her mistake was reasonable. The High Court referred to this as a "basic and complicating conceptual anomaly",[50] an inconsistency that had to be removed. A further problem with the doctrine of excessive defence, as formulated in *Howe*, had to do with the difficulty in applying in excessive defence cases an objective test such as the one that applies in the context of provocation. The Court recognised, however, that although the doctrine of excessive defence no longer applies, the jury are still entitled to return a compromise verdict of manslaughter in such cases.[51] Moreover, the fact that in Australian law murder no longer entails a fixed penalty of life imprisonment is seen as mitigating further the effects of the High Court's decision in *Zecevic*. The decision of the High Court of Australia has been criticised on the grounds that a doctrine that was in principle correct should not have been so easily abolished because of the inability of the judges to state the law in a form understandable to the jury.[52]

---

48    (1987) 71 ALR 641.

49    According to Mason C.J., "The doctrine enunciated in *Howe* and *Viro* expressed a concept of self-defence which best accords with acceptable standards of culpability, so that the accused whose only error is that he lacks reasonable grounds for his belief that the degree of force used was necessary for his self-defence is guilty of manslaughter not murder", Ibid at p. 646. In the same case Gaudron J. stated: "The proposition that it is manslaughter, not murder, where self-defence in relation to homicide fails by reason only that disproportionate force was used, is consonant ...with the definitional difference between murder and voluntary manslaughter involving the presence or absence of malice aforethought", (at p. 669).

50    Ibid, at p.666.

51    "There is no rule which dictates the use which the jury must make of the evidence and the ultimate question is for it alone", Ibid at p. 653. See also *Tajbor* (1986) 23 A Crim R 189 at 201.

52    For a critical look at the High Court's decision in *Zecevic* see P.A. Fairall, "The Demise of Excessive Self-Defence Manslaughter in Australia: A Final Obituary?" *Criminal Law Journal* 12 (1988), 41. S.M.H. Yeo, "The Demise

It should be noted, however, that in England the Criminal Law Revision Committee adopted the view that the doctrine of excessive defence, as expressed in *Howe*, was right in principle and recommended its introduction in the context of self-defence and related defences. The Committee proposed that

> Where a person kills in a situation in which it is reasonable for some force to be used in self-defence or in the prevention of crime but the defendant uses excessive force, he should be liable to be convicted of manslaughter not murder if at the time of the act he honestly believed that the force he used was reasonable in the circumstances.[53]

The above position was adopted in the light of the Committee's recommendation that murder should be retained as a distinct offence category comprising the most heinous forms of homicide. A person who believes that his actions are justified does not deserve to be stigmatised as a murderer, mo matter how unreasonable his belief may be. The Committee's proposal has been endorsed by the Law Commission which, in cl. 59 of its Draft Criminal Code, has also recommended the introduction of a defence of excessive defence leading to the reduction of murder to manslaughter.[54]

It was said above that, under the excessive defence doctrine, where an accused has killed by exceeding the limits of necessary force in defence, he may be able to rely on a partial defence if the jury are satisfied that the accused honestly believed that the amount of force he used was reasonable in the circumstances. What connects the defence of excessive force with self-defence and related defences is that for the former defence to apply it is required that there should initially have been a situation in which the accused would have been justified in using force in defence of himself or another, or in the prevention of crime. From the point of view of the excuse theory it is not clear, however, whether this connection is enough to justify the introduction of a separate partial defence to murder. To put it otherwise, treating excessive defence as an independent defence in its own right may be taken to imply that the mere fact that the accused was acting (or believed that he was acting) in defence has something to do with the

---

of Excessive Self-Defence in Australia" (1988) 37 *International and Comparative Law Quarterly* 348; "Proportionality in Criminal Defences", (1988) 12 *Criminal Law Journal* 211; D. Lanham, "Death of a Qualified Defence?" (1988) 104 *Law Quarterly Review* 239.

53   CLRC, Offences Against the Person, 14th Report, Cmnd 7844 (1980), para. 288.

54   See also the Report of the House of Lords Select Committee on *Murder and Life Imprisonment* (1989), HL Paper 78.

reduction of culpability for homicide. Unless one is prepared to accept that the accused's response was partially justified by the fact that he was defending himself against unlawful aggression, such cases should more properly be treated under different excuse-based criminal defences. A killing that results from the use of excessive force in self-defence may be partially excused on different grounds, such as provocation, mistake, or a partial defence of extreme emotional disturbance. An excuse-based defence could be raised following the rejection of the accused's claim of justification and would be aimed at denying that the killing manifests the degree of culpability required for a conviction for murder.

Where there is evidence suggesting that the victim's attack provoked the accused to lose his self-control and kill by knowingly using excessive force, his offence may be reduced to manslaughter on the grounds of provocation.[55] The same defence may be relied upon, where the accused's plea of self-defence fails on the grounds that he could have avoided the need of using deadly force in defence by taking an opportunity to retreat. The mere apprehension of an attack may be sufficient to support a plea of provocation here. When provocation is pleaded as a partial defence to murder, following the rejection of the defence of self-defence, the accused admits that he intentionally killed his attacker, but claims that this was the result of his being carried away by angry passion. The first question for the jury to consider would be whether there was a reasonable possibility that the accused was provoked by the victim's attack to lose his self-control.[56] As was explained in chapter 4, the provoked person is not required to have lost his self-control in an absolute sense for the provocation defence to succeed. His or her actions may be entirely impulsive or controlled to some extent but in both cases the actor can be said to be acting morally involuntarily. When a provoked person loses self-control and overreacts, he judges that more retaliation is appropriate than is in fact justified by the seriousness of the provocation — here the actual or threatened attack of another. This misjudgment is excusable, depending on its severity, because people are fallible and sometimes

---

55   As was stated in *McInnes* [1971] 1 WLR 1600, 3 All ER 295, "the facts upon which the plea of self-defence is unsuccessfully sought to be based may nevertheless ... go to show that [the accused] acted under provocation". And see *De Freitas v The Queen* [1960] 2 WLR 533; *Shannon* [1980] Cr App Rep 192.

56   *Duffy* [1949] 1 All ER 932n; *Davies* [1975] QB 691; *Cocker* [1989] Crim L R 740; *Ibrams* (1981) 74 Cr App R 154.

leap before they look, especially when they are conquered by anger.[57] As we saw in chapter 3, besides the subjective question (did the accused lose his self-control?) the jury will also have to consider the objective one of whether a reasonable or ordinary person may have been provoked by the victim's conduct to lose his self-control and do as the accused did. In an excessive defence case  this would be relatively easy to accept, for a physical assault possibly involving a threat to life or limb has traditionally been regarded as conduct most likely to support a claim of provocation in law.

Besides provocation, an accused charged with murder whose plea of self-defence has failed on the grounds that he used more force than was reasonably necessary may be able to rely on the excuse of mistake. If the accused's mistake as to the degree of force needed to repel the (real or imaginary) attack is a reasonable one in the circumstances, the accused should be entitled to full acquittal. Where, on the other hand, the accused's mistake is unreasonable but nevertheless honest it may be taken to provide the basis for a partial defence to murder, reducing that offence to manslaughter. This is, in essence, a reformulation of the defence of excessive force, as defined in *Howe*, with the emphasis now clearly placed on the element of mistake rather than on the fact that the accused was acting in defence. Such a partial defence of mistake would be available only where the accused is charged with murder and would operate on the assumption that an honest mistake, unreasonable though it may be, eliminates the degree of culpability required for a conviction of murder.[58] The fact that the accused honestly believes that what he does is justified makes him less culpable than when he does the same thing being aware that it is wrong. As long as a mistake blocks the inference of the degree of culpability required for murder, it should make no difference how unreasonable the mistaken belief may be. A mistake is unreasonable if it may be avoided by the exercise of reasonable care so an unreasonable mistake constitutes negligence. Such a mistake does not

---

57   From the point of view of the provocation defence, the provoked person's claim for extenuation  has to do with his loss of self-control as the cause of a mistaken judgment.

58   As P. Smith  has remarked, "The moral culpability of the man who honestly believes  that  he needs to use lethal force to defend himself — no matter how mistaken  his  belief — is surely very much less than that of a man who kills deliberately  and in cold blood. It is submitted that society ought to reserve its major condemnation  for the  cold-blooded killer, and to have the mistaken victim of  an attack convicted of the same crime tends to weaken this condemnation", "Excessive Defence — A Rejection of Australian Initiative?", *Criminal Law Review* [1972], 533, pp. 533-4.

preclude the attribution of blame and thus it cannot prevent conviction for the lesser offence.

A partial defence of mistake may be available in a situation where there is no basis at all for the defence of provocation to be raised. Indeed, in some cases there may be an element of inconsistency between an honest, although unreasonable, belief that deadly force is necessary in self-defence and the loss of self-control as a basic requirement of the provocation defence. What distinguishes mistake, as a partial excuse, from provocation is that, in the former case, the accused's plea for extenuation focuses upon his honest belief as to the need to use deadly force in the circumstances. Loss of self-control, in the sense of acting in the heat of passion, is not here in issue. In provocation, on the other hand, the acccused's plea focuses on his loss of self-control as a result of the victim's attack — taken here to constitute provocation — rather than on mistake. Although both defences are excusative in character, they are based on clearly different presuppositions.

# 7 Concluding Note

Provocation has been a source of controversy in criminal law theory. Some commentators have been calling for the total elimination of provocation as an independent defence, while others have been arguing for its expansion to criminal offences other than murder. This controversy issues, in part, from the confusion that has long dogged the law of homicide and, in particular, the definition of murder, with which the defence has traditionally been associated. Besides that, however, there are questions peculiar to the nature of provocation and the moral basis of the ensuing plea for mitigation that need to be dealt with before a coherent approach to the defence in law can be formulated. The starting point of this book was that many of the questions besetting criminal law doctrine might prove more decipherable if examined from the point of view of the theory of justification and excuse. It was noted that, although the formal classification of criminal law defences on this basis may not be easy, or even desirable, examining the rationale and function of criminal law defences in the light of the justification-excuse distinction may prove helpful in eliminating some of the confusion surrounding criminal law doctrine.

For a plea of provocation to succeed the jury must be satisfied that the accused was deprived of his self-control at the time of the killing (the subjective test) and that this was the result of conduct capable of amounting to provocation in law (the objective test). If there is no evidence to support a finding of provocation, the defence will fail, whether the accused lost his self-control or not. Moreover, even if the victim's conduct was such as to amount to provocation in law, the defence cannot be relied upon if evidence shows that the accused did not lose his self-control as a result. The interconnection of excusative (loss of self-control) and justificatory (rightful indignation at the provoker) in provocation has given rise to the question of whether the defence operates as a partial excuse or as a partial justification. At an earlier stage in the development of the provocation defence the justificatory element has played an important role. This accounts, for example, for the requirement that only certain wrongdoings, regarded as particularly grave, could amount to provocation in law, or the requirement that, for the defence to be accepted, the provocation had to come from the victim. Moreover, the requirement that the accused's mode of retaliation must be reasonably proportionate to the provocation offered is more consonant with the idea that provocation operates as a partial justification. As was pointed out, however, the introduction of the Homicide Act 1957 marks a shift towards treating provocation as a partial excuse. This shift is manifested by the gradual removal of requirements of the defence which laid emphasis on its justificatory aspect. Although some modern commentators have expressed support for the idea that provocation operates as a partial justification, it has been argued that the defence is correctly to be treated as a partial excuse. It was pointed out that none of the three major theories of justification (the lesser evil theory, the forfeiture theory and the theory of the vindication of autonomy) can buttress the position that provocation should be viewed as a justification-based defence. Such an approach to the defence is inconsistent with important moral principles pertaining to the sanctity and inviolability of human life; it is, moreover, incompatible with the rationale of justification-based legal defences.

The defence operates as an excuse on the assumption that provocation is capable of raising in an ordinary person such a degree of psychological pressure, in the form of angry passion, as to deprive him of his ability to exercise control over his conduct. The emphasis is now placed on the actor's loss of self-control and his inability to act morally voluntarily as a factor reducing his moral culpability for his wrongful actions. Nevertheless, this sort of pressure can only support a claim for extenuation, not exculpation, for the actor has failed to live up to community standards which demand us to exercise self-control even under pressure. The provoked killer remains blameworthy, but not blameworthy enough to justify his conviction as a murderer. Although a successful plea of provocation negatives the degree of culpability required for murder, it cannot prevent conviction for the lesser offence of manslaughter for a provoked killing still manifests a socially undesirable disposition or trait of character.

From the point of view of the excuse theory, the "reasonable person" test is relied upon in answering the question of whether the provocation offered was serious enough to raise such a degree of angry passion as to be likely to deprive a person of his self-control. Provocation is relevant to establishing a good or acceptable reason for the accused's loss of control as a basis for excusing. In answering this question the jury is directed to take into account those of the accused's characteristics that may bear upon the gravity of the provocation which he or she received. It has been argued that in assessing a plea of provocation one need not speculate about how exactly a "reasonable person" would have responded, for what matters is whether the victim's conduct was sufficient to provoke a "reasonable person" (with the accused's characteristics) to lose his self-control to such a degree as to be likely to form an intention to kill. If it is established that the accused was provoked, what needs to be considered is whether he lost his self-control as a matter of fact (the subjective question). In answering this latter question the jury may consider the accused's mode of retaliation as providing important evidence. The accused's mode of retaliation may also be taken into account in determining the appropriate amount of punishment to be imposed for the lesser offence.

The fact that the accused did not act entirely impulsively in some cases of cumulative provocation, especially in cases involving domestic violence, may be taken to militate against the availability of the provocation defence. It has been suggested that, as loss of self-control is a matter of degree, the fact that the accused appears to have retained a degree of self-control should not necessarily preclude the defence in such cases. On the other hand, where there is no evidence suggesting that the accused was sufficiently provoked, or that he acted in the heat of passion as a result, as required for the provocation defence to apply, the accused may still be entitled to a partial defence on different grounds, such as diminished responsibility or a defence of extreme emotional disturbance. If evidence suggests that the accused suffered from an abnormality of mind and was provoked, provocation and diminished responsibility may be pleaded together. Such a combined defence may be accepted either on the basis of provocation or on that of diminished responsibility or, possibly, on both. The latter should be the case where the requirements of both defences appear to be satisfied.

Finally it was noted that provocation may be relied upon as a partial excuse in some cases where the accused's plea of self-defence is rejected on the grounds that the accused used more force than was reasonably necessary to avert a (real or imaginary) attack. In so far as killing by using excessive force in defence cannot be said to be partially justified, such cases may be treated under either provocation or, perhaps, under a partial excuse of honest mistake relating to conditions of justification. The latter defence — if such a general defence were to be introduced — should rest on the assumption that a mistaken belief as to the amount of defensive force needed, unreasonable though it may be, eliminates the degree of moral culpability required for murder.

Having outlined the main themes of this book, I should point out that the book was not meant to cover all aspects of current criminal law relating to partial defences, nor to provide an exhaustive account of the relevant case law. I have not attempted to treat all possibly relevant issues commonly discussed in criminal law textbooks. The book was limited to the discussion of standards of liability and responsibility issues in the context of provocation and related defences from the point of view of the theory of justification and excuse. It has been argued that this theory offers a viable normative model which can achieve and maintain coherence among criminal law defences and secure community understanding and acceptance of the presuppositions upon which the criminal law system operates. This is because the very focus of the theory is on the question of rightness or wrongness of actions and society's expectations in dealing with the authors of such actions. Attention to the theory of justification and excuse will warrant the legitimacy and institutional efficacy of the criminal law system as a system which derives its aims and guiding principles from the society which it serves.

# Bibliography

Ackrill, J.L. (ed.) (1973), *Aristotle's Ethics*, Faber and Faber, London.

Alldridge, P. (1983), 'The Coherence of Defences', *Criminal Law Review*, p. 665.

Alldridge, P. (1991), 'Self-Induced Provocation', *Journal of Criminal Law*, 55, p. 94.

Allen, H. (1988), 'One Law for All Reasonable Persons?', *International Journal of Sociology of Law*, 16, p. 419.

Archibald, T. (1985 - 86), 'The Interrelationship Between Provocation and Mens Rea: A Defence of Loss of Self-Control', *Criminal Law Quarterly*, 28, p.454.

Arenella, P. (1994), 'Character, Choice and Moral Agency: The Relevance of Character to Our Moral Culpability Judgments', in M. L. Corrado (ed.), *Justification and Excuse in the Criminal Law*, Garland Publishing, New York and London, p. 241.

Aristotle, *Nicomachean Ethics*, W. D. Ross (trans.) in Aristotle's Ethics, J.L. Ackrill (ed.) (1973), Humanities Press, New York.

Ashworth, A. (1973), 'Self-Induced Provocation and the Homicide Act', *Criminal Law Review*, p. 483.

Ashworth, A. (1975), 'Reason, Logic and Criminal Liability', *Law Quarterly Review*, 91, p. 102.

Ashworth, A. (1975), 'Self-Defence and the Right to Life', *Cambridge Law Journal*, 34, p. 282.

Ashworth, A. (1975), 'Sentencing in Provocation Cases', *Criminal Law Review*, p. 553.

Ashworth, A. (1976), 'The Doctrine of Provocation', *Cambridge Law Journal*, 35, p. 292.

Ashworth, A. (1991), *Principles of Criminal Law*, Oxford University Press, Oxford.

Austin, J. L. (1968), 'A Plea for Excuses', in A. R. White (ed.), *The Philosophy of Action*, Oxford University Press, Oxford, p. 19.

Bacon, F. (1630), *The Elements of the Common Laws of England*, printed by the assignees of John More, London.

Barnes, J. (1984), *The Complete Works of Aristotle*, Princeton University Press, Princeton.

Bayles, M. (1982), 'Character, Purpose and Criminal Responsibility', *Law and Philosophy*, 1, p. 5.

Bedau, H. (1968), 'The Right to Life', *Monist*, 52, p. 550.

Bentham, J. (1789, 1948), *An Introduction to the Principles of Morals and Legislation*, Hafner, New York.

Berger, R. (1967), 'Provocation and Involuntary Act', *McGill Law Journal*, 12, p. 202.

Blackstone, W. (1769, 1966), *Commentaries on the Laws of England*, 4 vols, Clarendon Press, Oxford; reprint. ed., Dawsons of Pall Mall, London.

Brandt, R. (1969), 'A Utilitarian Theory of Excuses', *Philosophical Review*, 78, p. 337.

Brandt, R. (1970), 'Traits of Character: A Conceptual Analysis', *American Philosophical Quarterly*, 7, No 1, p. 23.

Brandt, R. (1994), 'A Motivational Theory of Excuses in the Criminal Law', in M. L. Corrado (ed.), *Justification and Excuse in the Criminal Law*, Garland Publishing, New York and London.

Brett, P. (1970), 'The Physiology of Provocation', *Criminal Law Review*, p. 634.

Bronaugh, R.N. (April 1964), 'Freedom as the Absence of an Excuse', *Ethics*, 74, p. 163.

Clarkson, C. (1987), *Understanding Criminal Law*, Fontana, London.

Coke, E. (1644), *The Third Part of the Institutes*, reprinted in *Classics of English Legal History in the Modern Era*, D. S. Berkowitz & S.L. Thorne (eds), Garland Publishing, New York.

Colvin, E. (1991), *Principles of Criminal Law*, A Carswell Publication, Canada.

Coval, S.C. and Smith, J.S. (1986), *Law and its Presuppositions: Actions, Agents and Rules*, Routledge and Paul, London.

Crompton, R. (1606), *L'Office et Auctority de Justices de Peace*, 2nd ed., London.

Davidson, D. (1980), *Essays on Actions and Events*, Oxford University Press, Oxford.

Devlin, P (1965), *The Enforcement of Morals,* Oxford University Press, London.

Dix, G.E. (1971), 'Psychological Abnormality as a Factor in Grading Criminal Liability: Diminished Capacity, Diminished Responsibility and the Like', *Journal of Criminal Law, Criminology and Police Science*, p. 313.

Dressler, J. (1982), 'Rethinking Heat of Passion: A Defence in Search of a Rationale', *Journal of Criminal Law and Criminology*, 73, p. 421.

Dressler, J. (1984), 'New Thoughts About the Concept of Justification in the Criminal Law: A Critique of Fletcher's Thinking and Rethinking', *University of California at Los Angeles Law Review*, 32, p. 61.

Dressler, J. (1987), 'Justifications and Excuses: A Brief Review of the Concepts and the Literature', *Wayne Law Review*, 33, p. 1155.

Dressler, J. (1988), 'Provocation: Partial Justification or Partial Excuse?", *Modern Law Review*, 51, p. 467.

Dressler, J. (1988), 'Reflections on Excusing Wrongdoers: Moral Theory, New Excuses and the Model Penal Code', *Rutgers Law Journal*, 19, p. 671.

Dworkin, R. (1977), *Taking Rights Seriously*, Duckworth, London.

East, E.H. (1803), *A Treatise of the Pleas of the Crown*, Butterworths, London.

Edwards, J. (1951), 'Compulsion, Coercion, and Criminal Responsibility', *Modern Law Review*, 14, p. 297.

Elliot, I. (1973), 'Excessive Self-Defence in Commonwealth Law: A Comment', *International and Comparative Law Quarterly*, p. 727.

English, P. (1973), 'Provocation and Attempted Murder', *Criminal Law Review*, p. 727.

Eser, A. (1976), 'Justification and Excuse', *American Journal of Comparative Law*, 24, p. 625.

Fairall, P. A. (1988), 'The Demise of Excessive Self-Defence Manslaughter in Australia: A Final Obituary?', *Criminal Law Journal*, 12, p. 41.

Feinberg, J. (1970), *Doing and Deserving*, Princeton University Press, Princeton, N.J.

Fingarette, H. (1980), 'Rethinking Criminal Law Excuses', *Yale Law Journal*, 89, p. 1002.

Fitzgerald, P.J. (1962), *Criminal Law and Punishment*, Clarendon Press, Oxford.

Fletcher, G. (1974), 'The Individualization of Excusing Conditions', *Southern California Law Review*, 47, p. 1269.

Fletcher, G. (1975), 'The Right Deed for the Wrong Reason: A Reply to Mr Robinson', *University of California at Los Angeles Law Review*, 23, p. 293.

Fletcher, G. (1978), 'Proportionality and the Psychotic Aggressor: A Vignette in Comparative Criminal Theory', *Israel Law Review*, 8, 367.

Fletcher, G. (1978), *Rethinking Criminal Law*, Little, Brown & Co, Boston, Toronto.

Fletcher, G. (1979), 'The Right to Life', *Georgia Law Review*, 13, p. 1371.

Fletcher, G. (1985), 'The Right and the Reasonable', *Harvard Law Review*, 98, p. 949.

Foster, M. (1762), *Crown Cases*, Professional Books, Abingdon, Oxfordshire,1982.

Foster, M. ( 1762, 1982 ), *Crown Cases*, Professional Books, Abingdon, Oxfordshire.

Frankfurt, H.G. (1973), 'Coercion and Moral Responsibility', in T.Honderich (ed.), *Essays on Freedom of Action*, Routledge and Paul, London, p. 63.

Goff, R. (1988), 'The Mental Element in Murder', *Law Quarterly Review*, 104, p. 30.

Gordon, G. H. (1978), *The Criminal Law of Scotland*, W. Green and Son, Edinburgh.

Green, T. A. (1972), 'Societal Concepts of Criminal Liability in Medieval England', *Speculum*, 47, p. 669.

Green, T. A. (1976), 'The Jury and the English Law of Homicide, 1200-1600', *Michigan Law Review*, 74, p. 413.

Green, T. A. (1985), *Verdict According to Conscience*, University of Chicago Press, Chicago.

Greenawalt, K. (1984), 'The Perplexing Borders of Justification and Excuse', *Columbia Law Review*, 84, p. 1898.

Greenawalt, K. (1986), 'Distinguishing Justifications from Excuses', *Law and Contemporary Problems*, 49, p. 89.

Griew, E. (1988), 'The Future of Diminished Responsibility', *Criminal Law Review*, p. 82.

Gross, H. (1979), *A Theory of Criminal Justice*, Oxford University Press, New York.

Hale, M. (1678, 1736 ed.), *The History of the Pleas of the Crown*, Vol. 1, Professional Books Ltd, London, 1972.

Hall, J. (1960), *General Principles of Criminal Law*, Bobbs-Merrill, New York.

Hall, J. (1976), 'Comment on Justification and Excuse', *American Journal of Comparative Law*, p. 638.

Hart, H.L.A. (1961, 1994), *The Concept of Law*, Clarendon Press, Oxford.

Hart, H.L.A. (1968), *Punishment and Responsibility*, Clarendon Press, Oxford.

Hawkins, W. (1716), *Treatise of the Pleas of the Crown*, London.

Heintz, L. (1981), 'The Logic of Defences', *American Philosophical Quarterly*, 18, p. 243.

Hirsch, A. von and Jareborg, N. (1987), 'Provocation and Culpability', in F. Schoeman (ed.), *Responsibility, Character, and the Emotions*, Cambridge University Press, Cambridge.

Hoekema, D. (1986), *Rights and Wrongs*, Assoc. University Presses, Toronto.

Horder, J. (1990), 'Cognition, Emotion and Criminal Culpability', *Law Quarterly Review*, 106, p. 469.

Horder, J. (1992), *Provocation and Responsibility*, Clarendon Press, Oxford.

Horowitz, D. (1986), 'Justification and Excuse in the Program of the Criminal Law', *Law and Contemporary Problems*, 49, p. 109.

Howard, C. (1964), 'An Australian Letter: Excessive Defence', *Criminal Law Review*, p. 448.

Howard, C. (1968), 'Two Problems of Excessive Defence', *Law Quarterly Review*, 84, p. 343.

Howard, C. (1990), *Criminal Law* (5th ed.), The Law Book Company, Sydney.

Hume, D. (1955), *An Inquiry Concerning Human Understanding*, Charles Hendel (ed.), Indianapolis, Ind.

Hume, D. (1978), *A Treatise on Human Nature*, L.A. Selby-Bigge (ed.), Oxford University Press, Oxford,

Husak, D. N. (1987), *Philosophy of the Criminal Law*, Rowman and Littlefield, Totowa, N.J.

Irwin, T. (1980), 'Reason and Responsibility in Aristotle', in A. Rorty (ed.), *Essays on Aristotle's Ethics*, University of California Press, Berkeley, California.

Kadish, S. (1976), 'Respect for Life and Regard for Rights in the Criminal Law', *California Law Review*, 64, p. 871.

Kaye, J. M. (1967), 'The Early History of Murder and Manslaughter',*Law Quarterly Review*, 83, pp. 365 and 569.

Kosman, L. (1980), 'Being Properly Affected: Virtues and Feelings in Aristotle's Ethics', in A. Rorty (ed.), *Essays on Aristotle's Ethics*, University of California Press, Berkeley, California.

Lacey, N (1988), *State Punishment*, Routledge, London.

Lambarde, W. (1581), *Eirenarcha*.

Lanham, D. (1988), 'Death of a Qualified Defence?', *Law Quarterly Review*, 104, p. 239.

Lindgren, J. (1987), 'Criminal Responsibility Reconsidered', *Law and Philosophy*, 6, p. 89.

Lyons, W. (1980), *Emotion*, Cambridge University Press, Cambridge.

MacKay, R. D. (1988), 'Pleading Provocation and Diminished Responsibility Together', *Criminal Law Review*, p. 411.

Maier, N. R. F. (1956), 'Frustration Theory: Restatement and Extension', *Psychological Review*, 63, p. 370.

McAuley, F. (1987), 'Anticipating the Past: The Defence of Provocation in Irish Law', *Modern Law Review*, 50, p. 133.

Mele, A. (April 1985), 'Self-Control, Action, and Belief', *American Philosophical Quarterly*, 22, 2, p. 171.

Mewett, A. W. (1984-85), 'Murder and Intent: Self-Defence and Provocation', *Criminal Law Quarterly*, 27, p. 433.

Montague, P (1981), 'Self-Defence and Choosing Between Lives', *Philosophical Studies*, 40, p. 215.

Moore, M. (1985), 'Causation and Excuses', *California Law Review*, 73, p. 1091.

Moore, M. (1994), 'Choice, Character and Excuse', in M. L. Corrado (ed.), *Justification and Excuse in the Criminal Law*, Garland Publishing, New York and London, p. 197.

Morris, N., and Howard, C. (1964), *Studies in Criminal Law*, Oxford University Press, Oxford.

Morse, S.L. (1984), 'Undiminished Confusion in Diminished Capacity', *Journal of Criminal Law and Criminology*, 75, p. 1.

Nicolson and Sanghvi, 'Battered Women and Provocation: The Implications of *R v Ahluwalia*', *Criminal Law Review*, p. 728.

Nowell-Smith, P. H. (1970), 'On Sanctioning Excuses', *The Journal of Philosophy*, 67, p. 609.

O'Regan, R.S. (1968), 'Indirect Provocation and Misdirected Retaliation', *Criminal Law Review*, p. 319.

Omichinski, N. (1987), 'Applying the Theories of Justifiable Homicide to Conflicts in the Doctrine of Self-Defence', *Wayne Law Review*, 33, p. 1447.

Perkins, R. (1957), *Criminal Law*, The Foundation Press, Brooklyn.

Pincoffs, E. L. (1973), 'Legal Responsibility and Moral Character', *Wayne Law Review*, 19, p. 905.

Pollock, F. & Maitland, F. W. (1898), *The History of English Law*, 2nd ed., Cambridge University Press, Cambridge.

Radzinowicz, L. (1948), *A History of the English Criminal Law*, Stevens, London.

Raz, J. (1986), *The Morality of Freedom*, Clarendon Press, Oxford.

Robinson, P. (1975), 'A Theory of Justification: Societal Harm as a Prerequisite for Criminal Liability', *University of California at Los Angeles Law Review*, 23, p. 266.

Robinson, P. (1982), 'Criminal Law Defenses: A Systematic Analysis', *Columbia Law Review*, 82, p. 199.

Robinson, P. (1984), *Criminal Law Defenses*, West Publishing Co, St. Paul, Minn.

Rorty, A. O. (1970), 'Plato and Aristotle on Belief, Habit, and Akrasia', *American Philosophical Quarterly*, 7, p. 50.

Ross, A. (1975), *On Guilt, Responsibility and Punishment*, University of California Press, Berkeley.

Sabini, J. and Silver, M. (1987), 'Emotions, Responsibility, and Character', in F. Schoeman (ed.), *Responsibility, Character, and the Emotions*, Cambridge University Press, Cambridge.

Samuels, A. (1971), 'Excusable Loss of Self-Control in Homicide', *Modern Law Review*, 34, p. 163.

Shute, S., Gardner, J., Horder, J. (eds) (1993), *Action and Value in Criminal Law*, Clarendon Press, Oxford.

Sistare, C. T. (1989), *Responsibility and Criminal Liability*, Kluwer Academic Publishers, Dordrecht.

Smith, J and Hogan B. (1996), *Criminal Law*, Butterworths, London.

Smith, J. C. (1989), *Justification and Excuse in the Criminal Law*, Stevens and Sons, London.

Smith, P. (1972), 'Excessive Defence — A Rejection of Australian Initiative?',

*Criminal Law Review*, p. 533.

Solomon, R. (1973), 'Emotions and Choice', reprinted in A. Rorty (ed.), *Explaining Emotions*, University of California Press, Berkeley, California.

Sparks, R. F. (1964), 'Diminished Responsibility in Theory and Practice', *Modern Law Review* 27, p. 9.

Stephen, J. F. A. (1883), *A History of the Criminal Law of England*, II, III, Macmillan, London.

Stephen, J. F. A. (1926), *A Digest of the Criminal Law*, (7th ed.), Sweet and Maxwell, London.

Taylor, C. (1982), 'Responsibility for Self', in G. Watson (ed.), *Free Will*, Oxford University Press, Oxford.

Ten, C.L. (1987), *Crime, Guilt and Punishment*, Clarendon Press, Oxford.

Turner, J. (1964), *Russell on Crime*, (12th ed.) Stevens, London.

Turner, J. (1966), *Kenny's Outlines of Criminal Law*, (19th edn.), Cambridge University Press, Cambridge.

Wasik, M. (1982), 'Cumulative Provocation and Domestic Killing', *Criminal Law Review*, p. 29.

Wasik, M. (1982), 'Partial Excuses in the Criminal Law', *The Modern Law Review*, 45, p. 516.

Wasserman, D. (1985), 'Justifying Self-Defence', *Philosophy and Public Affairs*, p. 356.

Wasserstrom, R. (1967), 'H.L.A. Hart and the Doctrines of Mens Rea and Criminal Responsibility', *The University of Chicago Law Review*, 35, p. 92.

Watson, G. (1982), 'Free Agency', in G. Watson (ed.), *Free Will*, Oxford University Press, Oxford.

White, A.R. (1985), *Grounds of Liability*, Clarendon Press, Oxford.

White, S. (1970), 'A Note on Provocation', *Criminal Law Review* , p. 446.

Wiggins, D. (1980), 'Weakness of Will, Commensurability, and the Objects of Deliberation and Desire', in A. D. Rorty (ed.), *Essays on Aristotle's Ethics*, University of California Press, Berkeley, California.

Williams, G. (1954), 'Provocation and the Reasonable Man', *Criminal Law Review*, p. 740.

Williams, G. (1961), *Criminal Law: The General Part*, 2nd ed., Stevens, London.

Williams, G. (1978, 1983),*Textbook of Criminal Law*, Stevens and Sons, London.

Williams, G. (1982), 'Offences and Defences', *Legal Studies*, 2, 3, p. 238.

Williams, G. (1982), 'The Theory of Excuses', *Criminal Law Review*, p. 732.

Yeo, S.M.H. (1990-91), 'Recent Pronouncements on the Ordinary Person test in Provocation and Automatism', *Criminal Law Quarterly*, 33, p. 280.

Yeo, S.M.H. (1988), 'Proportionality in Criminal Law Defences', *Criminal Law Journal*, 12, p. 211.

Yeo, S.M.H. (1988), 'The Demise of Excessive Self-Defence in Australia', *International and Comparative Law Quarterly*, 37, p. 348.

Yeo, S.M.H. (1990), *Compulsion in the Criminal Law*, The Law Book Company, Sydney.

Yeo, S.M.H. (ed.) (1991), *Partial Excuses to Murder*, Federation Press, Melbourne.

# Table of Cases

# Index